# The Past is not Past

# CULTURAL MEMORIES

VOL. 22

SERIES EDITOR

Dr Katia Pizzi
Institute of Languages, Cultures and Societies,
School of Advanced Study,
University of London

PETER LANG
Oxford - Berlin - Bruxelles - Chennai - Lausanne - New York

# The Past is not Past

## Confronting the Twentieth Century in the Hungarian-Austrian Borderlands

Frank N. Schubert

PETER LANG
Oxford - Berlin - Bruxelles - Chennai - Lausanne - New York

Bibliographic information published by the Deutsche Nationalbibliothek. The German National Library lists this publication in the German National Bibliography; detailed bibliographic data is available on the Internet at http://dnb.d-nb.de.

A catalogue record for this book is available from the British Library.

Library of Congress Cataloging-in-Publication Data

Names: Schubert, Frank N., author.
Title: The past is not past : confronting the twentieth century in the Hungarian-Austrian borderlands / Frank N. Schubert.
Description: Oxford ; Bern ; Berlin ; Bruxelles ; New York ; Wien : Peter Lang, 2024. | Series: Cultural memories, 2235-2325 ; volume no. 22 | Includes bibliographical references and index.
Identifiers: LCCN 2024007425 (print) | LCCN 2024007426 (ebook) | ISBN 9781803743592 (paperback) | ISBN 9781803743608 (ebook) | ISBN 9781803743615 (epub)
Subjects: LCSH: Hungary—History—20th century. | Borderlands—Social aspects—Hungary. | Collective memory—Hungary—History—20th century. | Memorialization—Hungary—History—20th century. | Memory—Political aspects—Hungary. | Hungary—Politics and government—20th century. | Hungary—Ethnic relations—History—20th century. | Schubert, Frank N.
Classification: LCC DB947 .S385 2024 (print) | LCC DB947 (ebook) | DDC 943.905—dc23/eng/20240328
LC record available at https://lccn.loc.gov/2024007425
LC ebook record available at https://lccn.loc.gov/2024007426

This book was originally published by the Holocaust Memorial Center, Budapest, Hungary, in 2022.

Cover image: The current Jeli grave marker, which replaced the weathered and worn original in 2021. Photograph by Balázs Őri.
Cover design by Peter Lang Group AG

ISSN 2235-2325
ISBN 978-1-80374-359-2 (print)
ISBN 978-1-80374-360-8 (ePDF)
ISBN 978-1-80374-361-5 (ePub)
DOI 10.3726/b21466


Published by Peter Lang Ltd, Oxford, United Kingdom
info@peterlang.com - www.peterlang.com



This publication has been peer reviewed.

*To the memory of my parents*
*With love and gratitude*

*Max (Miksa) Schubert*
*Kispaka, Hungary, 1907–Washington, D.C., U.S.A., 1964*

*Elizabeth (Erzsébet Redlich) Schubert*
*Pesterzsébet, Hungary, 1910–Silver Spring, Maryland, U.S.A., 1998*

*and*

*To Irene*
*without whom none of this would have been possible*

"One can tell a great deal about a country by what it chooses to remember: by what graces the walls of its museums, by what monuments are venerated, and by what parts of its history are embraced. One can tell even more by what a nation chooses to forget: what memories are erased and what aspects of its past are feared. This unwillingness to understand, accept, and embrace an accurate history, shaped by scholarship, reflects an unease with ambiguity and nuance—and with truth."

Lonnie G. Bunch III, "The Archive of Emancipation,"
*The Atlantic* (November 2023)

# Contents

# Figures

All maps reproduced in the volume were made by Béla Nagy, cartographer for the Hungarian Academy of Science.

# Acknowledgments

This book draws largely on research-centered short trips from our home in Győr to sites on both sides of the Hungarian-Austrian border. These excursions were made possible by dear friends with automobiles, broad knowledge of the region, and tolerance for my agenda. I thank them all for their patience, friendship, and help. They included long-time friend and colleague Dr. Erwin Schmidl and his wife, Elena, of Vienna; professional tour guide and friend Lajos Simon and his wife, Éva, of Szombathely; and our friends from Győr, Dezső and Ániko Jakabovits, István and Marika Nagy, and Ernő Tükovics and Erika Szenftner. They shared their knowledge of the region and its history, at coffeehouses or around dinner tables in their homes and ours. It was difficult to remember that I was actually working while traveling with these delightful people. The same applies to two most patient and tolerant taxi drivers who became dear friends, István Tűttő and Laci Komjáti.

In addition to accompanying me on research forays, István Nagy, Győr photographer and author of several books on regional history, helped me in myriad ways. He shared his knowledge, research, and connections. In addition, he as well as Erika Szenftner and Irene Schubert provided most of the photographs that appear in this book. All are used with their kind permission. During many pleasant encounters over coffee and pastry, mainly at the Bécsi Kávéház, István and I discussed my work and the local past. We did not always agree, particularly about whether I should publish the list of caretakers assigned by the city government to watch over residences taken from Jewish citizens in 1944, but he remained my friend and always went out of his way to be helpful.

I am also grateful for the professional support, friendly advice, and assistance of Michael Achenbach; Allan and Janet Akman; Tünde Csendes; Ella Davletshina; Dennis Deletant; Sándor Goják; my cousin Péter Hahner; Melody Herr; Manfred Imre; Dezső and Piroska Istántsuly; András Jókuti; Károly and Zsuzsanna Kopócs; Megan Lewis; Sándor Márkus; Gordon

Olson; András, Marta, and Attila Rajcsányi; Andrew Riemer; Tony Salgo; my son Max Schubert; Csaba Kiss and Suzanne Seet; Judith Summerfield; Balázs Szalay; Emöke Szalay; Dieter Szorger; Paul and Hajni Tinsley; Imre Tóth; György and Gábriella Vámos; Rabán and Zsofi Vántus; László Veres; István Vida; Tibor Villányi; and Petra Weiss.

At the Holocaust Memorial Center in Budapest, which published the original version of this book, I want to thank director Tamás Kovács for his interest in my work; educator Marta Goldmann for her friendship, support, and examination of the text in the Hungarian version; and librarian Zsuzsanna Bittner Temesi, who also worked on translation-related issues.

Above all, my wife, Irene, made possible our sojourn in Hungary as well as this book. Willing to try life in a country to which she had no connection, she brought to fruition my dream of a residence in Hungary and turned a barren four-room flat into a bright and comfortable home. She also participated in the preparation of this volume, documenting our travels with her meticulous photography, reading multiple drafts of the narrative, and enduring my occasional rants. After 15 wonderful years together in Győr, she was also the first to see that it was time to leave. None of this would have happened without her.

Frank N. Schubert
Mount Vernon, Virginia, U.S.A.

# Introduction

## Jeli: Death in the garden

After some years of visiting border towns in search of commemorations of the many catastrophes of the century gone by, Irene and I thought we knew what to expect. Almost all Hungarian towns, even the most minuscule, have memorials to the Treaty of Trianon, which the Allies imposed after the Great War of 1914–18. Hungarians regard this instrument as the nation's seminal modern catastrophe. It resulted in the truncation of the country and the physical separation of millions of Magyars into often hostile neighboring states. Monuments to the local fallen of the Great War, later edited to incorporate the military dead of World War II, also abound. Then there are the Holocaust memorials that sometimes shy away from explicit acknowledgment of the overwhelmingly Jewish nature of the catastrophe or of Hungarian culpability. Other calamities—lynchings, uprisings, deportations, and systematic oppression—also get attention. Pogroms get no attention, though there were at least two, and some important sites go unmarked and have become unknown. There are also the more positive reminders of the deliriously happy events of 1989 that brought the end of Soviet dominance, the People's Republic, and the despised Iron Curtain.

Jeli promised to be different. In 1922, Dr. (Count) István Ambrozy-Migazzi (1869–1933), a lawyer and botanist with a keen interest in Mediterranean microclimates, founded this arboretum just inside the community of Kám about 26 kilometers (16 miles) southeast of Szombathely. Before World War I, Ambrozzy-Migazzi represented the Felsőőr district, part of Austria since Trianon, in the Hungarian parliament. He devoted the last 12 years of his life to the establishment and development of Jeli.

On a clear day in May the arboretum, in a protected area of more than 260 acres, embodies peace and tranquility. Parking is free and admission fees are modest, 1,000 Hungarian forints or under four dollars at the 2017 exchange rate for an adult, 700 for an old guy like me. A lookout tower offers a fine view of the surrounding woods and fields. The park is far enough from the highway that only tourist foot traffic and the songbirds provide a backdrop to the serenity. Visitors stroll the paths through the pines, listen for the tapping of a woodpecker, and watch the stream reflect the sunlight. Maybe they exert themselves by climbing the stairs of the lookout tower, but mostly they meander among the lush plantings, dominated by rhododendrons and azaleas. The pastel blossoms underscore the tranquil feeling of the park, its remoteness from modern pressures, dissonances, and tensions.

This is the last place where you would expect the horrors of the past century to intrude, but still they do. Amid this sweet verdant setting, it is easy to walk right past the grave marker. In fact, I did, but Irene noticed it. We saw no sign calling attention to its presence or its symbolic importance. But there it was, a jolt to the visitor, the resting place of a soldier under a lush rhododendron bush, marked "Ismeretlen" [Unknown]. The marker followed a standard design found in military cemeteries throughout Hungary [Magyarország, or "Land of the Magyars" in Hungarian]. It was a worn and cracked wooden cross partially protected from the elements by two slabs of wood that meet at the peak of the cross to form a roof. In 2021, a sleek modern version replaced the weather-beaten original that we had seen. But the design is barely changed, the marker is not even a meter tall, and the inscription in Hungarian still says only "Itt nyugszik egy ismeretlen katona" [Here lies an unknown soldier]. It is dated 1945, probably from the time of the Soviet offensive from the east, and doesn't even say whether he was Hungarian or not. From this perspective of more than 70 years, maybe it doesn't matter.

Most likely, the soldier died at the very end of March. The Red Army arrived at the eastern border of Vas County on March 26, 1945, and reached the county seat of Szombathely on the 28th. He probably fell then or shortly thereafter, in the very last days of the war, and was buried where he died. Now the marker, a discordant note amid the blossoms, reminds us of the dark recent past and its ability to seep into all corners of life in the border region, underscoring its pervasiveness.

Important and often terrible events took place along both sides of the border between Austria and Hungary. They started with the defeat in World War I and the dismemberment of the Habsburg Empire and extend beyond the heady days of breaching and rolling up the Iron Curtain and the Soviet departure to the current refugee migrations. In between, there were the short-lived Communist republic; the so-called red and white terrors; the peace treaty at Trianon; the western Hungary uprising and political turmoil in Austria; the German annexation of Austria; World War II, the Allied bombings, and construction of the Third Reich's East Wall with largely Jewish slave labor; the dispossession, deportation, and murder of the Jews; the removal and murder of the Romani; postwar banishment of the ethnic Germans; and the Soviet-dominated era with its occupation turning into long-term control, a militarized and lethal border regime, the 1956 revolution and refugee crisis, and the Cold War. If there ever was a time of which it could be said that history was one damn thing after another, this was it. Marked or ignored, described accurately or evasively, sites reflecting and illuminating the complex and largely grim events of the period are everywhere.

## Family connections

My perspective on this recent past is conditioned by my own deep and ultimately ambivalent connections to Hungary and nearby lands. My parents fled their native Hungary early in 1939, just months before Germany invaded Poland and started the war and the systematic destruction of Europe's Jews, including members of both of my parents' immediate families. Through the years, my father said almost nothing about his experience as a child and young man, particularly about how he came to decide that he had to leave Hungary, and then managed to do so. My mother, who reluctantly accompanied him to the United States, said too much. Her repeated tales of family tragedy and personal victimhood became tiresome and irritating. And I was too absorbed in becoming and being an American kid to care anyway. So, there we were: a Jewish

American family that annually celebrated the Passover with its ritual focus on the story of the Exodus from Egypt, while failing to articulate and pass down our own exodus story. The boy didn't think to ask, the father kept silent, and the mother focused on her own pain.

It was only toward the end of the Cold War that I discovered that Hungary mattered to me. Born in the United States and absorbed in my family, my profession, and my American life, I never expected to travel there. Irene and I talked about going early in the 1980s, but when my mother, who had been back more than once, indicated that she wanted to go with us, and a cousin chimed in that she too would be happy to join us, we decided to go to Egypt instead. I was not willing to organize a family tour, and certainly not ready to encounter Hungary with my mother. Ultimately though, I came to understand that if Irene and I were to go, we would have to go separately, each with my mother, before we could go together. And so, Irene went with her in 1987, and I followed in 1990.

Although I did not crave my mother's company, I respected her bravery in returning to a place that seemed to her to be haunted. There were indeed ghosts there, memories of poverty, illness, and murder. She faced these reminders of her past, albeit with her occasionally histrionic flair, and came back from her first return visit in the 1970s, impressed with the progress she had seen. She had been one of six children, brought up by their war-widow mother in dire circumstances. They shared a tiny Pesterzsébet space consisting of one room and a pantry, with neither electricity nor plumbing. When she returned from her first visit, she reported that her old neighborhood was electrified and that there were indoor toilets. What she had seen, she said, eyes wide with astonishment, was not Communism. It was Socialism. And it was good.

Going to Hungary with my mother meant visits to relatives, both alive and dead. I anticipated this and looked forward to encountering relations I had until then not expected to meet. I met my cousin Marika Vas, the daughter of my mother's sister, who was married to a recently retired lieutenant colonel in the Hungarian People's Army. I also met Peter Hahner, the grandson of the same sister and a historian and university professor whose specialty was the age of the Enlightenment. By then Peter had written a biography of George Washington, whose Mount Vernon home is barely more than a mile from our own house. So he and I were more than relatives. We were also colleagues and came to be friends. I met my father's sister, Aranka, who was one of his three siblings, all of whom had survived the war. The other two were my uncles, half-brothers to my father, and had different experiences. One hid on an acquaintance's farm; the other toiled in the Hungarian army's labor service. One uncle fled Hungary with his wife and son after the 1956 revolution and lived in the Washington area. However, I did not see him for many years, after he and my mother had an argument about which of them was the worse parent. In Budapest, I visited cemeteries and saw the name of one of my mother's siblings engraved with those of other Holocaust victims on the silver-leaved memorial tree in the courtyard of the Dohány Street synagogue.

But the most memorable experience in Budapest took place on the street. When I left the hotel for my first morning walk, I heard the language of my early childhood—everywhere. And I was nearly overwhelmed by the feeling that I had come home. Since then, I have read novelist and essayist Sandor Márai's memoir of his departure from Hungary and have come to appreciate his claim that the Hungarian language—not the land, not the cuisine—was his home. When we were in Budapest during that autumn of 1990, the red star of the People's Republic still adorned the parliament building, but mayoral elections were underway. There was excitement in the air beyond my personal turmoil. Although I comprehended only a little of what was being said, I did understand one big thing: in some primordial strange way, I had come home.

Amid a blurred week of family and cemetery visits mixed in with museum tours, one additional experience stood out—breakfast with my mother at our hotel. The hostelry, like the country, was in a transitional mode. It was still called the "Béke" [Peace] Hotel, a typical Communist-era name, but it had a modern capitalist feel and was about to be absorbed into the Radisson chain. Breakfast was a lavish buffet, and my mother accompanied the feast with a cup of freshly brewed tea, served by a respectful, even obsequious waiter. The performance came at the end of the meal. With her purse in her lap, she beckoned the waiter by crooking a finger. He came, bowed slightly, and said the Hungarian equivalent of "yes, my lady?" My mother opened her purse, pulled out a single one-dollar bill, and while looking up at the waiter placed it on the table, watching and listening while he mumbled his thanks. Clearly, she was getting her revenge for a childhood filled with deprivation and for the murder of relatives left behind.

While she orchestrated this bit of homecoming theater, I decided to opt out of witnessing further performances, and jogged while she took breakfast during the rest of our stay. But I have come to regard my experience on this trip with my mother as critical to the development of my own view of Hungary and my ambivalent connection to a society that treated my family horribly and ultimately compelled my parents to seek lives elsewhere. Though born in the United States, I came from this place. I inherited a feeling for the language, which I spoke until I went to kindergarten and decided that I was an American kid, and a fondness for the food, which my mother skillfully prepared. Still, I knew there were ghosts here, lingering reflections of the evils visited on my family and people like us. A little like the grave hidden among the flowers of Jeli, a hospitable table laden with cheese-crusted *pogi* [little biscuits] and clear fiery *palinka* [fruit brandy] could obscure an ugly underlying past that is still unevenly acknowledged and confronted. Encountering the language and witnessing my mother's low-budget act of revenge set the tone for an emerging love-hate relationship.

As I explained in my earlier book *Hungarian Borderlands*, the specific quirks of regional borderland history had an important and inadvertent role in my parents' ability to get out of Hungary just before World War II erupted and thus in the great good fortune of my birth in the United States. More recently, I have returned with Irene to Hungary, and since 2004 have lived part-time in Győr, the largest city of the border region, where we bought a flat. We have also traveled through the towns and settlements on both sides of the border with Austria, photographed monuments and memorial tablets, attended memorial gatherings, and spoken with residents. My Jewish Hungarian background and my personal experience in the region has driven much of this enterprise and form the basis of a relationship with Hungary that goes beyond my interest as a historian. Ultimately, through exploration of Hungary's recent past as a historian, and as a part-time resident, I would develop a long-term relationship with the country and find my own revenge. I have tried in this book to blend my narrative of sites pertinent to this horrible century just past with discussion of my own personal encounters with this recent past and its physical and documentary traces.

## Recent borderlands history on exhibit

When my friend and colleague Erwin Schmidl, a senior historian in the Austrian Ministry of Defense, suggested a guidebook to important Cold War sites in the border region of Austria and Hungary, I thought of expanding the project to cover the entire twentieth century. So I set out to compile a guidebook to the two westernmost Hungarian counties of Győr-Moson-Sopron and Vas and the Austrian state of Burgenland, with a focus on how the twentieth century's rolling catastrophe has been commemorated, interpreted, obscured, and ignored. The ground on both sides of the national border has provided the locations where international politics, wars, treaties, and revolts have been acted out. Decisions in many cases were made in Vienna, Paris, Berlin, Budapest, Moscow, or Brussels, but they were implemented as well as resisted, endured, or celebrated in the towns and farmlands on both sides of the border. Other choices and movements that washed over the borderlands were not remotely generated, and they too left bloody traces on the region and its people.

Memorialization of the calamity that started with World War I and the collapse of the Habsburg Empire and continued for a century remains complicated and contentious. Austria, designated by the Allies as "the first victim" of the Third Reich, got a pass for culpability for what was inflicted on Jews and Romani by willing and even zealous local participants in the Hitler regime. The murderous practices of seizing or raiding and destroying synagogues, homes, businesses, schools, and cemeteries could be explained away as matters involving Germans and Jews, rather than Austrians. As recently as 2006, an employee of the Salzburg Seminar, giving a tour of the seminar's center in Schloss Leopoldskron, could say that the castle, formerly the home of renowned theater director Max Reinhardt, had been appropriated during World War II and made into an office of "the German Nazis," ignoring the likelihood that some of the Nazis of Salzburg were Austrians.

The flip side of remembrance is forgetting, including willful and deliberate refusal to confront certain events and outrages. The Austrian myth of the first victim of Nazism slowly unraveled following revelations concerning the nature of the Wehrmacht service of Kurt Waldheim, former secretary-general of the United Nations. At first, Austrians were so unaffected by these revelations that they elected Waldheim president. Perceptions have slowly changed. The Austrians have acknowledged their culpability in the murder of Romani, and stolen paintings have been restored to rightful owners. Irene and I have watched this process unfold, viewing the famous Klimt portrait of Adele Bloch Bauer first in the Vienna Belvedere, then in its new home at the Neue Galerie in New York.

In Hungary, the Communist regime suppressed manifestations of independent Hungarian nationalism and recognition of ethnic strife. This official refusal to face a contentious past had two opposite outcomes. The policy stifled Hungarian desires to mourn the national defeat, dismemberment, and humiliation that dated back to the first war and was exacerbated in the second war, which added physical devastation to the damages. Meanwhile official silence sustained the Hungarian disinclination to recognize that Jewish dispossession and suffering had taken place largely at Hungarian hands. As psychiatrist and survivor Ervin Várga wryly observed, "most Hungarians distrusted everything that the Communist Party said except for one well-chosen slogan, 'The people were not fascists; they were only misled by the fascists.'"[1] This they believed.

Beginning in the 1990s, with the disintegration of the Communist regime in Hungary, the unleashing of previously stifled nationalist impulses generated large numbers of memorials and monuments. To be sure, Trianon and the dismemberment of Hungary were never forgotten, as evidenced by the disastrous alliance with the Third Reich in return for German help with restoration of lost territory. After decades of Communist hostility to

1 Ervin Várga, *Living and Dying in Hungary: Jewish Psychiatrist Looks Back* (Bloomington, IN: Xlibris, 2012), p. 104.

commemoration of the post–World War I settlement, a virtual tsunami of Trianon memorials came after the collapse of the Iron Curtain. Over the following 25 years, they spread over the country to such an extent that it would be easier to list the towns that do not have Trianon memorials than to enumerate those that do. The message of these memorials is nowhere more clearly expressed than at tiny Mórichida, population just over 800, about 20 kilometers southwest of Győr: "Those who are Hungarian feel the pain of Trianon."[2] Memorials to the 1956 revolution proliferated too, albeit less widely, while ignoring the lynching of state security agents and the resurgence of anti-Semitism that accompanied the struggle for freedom.

International pressure and financial support from descendants of Hungarian survivors of the Holocaust helped propel the commemoration of the former Jewish presence and their disappearance. Memorials to the Romani catastrophe also started to appear, albeit more slowly and less widely than markers of the Jewish Holocaust. The few memorials to the latter calamity have tended to be more forthright in Austria than in Hungary. Commemorations of wartime Allied bombing also began to take place, with annual observances as well as wall plaques, statues, and memorials. The emphasis in these towns and observances on Hungarian victimhood sharply differed from the German approach. In Germany, as a *New York Times* reporter observed, there are no major commemorations to the approximately half million Germans who died because of Allied bombings. The Germans have stayed clear of emphasizing their own losses, avoiding an appearance of asserting equivalence with the mass murders committed under the Reich.[3] Hungarians are not reluctant to push forward

2 In Hungarian the text reads, "Az a Magyar, Akinek Fáj Trianon." My thanks to photographer and historian István Nagy for calling my attention to this monument.

3 Sabrina Tavernise, "When History's Losers Write the Story," *New York Times*, "Sunday Review" (September 17, 2017, published online September 15, 2017). The basic text regarding German disinclination to commemorate city destruction is W. G. Sebald, *On the Natural History of Destruction*, trans. Anthea Bell (New York: Modern Library, 2003). German acknowledgment of responsibility for the Holocaust came slowly and at different rates on both sides of the Berlin Wall. The key early text concerning culpability was a 1945 lecture at Heidelberg University by philosopher Karl Jaspers called *Die Schuldfrage* [*The Question of German Guilt*] and first published in 1947. Susan Neiman's *Learning from the Germans: Race and*

claims asserting or implying that all were similarly unfortunate sufferers. The recent and highly controversial monument to all the war dead at Szabadság tér in Budapest is the primary example of this. Austrians, generally avid partners with the Germans in the slaughter, took the Hungarian approach in commemoration rather than the German. So in the Burgenland town of Pöttsching, near Wiener Neustadt, there is an all-encompassing memorial to the victims of violence from 1934 to 1945. One memorial fits all.[4]

Generally, except in cases where the perpetrators of murder, deportations, and expropriations were Communist, marked victim sites are easier to find than perpetrator sites, such as Gestapo, Arrow Cross, and Nazi Party offices. The victim sites themselves are designated at times in incomplete, disingenuous, and deceitful ways. Sometimes they play more to the general sense of Hungarian victimization and ignore the specific group with whom the site is nominally associated. Temporizing, pulling punches, stopping short of explicit identification of victims and perpetrators all serve to support a positive national image, appearing to recognize the terrible past by installing memorials that avoid explicit recognition of the particular victims or perpetrators. In Budapest a memorial tablet on the wall of the current British Embassy notes the humanitarian efforts of Swedish diplomat Raoul Wallenberg. It neglects to mention that the people he tried to rescue were Jews. Hostility to certain categories of memorialization also leads to vandalism, with attempts to erase, deface, or remove markers. While this failure to note the singularly Jewish nature of the Holocaust is not uncommon in Hungary, it has recently appeared in North America as well, in President Donald Trump's proclamation of International Holocaust Memorial Day in January 2017 and in the autumn of the same year with the unveiling of a Canadian Holocaust memorial in Ottawa.

Victimhoods tend to clash and compete, emphasizing the tragedy of one group while downplaying or ignoring the horrible experience of another, for example the privileging of the unfortunate but much less vicious

---

*the Memory of Evil* (New York: Farrar, Strauss and Giroux, 2019) is an excellent account of the development of this awareness.

4 Herbert Brettl and Michael Hess, *NS-Euthanasie im Burgenland*, Wissenschaftliche Arbeiten aus dem Burgenland, Band 136 (Eisenstadt: Burgenlandischen Landesregierung, Abteilung 7-Landesmuseum, 2015), p. 76.

relocation of the Germans after World War II over the deportation of the Jews to death camps. Then there is the tendency of travel literature to ignore most or all the local involvement in recent horrors, especially the crimes and brutality of Hungarians, of which there were plenty. Books ranging from locally produced Hungarian pamphlets to major English-language guidebooks tend to emphasize the bland, the charming, and the chronologically remote, as do most examples of the genre.

While considering these attributes of memorialization and travel literature, I started to think about cities as museums. Like museums, towns contain objects, in this case buildings and sites, that are on public display, labeled by tablets and historical markers which explain their significance, in ways that are sometimes satisfactory and sometimes not. The city as museum also contains a wide range of memorial sculpture, commemorating, celebrating, or distorting the meaning of past events. Taking this idea a little further, I suggest that places that are marked and thus on display as historical sites are like museum exhibits, while unmarked places are like the part of the museum collection that is in storage, that visitors don't see, but that are still always there.

The comparison is not perfect, of course. Above all, there is the inescapable fact that visitors enter museums voluntarily, because they want to. They consider the contents selectively, again, because they choose to. The city houses collections of historically important sites, but residents work there, play there, live there. They don't approach their city as tourists. Structures, memorials, and places that reflect the past, perhaps known to some if not all inhabitants, may represent a past that is glorious or grim. All of them are part of the background of their lives, whether they seek them out and ponder their significance or not.[5]

In addition to this basic contextual difference between city and museum, the collection housed in the museum diverges widely from that distributed through the city. The stored portion of the museum collection is organized, catalogued, and housed in an environment intended

5 András Lénárt, "Csillagos házak Budapesten, 1944–2014," in Judit Molnár, ed., *A Nagypolitikától a Hétköznapokig: A Magyar Holokauszt 70 Év Távlatából* (Szeged: Balassi Kiadó, 2016), p. 385.

to preserve the individual pieces. The sites that are stored in towns are often unpreserved, obscured, and in some cases unknown. For example, it is known that the Arrow Cross regime's Ministry of the Interior had its headquarters at Sárvár during the westward retreat in the waning months of the war, but local historians in the castle at the city center have no idea where it might have been.[6] Other sites that are known, such as the Orthodox synagogue in Körmend, are visible—but only if you happen to stumble on them. If you do, there is nothing, no marker or tablet, to help you identify the building, which is rotting and in a state of near collapse. A third element rounds out the urban collection of sites, structures, and memorials. This category includes those that museum curators might consider to have been deaccessioned. These have been removed, demolished, or changed beyond recognition, inadvertently as well as deliberately. No current map of the city includes them because they no longer exist. They have left no overt trace, only scattered and obscure files of building plans and permits, newspaper references, and historical maps.[7]

Centrally located coffeehouses offer tourists wishing to consider the city as museum opportunities similar to museum cafés. Sitting with an espresso in a well-positioned downtown coffeehouse, gazing at a map showing local sites of interest and considering the city as part memory museum and part amnesia museum can resemble relaxing in a museum café with an exhibit guide, noting what sites are nearby and whether they are worth seeing. This view of the city as a historical museum both on display and in storage veers away from the classic flaneur's conception of urban space. Walter Benjamin's flaneur and flaneuse, urban citizens of leisure who saw

6 As it happens, this is knowable. The ministry spread over five downtown sites, including the very castle where those historians worked. Minister of the Interior Gábor Vajna had his office in city hall, just south and across the street from the historians in the castle. See Zoltan András Kovács, "A Szálasy Kormány Belügyministeriuma: Rendvédelem, Állambiztonság, Közigazgatás A Nyilas Korszakban" (Ph. D. Dissertation, Pécsi Tudományegyetem-Bölcsészettudomanyi Kar, 2008), pp. 248–9.

7 Andrew Lichtenstein and Alex Lichtenstein, *Marked, Unmarked, Remembered* (Morgantown: West Virginia University Press, 2017), use a similar typology in considering sites relating to oppression of African Americans, Native Americans, and workers seeking better remuneration and trying to organize.

the city as unfolding theater, considered the coffeehouse as their office,[8] a comfortable place for an ongoing examination of what was taking place before their eyes. Benjamin's urban theater was forever changing, transient, ephemeral, and unpredictable. The historical observer's urban museum, on the other hand, tends in the short term to be static and stable except for occasional deaccessioning. Yet, for both the historically minded who view the city as a museum-like storehouse of memories and the traditionally engaged observer of city life, the coffeehouse remains the starting point for a leisurely inquiry.

For contemplation of the horrors of the twentieth century, the coffeehouse setting is a jarringly ironic one, given its safety and comfort, in stark contrast to the bloody nastiness of the recent past. Coffeehouses in this border region often retain some of their traditional charm with shimmery upholstery, cut-glass chandeliers, and round marble-top tables that at times evoke the cafés of the imperial era with their "amiable Habsburg tranquility."[9] Despite their similarity, they no longer symbolize the cohesion that once marked the Empire. Located within sight, around the corner, or atop reminders of the ugly recent past, they offer opportunities to contemplate in comfort the outrages that took place nearby. But visitors in 2017, sipping cappuccino after visiting a Tourinform office and flipping through the booklets "Western Hungary" or "The Treasures of Kőszeg," will learn nothing about the compelling and terrible recent events that took place within meters of their pleasant surroundings.

The official tourist guide to Győr-Moson-Sopron County illustrates well the general disinclination in such publications to confront the recent past. Available at the "Tourinform" website or offices in the county's more prominent towns, among them Győr, Sopron, and Mosonmagyaróvár, the brochure covers attractions in the entire county. The introduction to the currently available edition by Dr. Imre Szakács, president of the county General Assembly, promotes towns "rich in historical and architectural

8 "The Fascination of the Metropolis," *Lost in the City: Urban Life in the IVAM* [Institut Valencia d'Art Modern] *Collection*, May 18, 2016–June 4, 2017, p. 3 (https://ivam.es/en/exposiciones/lost-in-the-city-urban-life-in-the-ivam-collection/)

9 Claudio Magris, *Journeying*, trans. Anne Milano Appel (New Haven: Yale University Press, 2018), p. 184.

sites," and "romantic natural and water worlds," as well as festivals and folklore attractions. Győr has "churches, palaces, museums, characteristic corner balconies and narrow passages." Sopron, at the far western tip of Hungary and not far from Győr, has the Goat Church, site of coronations and Parliament sessions in the seventeenth century. But the Tourinform brochure omits mention of sites relating to the dark recent past, such as the Sopron monument to Pál Prónáy, a virulent and violent anti-Semite and leader of a murderous right-wing gang of the post–World War I period, a site of pilgrimage for modern irredentists and right-wing anti-Semites.[10]

And so it goes. Hegykő has a thermal bath "recommended for curing locomotive and gastric disorders." But there is also a replica section of the lethal Cold War border that was the site of poet György Faludy's second escape from the Communist "prison" that was Hungary, commemorated in his poem "Exodus." And Hegyeshalom, the main border crossing on both the highway and railroad to Vienna, boasts a thirteenth-century Gothic-style church with frescoes from the Middle Ages. It also has an unmarked site on a street by the train station where Jewish slave laborers who had survived into the spring of 1945 were murdered three days before Soviet troops arrived.

This book goes beyond official and conventional travel literature. It is a travel guide to the dark side, and it focuses on sites and traces of political drama, tension, and brute violence that are part of the region's recent past. The streaming service Netflix played to this interest with an eight-part series called *Dark Tourist* that was released in 2018, and the authors of a historical travel guide called *The Time Traveler's Companion* quipped, "History repeats itself, first time as tragedy, second time as vacation."[11] This

10 Krisztina Rimany, general editor, *border(hi)stories 1914–2022*, a trilingual volume (English, German, Hungarian) published jointly in 2022 by Austrian and Hungarian authorities with European Union support, contains photographs and text regarding some of the places and episodes explored in this book. It does not consider specific memorials and the motivations behind them and generally shies away from analysis and criticism.

11 Quoted in Henry Alford, "Return Trips," review of *The Time Traveler's Handbook: 18 Experiences, From the Eruption of Vesuvius to Woodstock*, by James Wyllie, Johnny Acton, and David Goldblatt (New York: Harper Design/Harper Collins, 2016), *New York Times Book Review*, June 5, 2016, p. 18.

volume may indeed appeal to travelers interested in what is now known as "dark tourism" or "death tourism."[12] Tourists connect to sites of human brutality or stupidity, especially those which may have been scenes of personal or family catastrophes. But the reason for that attraction is not just in vogue among tourists or those who write about travel. It is in the nature of the century just gone by. An inquiry into locations connected to the border region's recent past inevitably dissolves into dark tourism, and the literature does more than cater to current interests in the abundant sites of horrible deeds. It provides a corrective to the habitual cheeriness of guidebooks, adds balance to the perspective of a traveler, and ultimately leads to a fuller understanding of the recent past. Broadly, whether sites are seen through the lens of cities as museums with collections on display, in storage, or deaccessioned, they reveal much about a society itself. As Magdalena Neumüller observed in a study of a Burgenland town's approach to this matter, memorials reveal the self-perceptions and interests of a society.[13] Towns and nations represent and reveal themselves through their monuments. Their quality, materials, location, and sponsorship, as well as the timing of their erection and their number all illuminate, in ways that are inadvertent as well as intended, what is important, what is dismissed, and what is troublesome.

Finally, a word about why this is important. The landmarks and memorials to the events of the twentieth century are reminders of past regimes and systems, victims and perpetrators, heroes and scoundrels, all of whom cleared, shaped, built, and maintained the path to the present. This is true of all the horrors of the past century, whether committed in the name of ideologies of the left or right, whether out of fear, racism, or

12 On dark tourism, see Brigitte Sion, "Introduction," in Sion, ed., *Death Tourism: Disaster Sites as Recreational Landscape* (London: Seagull Books, 2014); Kate Brown, *Dispatches from Dystopia: Histories of Places Not Yet Forgotten* (Chicago: University of Chicago Press, 2015). The Lichtenstein volume cited above also fits into this category.

13 Magdalena Neumüller, "Erinnerung in Rechnitz—Mikrostudie über den Umgang mit Toten" ["Remembrance in Rechnitz—Micro Study on Dealing with the Dead"], in Walter Manoschek, Hg., *Der Fall Rechnitz: Das Massaker an Juden im März 1945* (Vienna: Braumüller, 2009), pp. 199–219.

an acquisitive urge. This book is not just for people who lived it, loved or loathed it, or feared it. It is for the young too, because it illuminates who we are and how we got this way. And it is also for our own future: we will be remembered for what we remember, and for what we distort, obfuscate, ignore, and forget.

# PART I

# Eight Towns

Figure 0.1 The Hungarian-Austrian border region in the twentieth century [Map 1].

CHAPTER 1

# Szombathely: Coffee at Ground Zero

Irene and I visited Szombathely in the spring of 2014. We had been there previously with friends from Győr, seen the ruins of the Roman customs house, and visited the history museum. At least we had tried to. The posted hours clearly indicated the museum was open. The locked door said otherwise. This was not our last such experience in Hungary, and ultimately we learned to check websites and call ahead. In 2014, we were looking for places emblematic of the dark, more recent past and we were looking at the entire city as a museum. Our friend and colleague Erwin Schmidl came from Vienna, and our Szombathely friend Lajos Simon, an experienced professional tour guide, showed us around.

Together we went to the cemetery on the southwest edge of the city. The military section, reachable through the civilian cemetery, is at the top of a modest hill in the northeast quadrant of the complex and dates from 1920. There are graves of soldiers from both world wars who fell while serving in the armies of six different states, friend and foe alike. Long-standing taboos imposed during the Communist years were broken by the memorials at the cemetery to the uprising in western Hungary during 1921 and to the 1956 revolution. Both memorials are just inside the cemetery, south of the northern edge formed by Ferencsy István Street. Gábor Veres designed the 1956 memorial, a massive sheet of rusted steel armor plate emblazoned with the number "56" and a hole blasted through the center by a tank round, with a stainless-steel cross alongside. Dedicated in 2010, it clearly associates the revolution with Christianity.

The nearby monument to the western Hungary uprising, the work of Sándor Mayer and named "the Unknown Rebel," was dedicated in 1992. Its style resembles the socialist realism of the Communist period—an upright muscular fighter with sleeves rolled up, rifle barrel in his hand, and the broken stock of the weapon on the ground before his feet. It's the favorite memorial of many locals.

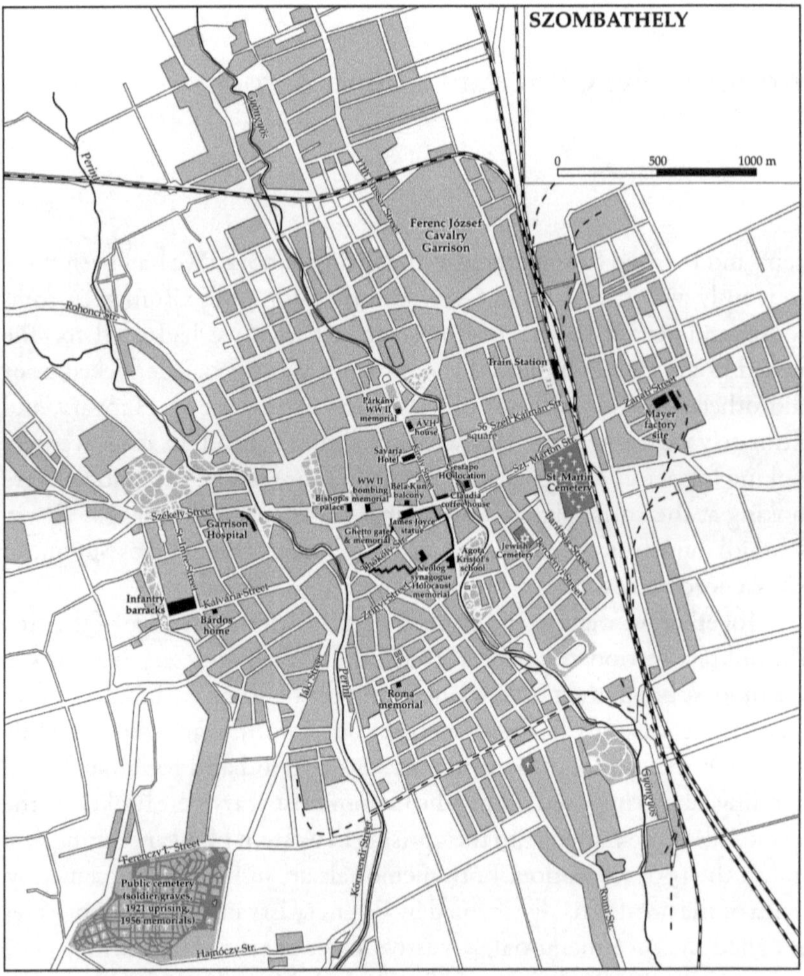


Figure 1.1 Szombathely [Map 2].

Figures 1.2 and 1.3 (see overleaf) The memorial to the 1956 revolution in Szombathely was not unique. Installations commemorating the 1956 revolution often have Christian design motifs. The October 26 massacre of demonstrators by security troops firing from their garrison in Mosonmagyaróvár was by far the bloodiest clash in the border counties during the revolution. The monument shown here, was erected in 2001 on Gyász Square near an industrial park on the western side of the city, at Határőr Street, which runs between Alkotmány and Bártok Streets. The pietà scene is the central element of the memorial, which covers the entire park, with individual markers for those shot by the security forces from the borderguard barracks across the street.

Figure 1.4 The Unknown Rebel.

The dominant memorial in terms of size, a trumpeter from the Árpád era created by István Rumi Rajki in 1928, announces the resurrection of Hungary, a rejoinder to the losses of territory and population incurred at Trianon and another Christian allusion. There is also a chapel built by prisoners of war from a nearby camp and a monument to Soviet forces of

World War II, that was banished here in 2001 from a location near the center of the city in Pelikán Park. Nearby to the north on Kálvária Street stands a monument to the Eighty-Third Infantry Regiment of World War I, whose home garrison was on the north side of the street. With so much of the carnage of the twentieth century, state sanctioned and otherwise, memorialized in the military cemetery, there is no better place to get an introduction to the terrible recent past.

After our tour of the cemetery, we walked past the home of Jewish classical violinist Alice Bárdos, a bit to the east and across Kálvária Street at number 47. Bárdos was among those deported to their deaths in 1944. The house bears a plaque in her memory.

Then we returned to Fő tér, the main square. Our energy had started to flag, and it was time for coffee. The four of us took an outdoor table at the Claudia coffeehouse on that fine April afternoon and started to discuss what we had seen. We were drawn to the Claudia, which has been in operation since 1923, by its centrality and its specific history and location. The café itself is ground zero for contemplating the ugliness of the century gone by. It stands on the site of the former Palace Hotel, which may have housed some of the Gestapo staff who worked down the street at another unmarked historical site, the current location of the Borostánykő áruház (the Chinese-owned "Amber Department Store") and a Spar supermarket, east on Szent Márton and right across the Gyöngyös. Whether the hotel was in fact home away from home for Gestapo employees, it was destroyed in an Allied bombing raid during 1944–5, making the Claudia itself an unmarked memorial site of the war.

While we sipped coffee and nibbled pastry, I thought about what had existed all around me. Near the Claudia, with its array of pastries under glass and its cozy warmth, a number of sites reflect the horrors of recent Hungarian history. The Tourinform office, on the square directly across Király utca [Street], offers nothing on the subject, but nearby reminders of a nasty and brutal recent past abound. For starters, of course, there is the Gestapo site down the street. Also the zigzagging ghetto wall, outlined on the town map at the start of the chapter, once ran directly across the plaza from where we sat. Toward the northwestern end of the square was the house where Béla Kún, head of the short-lived and widely loathed Communist republic of 1919, had once drawn a crowd. The Kún site, at 15 Fő tér, is about

100 meters from the Claudia. From the wrought-iron balcony of this one-time officers' casino, Kún stirred up the masses during his brief tenure. The balcony remains in place, but the plaque commemorating his appearance has been removed in an effort to erase the memory of this episode. The only historical marker on the building, next to the one-time carriage entrance, notes that the building reached its current form in the nineteenth century.

Past the Kún site just outside the northwest corner of the square but facing west away from it at the southeastern corner of Berzsenyi Square, a historical marker recalls the horrific Allied bombings of World War II. The tablet was dedicated on March 4, 2005, the sixtieth anniversary of the devastating air raid that destroyed the building that had housed city hall and a theater, barely three weeks before the Soviets entered Szombathely.[1] Aladar Hauszmann designed the destroyed building as well as the garrison of the Eleventh Huszárs, north of the city center.

The marker for the bombing is diagonally across the square from the bishop's palace, which survived the war intact. When Charles IV, the last reigning Habsburg emperor, tried to reclaim the throne of Hungary in April 1921, he headed for the palace. He entered Hungary by air and landed at Dénesfa just inside the southern edge of Győr-Moson-Sopron County, reached Szombathely by auto, and sought lodging at the palace. His aide and chauffeur on this escapade was László Almásy (1895–1951), whose life inspired Michael Ondaatje's 1992 novel *The English Patient* and the film starring Ralph Fiennes that followed. Almásy was born in nearby Bernstein, now across the border in Austria, and served with the Eleventh Huszárs on the Russian front during the world war before becoming a pilot. For a short time toward the end of the war, he commanded the airfield at Parndorf. A personal friend of Bishop János Mikes, he served as his private secretary during 1922–6, living first in the palace and then at Gagarin Street 6. Almásy

1 On the bombing of Szombathely, see Czirók Zoltán, *"Tegnap istenitélet volt Szombathelyen ..." Légitamadások a vasi megyeszékhely ellen 1944–1945* (Szombathely: A Vasi Muzeumbarát Egylet, 2015). For Győr and Sopron, see István Nagy, *Húsvéttól húsvétig*. Első Kötet. *Győr harmincöt bombazása* (Győr: Győr-Moson-Sopron Megye Győri Levéltára, 2007); Ifj. Sarkady Sándor, *Légiharcok és Légiesemények 1944–1945-ben Sopron Vármegyében* (Sopron: Edutech Kiadó, 2004).

later gained renown as an explorer and cartographer and wrote several books about the North African desert. There is a memorial to the regiment's World War I dead, inside the compound of the Eleventh Hussar garrison, behind the buildings facing 11-es Huszár út [Avenue], and a plaque at Gagarin 6, west of the city center, marks it as Almásy's residence during that period.

Charles (Károly in Hungarian) already had a reputation for ineptitude, based on his failure to govern the monarchy in the period of crisis that followed the 1916 death of Franz Joseph. Ignacy Daszynski, leader of the Polish socialists in the Viennese parliament, called him "a weak man of an immature mind," adding that "sometimes he made the impression of being simply harmlessly stupid."[2] That judgment may be harsh given the intractability of the situation at the time. Regardless of his intellectual capabilities, he was certainly persistent. Although Admiral Miklós Horthy, the head of state, had him escorted out of the country, he returned in October, detraining in Győr and leading an unsuccessful march toward Budapest from there. After that failed coup, he was packed off to exile in Madeira, where he died the following year.

The poignant Holocaust memorial just north of the Imre Wesel house, where Bejczy tér meets Fő tér at today's city hall, almost faces the Kún site from across the square. Gábor Veres designed the memorial marking the location of the ghetto gate. The bronze sculpture, installed in 2014 on the seventieth anniversary of the deportation, shows a locked door with a little girl's winter coat on a nail. A stuffed animal protrudes from the right coat pocket, and a Star of David is visible on the left side of the coat. A historical marker is to the left of the coat.

Lawyer Imre Wesel, who lived at Szenczy (now Bejcsy) utca, just south of the Holocaust memorial, ran the Jewish council established in 1944 by the Germans from an office in his home. He tirelessly tried to help those deprived of livelihoods by the anti-Jewish laws and the families of those conscripted for slave labor, until his deportation to Auschwitz. Wesel's home has been marked since 2007 by one of the first four stumble stone

2 Adam Kozuchowski, *The Afterlife of Austria-Hungary: The Image of the Habsburg Monarchy in Interwar Europe* (Pittsburgh: University of Pittsburgh Press, 2013), pp. 58, 102, 163.

memorials [*botlatókövek*] in Szombathely. These are part of a project conceived and executed by German artist Gunter Demnig, who has installed thousands of these memorials in Germany as well as in more than 10 countries like Hungary, from which the Nazis and their local surrogates and helpers deported Jews to their deaths.[3] These installations address directly the condition from which Jewish German philosopher Günther Anders recoiled at Hiroshima in 1958, the absence of any sense that something was in fact absent. Naming the deported and murdered, identifying them directly in front of their former homes in an indelible manner, over and over again, in town after town, speaks directly to what is missing.

Figure 1.5 The stumble stone at the site of Imre Wesel's home.

3 On the Russian "last address" project, which resembles Demnig's work, see Sabrina Tavernise, "Russian Project Honors Stalin's Victims and Stirs Talk on Brutal Past," *New York Times*, September 20, 2015.

Demnig's project resonates beyond Europe. In the United States, the sites of nearly 4,000 lynchings of African Americans are largely unmarked, and there is no uniform approach to marking them. The nongovernmental organization (NGO) called the Equal Justice Initiative, considering ways to mark these places, is well aware of the stumble stones. American lynchings differ from what happened in Hungary and the rest of Europe during the Third Reich's dominance. They were crimes more like those of the later Communist regimes, meant to terrorize a population into submission rather than exterminate it and victimizing a total number that is lower than 1 percent of the Jewish Hungarians who were murdered in the last year of the war. But they represent a similar memorialization problem: how to mark a large number of sites relating to numerous victims while emphasizing the individual humanity of the victims.[4]

Behind our table at the Claudia, a five-block stretch northward on Király utca contains a string of important sites and memorials. The most

4 Campbell Robertson, "History of Lynchings in the South Documents Nearly 4,000 Names," *New York Times*, Tuesday, February 10, 2015; Equal Justice Initiative (EJI), "Lynchings in America: Confronting the Legacy of Racial Terror," 2015, <www.eji.org/files/EJI Lynching in America SUMMARY.pdf>, accessed April 1, 2016. The EJI report focuses on 3,959 documented "racial terror lynchings carried out in 12 southern states during the period 1877–1950." This represents a large portion of such crimes, but cases of racially motivated lynchings in other states are also known. On the EJI museum and memorial, which opened at the end of April 2018, see "National Memorial for Peace and Justice and Legacy Museum Receive National Attention," April 9, 2018, <www.museumandmemorial .eji.org>, accessed April 24, 2018, and Campbell Robertson, "A Lynching Memorial Is Opening. The Country Has Never Seen Anything Like It," *New York Times*, April 25, 2018. Another effort in the United States called the "Middle Passage Project" seeks to document places involved in the slave trade. See Charles V. Bagli, "Slave Memorial Unveiled in Camden," *New York Times*, November 28, 2017. These places and others connected to lynchings, especially in rural or wooded areas, are highly susceptible to vandalism, mainly defacement with swastikas and bullet holes. Markers at the cluster of sites relating to the murder of black teenager Emmett Till by the Tallahatchie River in Mississippi in 1955 remain favorite targets for vandals to this day. See Veda Shastri, "The Many Realities of a Lynching" and Audra D. S. Burch, "Decay, and Indelible Memory," both in *New York Times*, February 22, 2019.

distant, just across Eighteenth Honvéd Regiment Avenue at the end of Király, remembers the victims of World War II, all of them. This is the Péter Parkány Raab statue, with its central figure reminiscent of Christ taken down from the cross, installed in 1995 on March 15 Square. One might take issue with whether such a monument can legitimately commemorate Jewish victims.

Broadly speaking, the Parkány memorial was part of the proliferation of monuments in the 1990s, after taboos of the Communist years were lifted. The dismemberment of Hungary in the Treaty of Trianon, the defeat in World War II, and the 1956 revolution had gone uncommemorated for two generations, and the impulses to understand, explain, celebrate, and sometimes obfuscate these events had been stifled. This installation purported to honor soldiers killed in action, civilians who died in aerial attacks and from other war-related causes, and those deported to their deaths, mainly Jews but Romani as well. It erased distinctions among the personal and group catastrophes of the World War II period. A monument designed by Mihály Prónáy for Sopron's Deák Square and installed in 1993 (see chapter 5 on Sopron below) took a similar approach, remembering, on a monument with clearly Christian imagery, all who were deported and murdered. Parkány reprised and broadened this approach nearly 20 years later, in the widely known and fiercely debated installation on Szabadság Square in Budapest. Understandably, Jewish groups were at the forefront of those who objected to relativizing the Jewish catastrophe, implicitly equating the Holocaust with other war-related carnage, and to the Christian imagery. The approach taken in this widely known and passionately attacked memorial extended down to flyspeck villages like Győrsövényház, almost 20 kilometers west of Győr. There, one slab of black marble memorialized Hungarian soldiers killed in combat, Jews murdered during the Holocaust, locals shot by the Germans during the Soviet offensive, and even families who were resettled after the war. Remarkably, this memorial, installed in 2011, named all people who fell into all four of these categories. At least they did not remain anonymous. The approach taken in towns from Budapest to Győrsövényház differs widely from the one taken by the Germans, who have eschewed anything that approached relativization of the Holocaust.[5]

The Holocaust memorial at the ghetto gate could be said to supersede the Parkány creation as a Holocaust memorial. It was installed almost 20 years later, and through use of the child's coat as well as the Star of David clearly alludes to the singular character of the deportation. There are no false equivalences here between armed uniformed soldiers and innocent children with stuffed animals in their pockets, and there is no Christian imagery.

Back on Király, at number 14, on the left just before Malom Street heading back down toward the Claudia, the ÁVH house contained the office, jail, and torture rooms of the Államvédelmi Hatóság, the State Security Authority of the (Communist) People's Republic of Hungary. After the 1956 revolution, tortures and executions took place in the basement. Pedestrians on Király utca tended to cross the street and give it a wide berth when going past. Some still do. The building is shuttered, but it is possible to glimpse through a gap of one of the imperfectly sealed basement windows, the doors of the facing rows of cell doors, capturing something of the gloom and menace of the cellar.

The historical marker by the door was placed by the western Trans-Danubia branch of the association of survivors of the Recsk forced labor camp (in Heves County, east of Budapest), the county branch of the 1956 Association, and the city government. It shows a guard tower behind barbed wire and is dedicated to the memory of those tortured here. The verse at the top is by local poet Amy Károlyi, the wife of poet and translator Sándor Weöres.

> Time judges otherwise
> But it does not let go of the deed,

5 The persistent tendency to obfuscate the singularity of the Holocaust in memorialization and commemoration is not confined to Hungary. See Yair Rosenberg, "The Shooter Didn't Hate 'Religion.' He hated Jews," *Washington Post*, Outlook, Sunday, November 4, 2018, p. B4. In the wake of the massacre at Tree of Life synagogue in Pittsburgh, Pennsylvania, on Saturday, October 27, 2018, Rosenberg writes about "airbrushing anti-Semitism from the greatest mass murder of Jews on American soil."

Everything goes round and round,
Like burned out celestial bodies.

A little south and across the street from the AVH house stands the shuttered Savaria Hotel. It faces east across Király Street, down Széll Kálmán toward the train station. Now closed, the Savaria was once a model of Secessionist elegance. It was designed by Artúr Vida, built in 1914–15 as the Kovács Hotel, and renamed the Savaria by 1919. Most of its 90 guest rooms lacked en suite bathrooms, assuring the ultimate failure of the enterprise. It closed for good in 2005.

Figure 1.6 A postcard view of the coffeehouse at the Kovács, a classic example of an elegant provincial café of the late Habsburg years.

Pál Prónáy, an embittered veteran officer of World War I, and his right-wing extremist comrades used the Savaria and the Eleventh Huszár garrison as bases for their rampage against Communists and Jews, merged in their worldview as *judeobolsheviks*. Their activities, far bloodier than those of the Communist republic they loathed as "the Red Terror," became known as "the White Terror." With the tacit approval of Admiral Horthy's government of reactionary aristocrats, Prónáy planned the 1921 western Hungary uprising, a futile effort to prevent Austria from taking over Burgenland, from the hotel. He directed surveillance of Communists returning from Austria from here, with agents at border crossings and watchers in Vienna. His men kidnapped and smuggled some leftists into Szombathely and locked them in the cellars at the barracks. After interrogations, they moved their prisoners north to the fort at Komárom on the Danube.[6]

During World War II, the Savaria employed four slave laborers marched up from the Bor camp in Serbia. This odd turn of events did not involve any of the Jews brought up for manual labor on the East Wall, the Third Reich's desperate attempt in late 1944 to block the Red Army as it approached from the east. Members of small pacifist Christian sects, among them Jehovah's Witnesses, Seventh-day Adventists, and Nazarenes, worked in town, clearing rubble at the airport, occasionally on farms, and even in food preparation and service at the white-tablecloth hotel restaurant. They were allowed to move about the city freely, trusted not to steal, and sometimes received decent medical care and better places to stay than other labor service slaves. In Szombathely, their billets included stables on the site of the current Barátság Óvoda (kindergarten), at number 24 on Barátság utca. The street runs north-south on the west side of the Szent Márton cemetery, which goes back to the days of Roman Savaria.[7]

Outsiders from the Christian pacifist sects sometimes fared better than Jews or Romani but remained outcasts. In the last desperate days of World War II, some Jehovah's Witnesses were hanged for conscientious objection

6 For comparisons of the two terrors in the historical literature, see Kádár Gábor and Vági Zoltán, *A Végső Döntés: Berlin, Budapest, Birkenau 1944* (Budapest: Jaffa, 2013), pp. 108–12; Joseph Rothschild, *East Central Europe between the Two World Wars* (Seattle: University of Washington Press, 1974), p. 153; Randolph Braham, *The Politics of Genocide: The Holocaust in Hungary* (New York: Columbia University Press, 1981), I, pp. 16–18, 35. Also consider the judgment of novelist Magda Szabó, through the housekeeper Emerence: "When the Whites were in power, it was the Whites doing it, and when it was the Reds' turn, they did the same, and the speeches they made before killing them were the same, and the legs of the victims kicked out in exactly the same way, no matter which colour had strung them up." Magda Szabó, *The Door*, trans. Len Riz (New York: NYRB, 2005), p. 94.

7 Tamás Csapody, *Bortól Szombathelyig* (Budapest: Zrinyi, 2012), pp. 118–19, 160–2, 166–7.

to military service, at Körmend and Sárvár. At the latter town, Lajos Deli was hanged publicly on March 12, 1945, in the main square, in front of the Catholic church. Deli died because his beliefs precluded participation in war, and he suffered his very public death in the town center. Yet the memorial, installed 66 years later, on June 11, 2011, is on the southeastern edge of town, in the floodplain along the Rába, on an exterior wall of the locked Jewish cemetery, near the bodies of members of Hungary's ultimate outsider group, the Jews. So alongside the modern recognition that the catastrophes of individuals and groups singled out for persecution and murder in the twentieth century should be recognized, there is another message, about what kind of people belong to the society that makes up this town and who does not.[8]

The Szent Márton cemetery in Szombathely was not for outsiders. The historical summary on a metal plate by the entrance notes the nearby tombs of "prominent figures of Szombathely's history," including the Bárdossy family and the Istóczys. The Bárdossy markers do not bear the name of the László Bárdossy, who was prime minister for about a year in 1941–2. He presided over milestones in the disintegration of the war effort and the status of Jewish citizens. After the war and his execution as a war criminal in January 1946, a sealed coffin purported to contain his remains was returned to his family along with orders not to open it. Some say he is buried in the family plot. As if to add substance to that claim, annual commemorations have been held, even up to the present, at the site under sponsorship of the László Bárdossy Remembrance and Friends Association. Catholic clergy officiate, wreaths are laid, and the bishop refers inquiries to the parish priest, who cannot be found to comment. Also buried in Szent Márton is politician Győző Istóczy. A year after an 1882 duel with a Jewish fellow member of parliament, from which Istóczy emerged unscathed, he founded

8 A monument on the outer wall of the Roman Catholic church on Kossuth Square, the site of the Deli hanging, underscores the outsider status of Deli and his coreligionists. This tablet was installed on June 4, 2011, three days before the Deli plaque went up. About the same size but in its far more prominent position, the marker notes that the Polish soldiers who had found refuge at Sárvár prayed there for the liberation of their country, already occupied by Germany, and for the glory of Hungary, which was about to go to war on Germany's side.

the first explicitly anti-Semitic political party in Hungary. His influence resonated well into the twentieth century.

Another gravestone in a less conspicuous location marks the burial of nine members of the Pokmetz family, caught up in the slaughter that was World War II. On October 21, 1944, while stonemason József Pokmetz filled bomb craters at the Sopte military airfield north of town, a bomb struck his home and killed his wife and eight children, scattering body parts in a 200-meter circle. He buried them in six coffins and lived with his memories until 1988.

Shortly after the deaths of Pokmetz's family, the gendarmes and Arrow Cross government turned to the dispossession of the Romani and their assembly for deportation. On November 3, 1944, they surrounded the Roma quarter, in preparation for deporting them first to Pápa and Komárom, and thence shipping those they considered fit for work to Dachau, Mauthausen, and Hamburg. Those removed included villagers of neighboring Meggyeskovácsi, Ondód, Őriszentpéter, and Torony. The monument to this removal, a black marble slab, is in Városmajor Park on Jászai Mari utca, just south of Szent Florian kórut at the intersection with Krudy Gyula utca. It is in the former Roma quarter and was defaced with brown paint in the summer of 2013. Then the city installed a fence around it. The text on the monument is as follows: In memory of the suffering of hundreds of Vas County Gypsies assembled here in November 1944 and deported to slave labor and to concentration camps, on the fiftieth anniversary, by the citizens of Szombathely and Vas County. Nowadays an annual public commemoration at the site takes place on November 4.

Memorials to 1956 are immune from such defacement. The main one is straight down Széll Kálmán from the Savaria Hotel on Király utca toward the train station, two blocks to the intersection of Vörösmarty and 56 Square. A monument on the northeast corner commemorates the revolution and marks the location of the headquarters of the voluntary national guard, an organization made up largely of former police and military personnel who supported the revolutionary cause. It specifically remembers 12 members of the National Guard who were massacred at that spot before dawn on the bitterly cold morning of November 4. The victims were roused from their beds inside the building by the returning Russians and ordered downstairs. They emerged in various states of undress and were mowed down by automatic weapons fire. The 12 names are chiseled on the brown panel of the memorial.

Figure 1.7 The memorial to the massacre on 56 Square.

They reflect a variety of personal and family tragedies, but Karoly Magyari might stand for them all. He was 46 years old when volunteers for the guard were recruited. His friend Lajos Simon had been asked to join but could not. Simon's wife was trapped inside Budapest trying to deliver medical supplies to the embattled residents, and he had full-time work and two children at home. His friend Magyari stepped in and volunteered to take his place. Diagonally across from the monument is an elegant survivor of the 1944–5 bombing that later became the headquarters of the local Communist Party. Király utca was known locally as the Andrássy út of Szombathely, after the elegant avenue of the same name in Budapest.

Figure 1.8 Former Communist Party headquarters.

From 56 Square it is a short walk back to the Claudia for coffee and maybe a little reflection on what a fine perch the coffeehouse provides for contemplating the evils and excesses of the twentieth century. There are sites relating to twentieth-century brutalization, terror, and murder nearby in almost every direction. Even nearby literary locations indirectly reflected the excesses and nastiness of the past hundred years. Commemoration of James Joyce and Agota Kristof illuminate some of the baser impulses of the recent past.

The Joyce statue at Fő tér 40 shows the author either emerging from the facade or disappearing into it. His writings are not ordinarily listed among the horrors of the twentieth century, but at one time they were, first by Western critics who considered his works, especially *Ulysses*, obscene, then by U.S. postal authorities who tried unsuccessfully to keep his books out of the country, and later by the Soviet Communists who agreed with the Americans on the obscenity charge. Bloomsday, an annual celebration of Joyce and his novel, started in Dublin on June 16, 1954, the fiftieth anniversary of the ordinary day in the life of an ordinary man depicted in the story. The annual event and the statue call attention to Szombathely as the birthplace of *Ulysses* protagonist Leopold Bloom's father, Rudolph. Joyce knew southern Europe well. He lived and wrote in Trieste for a time and is memorialized in Pula on the western coast of Croatian Istria. Bloomsday, an alternative "all-arts" festival, first came to Szombathely in 1994, after the Soviet departure. The Blooms are of course fictitious, but a Jewish family named Blum did live at the site in the 1840s.

Joyce is not the only famous writer connected to Szombathely. Agota Kristof explored the darker side of human nature in the context of the savage Arrow Cross period in western Hungary in her novel *The Notebook* [*A Nagy Füzet*]. She attended the Dorottya Kanizsai secondary school, south of the Claudia down Aréna Street, and graduated in 1954. Not long afterward, in the wake of the 1956 revolution, she fled to Switzerland, where she wrote her novels in French.[9]

The Kanizsai school sits just beyond the southeast corner of the ghetto. The Claudia is at the northeast corner. The ghetto's eastern wall once ran on the western side of Aréna Street between the two. A number of structures and memorials connected to the once thriving Jewish community are nearby within the irregular boundaries of the ghetto. The most significant sites center on Batthyány Square, the location of the Neolog synagogue designed by Vienna architect Ludwig Schöne and dedicated on August 30, 1880. Schöne's work in Transdanubia included the Lutheran church along the river at Károly Gaspár tér in Szombathely and the Kálvária Catholic

9 Kristof's engaging little memoir, less than 10 percent the size of Joyce's opus, was published in English as *The Illiterate* by New Directions in 2023.

church overlooking Kőszeg. The two-towered Jewish house of prayer reflected the impact of the Dohány utca synagogue in Budapest.

Within five years of the end of World War II, the Jewish community got its real property back, but the population kept diminishing to the point where it could not maintain buildings. In 1959, a city residential maintenance association bought the Orthodox synagogue building on the north side of Thokoly Imre Street at number 48, just west of Arena. The stumble stone in front of number 46 marks the residence of Rabbi Mark Benedikt, who was eighty-six years old when he was deported and killed. In 1964, the city also acquired the Neolog synagogue building and reconfigured it as a concert hall a decade later. Other important community buildings are close by. Next door to the north of the synagogue stands the headquarters of the tiny Jewish community that now remains. It contains a museum, showing the interior of a typical Jewish home and objects related to the community and the Holocaust. Around the corner on Zrinyi Ilona Street stood the school, the matzoh bakery, and

Figures 1.9, 1.10, and 1.11 Reminders of 1944–5: A newspaper article reporting the large amount of money and valuables found in the ghetto after removal of the Jews for deportation; symbols of oppression (a Nazi pennant, an Arrow Cross armband, and a gendarme hat); objects found in a labor service mass grave outside of Kőszeg. These were photographed in the museum next door to the synagogue.

a modest-sized old-age home, with a basement soup kitchen. A kosher restaurant now offers lunches there. The superb exhibit *Szemtol Szembem* [Face-to-Face] tracing the history of the Jewish community through personal stories is on permanent display at Zrinyi 17.[10]

Two of the first four stumble stones that mark the residences of deported Jewish citizens are inside the bounds of the ghetto, Rabbi Benedikt's before the Orthodox synagogue and his home, and Imre Wesel's on Belczy Street. The other two are beyond the ghetto boundaries, one in front of elementary school teacher and principal Albert Gábor's home on Király, across from the Savaria Hotel at number 9, and the other before the residence of fish merchant and greengrocer József Mermelstein on the main square at number 5, just outside the ghetto gate.

The ghetto was not the last stop for Szombathely's Jews before deportation. Just as the Jews of Győr spent their last few days at a collection camp under conditions even worse than the ghetto (see chapter 7), so too was the Szombathely community removed to a collection camp at the abandoned and dilapidated former Mayer motorcycle works. Today there is no trace of the one-time factory or a memorial indicating its use in 1944. But if you stop by the railroad crossing on Vépi Avenue, you can look north along the tracks in the direction of the camp along Zanati Street and follow with your eyes the track as it goes toward the white fence that surrounds the industrial area. At one time, it led beyond, to a spur and a siding at the factory. Outward bound, the track came past where you are standing, and ultimately led to Auschwitz.

10 There is a superb companion volume, Krisztina Kelbert, *Szemtöl Szemben: Képek az elhurcolt szombathelyi zsidóság történetéből* (Szombathely: Savaria Megyei Hatókörű Városi Múzeum, 2014). In the spring of 2018, the exhibit was closed "for technical reasons," a catchall phrase used in Hungary to cover a multitude of problems.

CHAPTER 2

# Rechnitz: Murder capital of the Austrian side

The Gasthaus Schlossberger at Schlossbergergasse 2 is just across Bahnhof Strasse (Route 56), the main north-south road, from the memorial park and just south of the site of the Batthyány family castle. The gasthaus serves an excellent homemade apricot schnapps, and its central location makes it a suitable place for reflection on the ugly recent past. It also occupies the site of the birthplace in 1832 of Gustav Pick, who wrote the widely popular "Fiaker song," celebrating the horse-drawn coaches of Vienna. Pick came from a Jewish family, and the *Wikipedia* summary of his life goes so far as to call Rechnitz a "Jewish village." During the 1910 census, the last Hungarian census before the war that destroyed the Empire, about 25 percent of the 4,000 residents were Jewish. From that point the number of Jews declined, along with the town's economic importance, caused by industrial development elsewhere and the postwar border change that disrupted economic connections, until only 170 Jews lived in Rechnitz by 1934. After 1938 none remained. Four returned after the war; the last one died in 1980.

Herrengasse, once the center of Jewish commerce and society, is still the location of the cemetery west of the town center. About 180 grave markers remain, the only evidence of the existence of a Jewish community, and seven Hungarian Jewish slave laborers from 1944–5 are interred there. The cemetery was desecrated during the Nazi years and has been vandalized more than once in recent times, even since restoration by the Jewish community of Graz. The gate is locked, and entry can be arranged through city hall at Hauptplatz 40 during business hours. The telephone number is 92-3363-79202. The Loos family at Herrengasse 38, about 50 meters from the cemetery gate in the direction of town, can also provide access.

The synagogue site is on Badergasse north of the Hauptplatz and behind the Roman Catholic church. Local Nazis destroyed the temple,

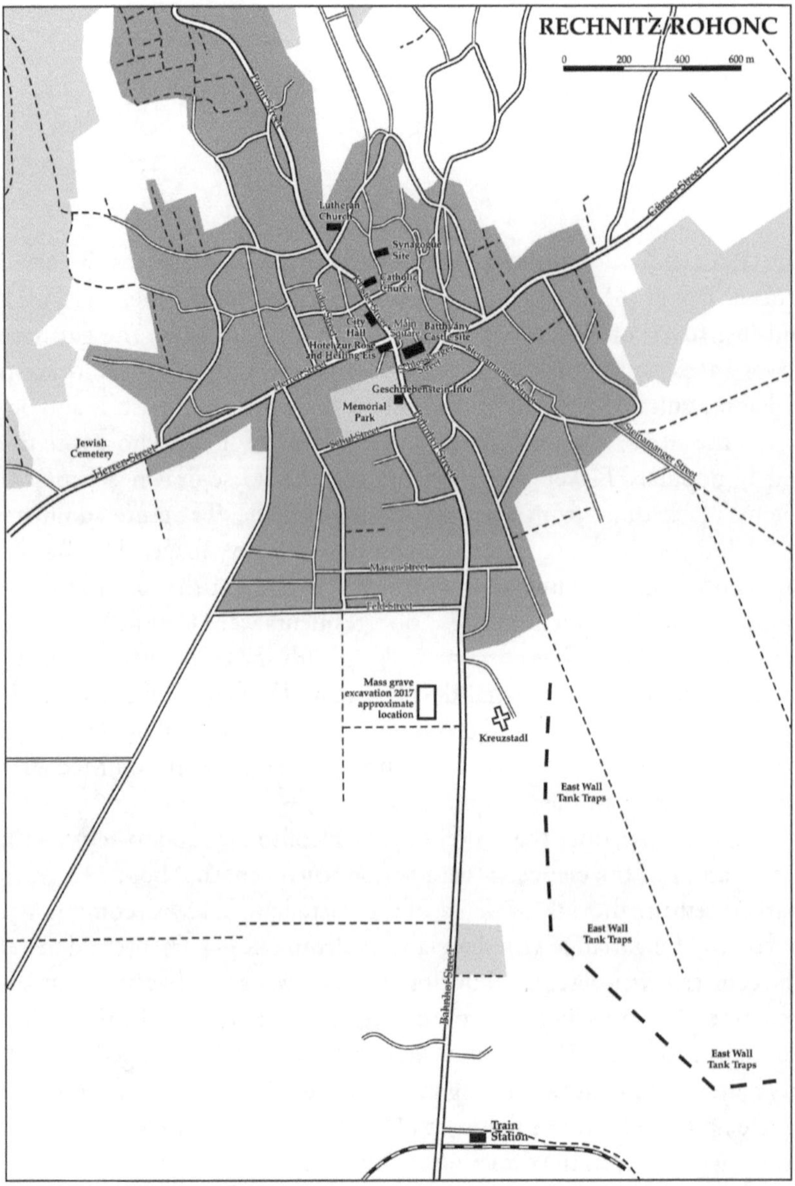


Figure 2.1 Rechnitz/Rohonc [Map 3].

established in 1729, in 1938. The location remained unmarked until 1991. Now there is a set of plaques on the facade of the building, which houses residences and medical facilities. Just as at the cemetery, the Jews of Graz paid for the initial commemorative tablet and drafted the text. The marker was installed quietly without fanfare or public participation, as the city kept its distance from observances or installations that recalled Jewish life in town. The site has been incorporated into a newly developed walking tour of Jewish life, but that was created by a private foundation going by the name of RE.F.U.G.I.U.S. (Rechnitzer Flüchtlings- Und GedenkInitiative Und Stiftung [Rechnitz Refugee and Memorial Initiative and Foundation]). The foundation, which produced the walking tour of Jewish and Romani life in Oberwart, is a private organization dedicated to commemorating the victims of 1938–45, particularly those involved in construction of the Third Reich defenses in Burgenland. Meanwhile, Rechnitz's Jewish past remains a touchstone for a musical ensemble called "Rechnitzer Rejects," known to aficionados of Yiddish folk and klezmer music for their parody songs full of Yiddishisms referring to the old country and its cultural survivals in the United States, especially in the New York area.

Figure 2.2 "Out of sight but not out of mind." This motto is on panel 6 of the recently emplaced 10-panel walking tour of Jewish life in Rechnitz. The pamphlet for the Rechnitz tour is available in English and German at the Geschriebenstein Park office as well as in boxes at the individual panels.

Figure 2.3 Gustav Pick shown on panel 2 of the RE.F.U.G.I.U.S. walking tour of Jewish life in Rechnitz.

Gustav Pick and his family moved to Vienna when he was a teenager, and the songs he wrote remained famous there until the Third Reich banned them as Jewish. Tobias Portschy, on the other hand, was born in 1905 to a peasant Catholic family at Unterschützen, nestled between Routes 63 and

50 just north of Oberwart and 20 kilometers west of Rechnitz. Fiercely anti-Semitic and anti-Romani, he earned a law degree, joined the Nazi Party when it was still illegal, and wholeheartedly served Adolf Hitler's regime. He rose to be deputy Gauleiter, or lieutenant governor of the Gau, or region of Styria, which had been redrawn to include Rechnitz and southern Burgenland. He married Edith Holndonner, the head of the local branch of the League of German Maidens, and settled in Rechnitz after the war. Aside from an abbreviated prison term—he was pardoned by Austrian president Theodor Körner in 1951 after serving less than two years of a 15-year sentence for his role in the Nazi regime—Portschy lived a long, respectable, and comfortable life in Rechnitz, much of it on the main square, in the Hotel zur Rose, which he and his wife owned. He died in 1996. The arcs of these two lives, Pick and Portschy, help illuminate Nobel laureate Elfriede Jelinek's savagely ironic characterization of Burgenland during the Third Reich as "Strudelgau," part cozy comfort and part Hitler salute.

Portschy, whom Jelinek called "Commander of the legion of horror," had his home just north of today's memorial park and across the street from the site of the Batthyány Castle.[1] After being vacant for 15 years, by 2017 the former hotel building was renovated and the apartments above the coffeehouse awaited tenants. Plans included a police station on the ground floor. There was no sign indicating that Tobias Portschy once lived there. For that matter, there was no sign that it had once been called the Hotel zur Rose or that the evolution of the local Nazi Party from clandestine cell to mass movement could have been observed from there. The illegal organizational meeting of the local Nazi Party chapter, in which Portschy participated, took place in the hotel, then owned by his future in-laws, on July 12, 1931. In 1934, shortly after Hitler came to power in Germany, six uniformed Nazis, chanting, "Hitler Erwache! Dollfuss Zerkrache!", which roughly translates as "Hitler awakens! Dollfuss crashes!", marched by before defacing some Jewish homes with swastikas.[2] The climax came the day

1 Elfriede Jelinek, *Rechnitz and the Merchant's Contracts*, trans. Gitta Honegger (London: Seagull Books, 2015), p. 75.

2 Engelbert Dollfus was chancellor of Austria from 1932 until his assassination in July 1934.

after the Anschluss, on March 12, 1938. Three thousand people paraded on Bahnhof Strasse in front of the hotel to celebrate incorporation of Austria into the Reich. The merriment ended with an evening speech by Customs Office leader Dürmayer from Schachendorf and chants of "Ein Volk, ein Reich, ein Führer!"

The waitress at the Heiling Eis (Hauptplatz 18a) on the ground floor knew about the building's former identity, and the map on the back of the RE.F.U.G.I.U.S. pamphlet "Jewish Life in Rechnitz" shows the Hotel zur Rose. With the opening of Heiling Eis in mid-2017, the Gasthaus Schlossberger was superseded as the ideal perch for contemplating recent evils. At Heiling Eis, the coffee is Lavazza, the washrooms are immaculate, and the café looks across Hauptplatz and Bahnhof Strasse toward the castle. The Schlossberger house schnapps is still worth sipping, but visiting the Heiling is a little like going to the Győr McDonald's, with its Arrow Cross heritage (see chapter 7).

The outdoor museum at the Kreuzstadl massacre site south of town, one of the most savage of the myriad Nazi crimes in Austria, pulls no punches in text regarding Portschy. In German, Hungarian, and English, it calls him "one of the intellectual fathers and ideologues behind the persecution of the Romani [who] was also responsible for radicalizing the Austrian population following the Anschluss in 1938." This characterization refers at least partly to Portschy's 1938 pamphlet *Die Zigeunerfrage* [*The Gypsy Question*], in which he summed up the Romani as archaic and rootless parasites who lacked discipline. They were the antithesis of industrious, responsible, rooted Germans. Jews were little better, though they had managed to insinuate themselves into modern institutional structures, notably stock exchanges, banks, and the media. Erwin Schmidl interviewed Portschy at his Hotel zur Rose home in October 1984. He describes Porschy as a "very polite, well-educated and well-mannered old gentleman" who dearly loved his grandchildren and still referred to Jews as *Ungeziefer* [vermin].[3] In zealously asserting the Germanness of Burgenland, the eastern edge of the Third Reich, Portschy also threw Hungarians into the collection of

3 Email, Erwin Schmidl to author, May 6, 2016; conversation, Erwin Schmidl with author, October 13, 2018.

outsiders, but the local Magyars avidly shared his Nazism and attached themselves publicly to the movement. There was no keeping them out.

Figure 2.4 The former Hotel zur Rose. The front windows on the right look over the Hauptplatz to the site of the Batthyány Castle across Bahnhof Strasse.

The memorial park just down the street from Portschy's former home commemorates World War I and the many-faceted catastrophe of the World War II years in ways resembling other commemorations on both sides of the border. A massive cross set against the background of the marble slab at the center dominates the installation. A first glance at the current group, which was designed and installed in 2006–7, would make you think you were facing a Christian shrine. But the memorial purports to honor all the victims of the world wars, ranging from soldiers shown in uniforms of the Third Reich to Hungarian Jewish civilians slaughtered south of town at the Kreuzstadl. All the marble surfaces have gold inscriptions. The four memorials that flank the cross resemble each other but take different approaches to memorialization. The ones on the viewer's right note the deaths of 197 local civilians and soldiers and show the names and faces of

162, identified as *Unsere Gefallenen* [our fallen], almost all men and almost all in uniforms of the Third Reich. The ones on the left commemorate resisters who were killed, all four of them by name, with the years of their birth and death, and two groups of Jews, those who were deported and murdered in the wake of the Anschluss and those murdered at Kreuzstadl in March 1945. Both latter groups are numberless, nameless, faceless, and, of course, not Christian.

Historian Magdalena Neumüller assesses the peculiar topography of the memorial park well, noting that all these groups are presented as victims of the war, the soldiers as well as the various groups of civilians, and that the soldiers are pictured while the expelled and murdered Jews are not even named, even though as residents of the town their identities would have been easy to ascertain.[4] Essentially, she sees the monotonous linear design as expressing a desire for finality. OK, the community seems to say, every category of victim is noted. Let's move on from the past. Of course, for every victim there is a perpetrator, and the question of whether any of the uniformed men might have fallen into this category is ignored as is the exterminationist nature of the war in which they fought. Moreover, every category of victim is *not* recognized. Romani residents of the district, all of whom were taken to labor and concentration camps during Holy Week in 1943, go unmentioned.

4 Magdalena Neumüller, "Erinnerung in Rechnitz—Mikrostudie über den Umgang mit Toten" [Remembrance in Rechnitz—micro study on dealing with the dead], in Walter Manoschek, Hg., *Der Fall Rechnitz: Das Massaker an Juden im März 1945* (Vienna: Braumüller, 2009), pp. 199–219.

Figure 2.5 The memorial park.

Just down the street a tourism office promotes visits to Geschriebenstein (Irrotkő in Hungarian), a nearby nature park that overlaps the border. Once part of the Batthyány family holdings, the forested hills are crowned by the highest peak in Burgenland, where an observation tower looks out over both countries. The tower straddles the border, and a 1922 border marker on the floor of the tower proves it. A set of panels inside the tower illustrates the history of the border and focuses on the "western Hungary uprising," the conflict just after World War I over the territory ceded to Austria. A group of memorial slabs in a rest area on the way up toward the peak dates from 1961 and remembers the dead of both wars and the uprising, as well as the Red Cross, Gendarmerie, Customs Service, and Burgenland fire brigade.

Figures 2.6 and 2.7 The tower and the memorial park at Geschriebenstein.

Because we had come to Rechnitz up Routes 63 and 56 from the border near Szombathely, we had already visited the Kreuzstadl about three kilometers south of town. This remainder of an abandoned farm outbuilding, whose cross-like shape can be seen from the air, sits on the former Batthyány family estate just east of the road from Szombathely, across the highway from a Billa supermarket. Between the ruins and the road and roughly parallel to both, a gash in the hillside contains an outdoor museum that contextualizes and narrates a chilling story.

Here, late on the night of March 24, 1945, three days before the Red Army arrived from the east, something terrible happened. The evening started innocently enough, given the circumstances, with a social gathering hosted by Margareta (Margit) von Batthyány, born Margareta Thyssen-Bornamisza. She shared her castle with the local SS office and a branch of the Organization Todt, which managed construction of the defenses on the eastern edge of the Reich, the so-called East Wall. With the war practically over and the Russians nearing, she brought together for a last fling 30 to 40 of her friends before packing up and joining the westward exodus. The guests were all local Nazi luminaries, among them party officials, SS officers, and construction managers. The group included the heads of two sections of East Wall fortification construction, Josef Muralter of Rechnitz II section and Franz Podezin of Rechnitz I. According to Eleonore Lappin, Podezin was already a known murderer, having shot to death the seven sick slave laborers who are interred in the Jewish cemetery.[5] Also present was Hans-Joachim Oldenburg, an employee of Thyssengas, one of the family's many industrial enterprises and manager of the estate. Ludwig Grol represented Kreisleiter [district leader] Eduard Nicka, who had his office in Oberwart. Six years younger than Tobias Portschy, Nicka also came from Unterschützen and attended the same schools. He had been Kreisleiter since the inception of the Nazi regime in the spring of 1938, except for a period of service in the Waffen-SS. Margit Batthyány had at least one lover, maybe more, among this group. The partygoers were not alone in the castle. Below, the cellars housed 600 Jewish slaves who worked on local fortifications.

5 Eleonore Lappin, "Das Massaker von Rechnitz im Zeitgeschichtlichen Kontext," in Gregor Holtzinger, ed., *Das Drama Südostwall am Beispiel Rechnitz: Daten, Taten, Fakten, Folgen*, Burgenländische Forschungen, Band 98 (Eisenstadt: 2009), p. 107.

Figure 2.8 The castle on a postcard mailed in 1922, shown from the southwest corner, looking north up the street.

These fortifications comprised part of the barrier that was to stretch from Bratislava to the north down to the southernmost limits of Austria and the river Drava. It was a lunatic enterprise from the beginning. Earthen tank traps and precast concrete firing positions shaped like giant eggs, fabricated by Soviet prisoners of war in a plant at Potzneusiedl [Lajtafalu] and wrestled into hand-dug holes by slave laborers, were never going to stop the onslaught of the Red Army, in Jelinek's words "a gigantic stream that makes a racket like a buffalo herd pounding on tin."[6] Even if that was not fully appreciated when the project started at the end of 1944, it must have been obvious by the last days of March 1945. But from the beginning of the undertaking, it was never clear whether the true objective was to build the wall or to consume the workforce through overwork, starvation, illness, exposure, and violent death. The two purposes seemed to exist in tension with each other.

6 Jelinek, *Rechnitz,* p. 65.

While the evening entertainment continued at the castle, 200 slave laborers were dumped at the Kreuzstadl, to spend the night in the open air. The emaciated and exhausted Jews had just been brought to Rechnitz, part of a train load of about 1,000 people assigned to work on the East Wall. These wretched prisoners had been designated as unfit for work even according to the lax standards of the Germans and Hungarians, neither of whom had serious qualms about working people to death. The slaves trudged up from the train station about a kilometer to the south of the Kreuzstadl and on the same side of the road.

The location of the railroad station well outside the town was a little unusual and reflected the kind of conflict that often took place when the railroad came to a frontier town. Entrenched interests resisted bringing the railroad into the center of town; modernizers demanded it. Such disputes are portrayed in the Hungarian film *Mágnás Miska* of 1949, a popular remake of a 1916 silent film by Alexander Korda, based in turn on the operetta of the same name by Károly Bakonyi and Ándor Gábor. In Rechnitz, tradition won out over innovation. The Rechnitz depot building, now vacant, was a pub when we first visited in 2014. It is at the *Gewerbepark* [business park], just north of the *Lagerhaus* [warehouse] and Genol petrol station, south of the recycling center across Route 56.

Around midnight on March 25, the two groups came together, the starving shivering slaves and the guests from the castle. Well and appropriately fortified, as Nobel laureate Jelinek wrote, with "blood sausage and shots of schnapps," the partygoers decided around midnight to go out to the Kreuzstadl and entertain themselves by killing some Jews.[7] The well-armed perpetrators made short work of the slaves. Stefan Beiglböck, a guest known for his viciousness, later claimed he killed six or seven himself. When the shooting stopped and burial pits were dug, they went back to the castle, maybe to resume socializing or for another bite of blood sausage, maybe to pack their bags for the flight west, joining the retreating stream of Nazis and their sympathizers. It is not clear whether Margit Batthyány joined

7 Jelinek, *Rechnitz*, p. 138.

them at the Kreutzstadl or waited at the castle for their return. Still, she came out of the appalling episode known as the "hostess of hell."[8]

The next day, the 20 forced laborers who dug the mass grave(s) were killed too and the deed was done. The coda came a few days later, when the castle, which British journalist David Litchfield called "a vast, grey-stoned Kafkaesque monolith," burned to the ground.[9] Whether the retreating Germans and their friends did it as they destroyed records documenting their tenure, or whether the Soviets did it during a three-day firefight as they took the town, cannot be ascertained.

The motive for this horrible act is hard to imagine. With the Russians so near and the war clearly lost, maybe the murderers intended to dispose of evidence to their monstrous project. Yet they surely knew that some victims and bystanders and even perpetrators would remain to bear witness to the futile brutality of East Wall construction. Whether or not they thought this through, the result was an act that became emblematic of the East Wall and of the treatment of Jews in Rechnitz. The local population dealt with this event by denial and silence, leading to the development of what came to be called the shame of Rechnitz, the double shame in fact, stemming from being the site of this crime and the refusal over the years to come to grips with it instead of obstructing the search for the burial site. It is hard to resist seeing Rechnitz as the murder capital of the Austrian side of the borderlands, the macabre sister city of Kőszeg (see chapter 3 below).

After 70 years of research, publicity, and lobbying, the site of the murder today has a suitable memorial. The outdoor monument and museum, completed with support from the Austrian state, the European Union (EU), and private donors, was dedicated on March 25, 2012. President Heinz Fischer presided over the opening and pledged support for efforts to locate the mass grave. Austria had come some distance from the time of

8 Gunnar Mertz, "Rechnitz in den Medien: Ein Massaker als Partyvergnugen," *Das Drama Südostwall am Beispiel Rechnitz,*,in Johannes Reiter, ed., *Ein Manter Des Schweigens* (Köln, Germany: Bohlau Verlag, 2022), p. 107.

9 David R. L. Litchfield, *The Thyssen Art Macabre* (London: Quartet Books, 2007), p. 45. Also see Sacha Batthyanyi, *A Crime in the Family* (New York: DaCapo Press, 2017).

President Körner and his pardon of Tobias Portschy in 1951. The museum includes objects from nearby Kőszeg excavations and the text of eyewitness interviews. It is strange to see an outdoor display that includes textiles, specifically a jacket worn by one of the slave workers, next to a Jewish star, as well as copies of maps and documents, photographs, and narrative text that are not under cover, but the objects are well protected in their cabinets and the location is fitting. The slaves were kept outside, exposed to the elements and the cruelty of those who exploited their labor. The memorial is appropriately outside as well. If visitors experience a little discomfort on that account, it is no more than symbolic of the outrage that took place here.

Inside the Kreuzstadl there is a monument designed by sculptor Karl Prantl. A Catholic Burgenlander, born in Pöttsching, Prantl designed two Jewish memorials in Vienna, one on the south side of St. Stephen's Cathedral and another at the Akademisches Gymnasium just outside the Schubert Ring and behind the Ritz Carlton. His Vienna installations are difficult to find, let alone comprehend, but the Kreutzstadl block is unambiguous. It bears a fragment from the book of Jeremiah (16:4): "You must die in a very agonizing way; you will not be mourned or buried." Since 1995, however, they have been regularly mourned. The Kreuzstadl has been the site of an annual March commemoration organized by the Vienna or Graz Jewish communities with a delegation from the Jewish community from across the Hungarian border in Zalaegerség (Zala County) attending.

In the summer of 2017, it seemed possible that the burial site might have been definitively identified, at the west end of a field across the road from the massacre scene. By then Rechnitz had had a humane, decent mayor named Engelbert Kenyeri, now retired, who like many in Burgenland had a Magyar family name but spoke no Hungarian, and who was determined to try to wash away the town's collective guilt. He and anesthesiologist Dr. Gábor Vadász, whose father and uncle were among those killed at Kreutzstadl, led the effort to ascertain the location of the burials, found an aerial photograph made by the Americans, and determined the GPS coordinates that led ultimately to what seemed to be the probable location. At the end of October, an archaeological team was being assembled to verify the discovery. Vadász personally does not think disinterment is a good idea, that nothing would be gained by exhuming skulls and bones.

The goals are to verify the location, erect a proper monument, and get an apology from the Austrian state.

Three years before the possible discovery was announced, during our visit to Szombathely in April 2014, Irene and I met Sándor Markusz, the head of the tiny Jewish community, in his office at the synagogue on Batthyány Square. Before we departed, Irene asked Mr. Markusz whether there were any particular events or people that he would like to see covered in our book. He said there was one in particular: he wanted us to record the location of the mass grave at Rechnitz, where the remains of the 200 Jewish slave laborers had been dumped in the spring of 1945, something nobody in the town wanted to talk about. In the autumn of 2017, it seemed possible that this long-standing question might be solved, but by the end of November only traces of more tank traps and infantry trenches had been found, no more, not yet.[10] Another year of digging turned up little more than additional shell casings and fragments of barbed wire. The mass grave has yet to be discovered.[11] Nevertheless, these things do have a way of ultimately coming out, even in Strudelgau.

10 By the spring of 2018, Dr. Vadâsz speculated that the Soviets might have moved the bodies back across the Hungarian border to the town of Bozsok, where there were known to be other mass graves of Hungarian forced laborers. Why they might have gone to that trouble is not clear. János Pelle, "Áldozatok nyomában," *Élet és Irodalom*, 62 (April 20, 2018).

11 For a summary of efforts to find the mass grave, including the most recent excavations, see Szilvia Pais-H, "Hiába kutatták megint Rohoncon a brutális lemészárolt 180 magyar zsidó tömegsírjait – 16-odszor is teljes a kudarc," <www.nyugat.hu>, March 12, 2019.

CHAPTER 3

# Kőszeg: Murder capital of the Hungarian side

Kőszeg, almost up against the Austrian border and in the hills leading to the Geschriebenstein Nature Park, is known largely for an epic battle and campaign from 1532 to 1536, which slowed the Turks on their way to Vienna. With more than 12,000 residents, Kőszeg is the fifth largest town on the Hungarian side, smaller than Győr, Szombathely, Sopron, and Mosonmagyraróvár, and barely larger than Csorna. Like Sopron, Kőszeg was close enough to the border for the Communist regime to discourage economic expansion and population growth. It has grown only a little since 1940, when it had about 10,000 residents.

It was in Kőszeg that Irene and I concluded in 1996 that we might be able to live in Hungary. We came on a day trip from a conference in Vienna to view the site of the siege. As impressive as the fort was, we were more taken with the presence of a train station and an American Express office. We still argue about which of us saw the light first, but we boarded the bus for what turned out to be a pálinka- and Tokay-drenched lunch in Szombathely convinced that we could find a retirement home here.

By that time, Kőszeg was more than a post-Trianon border town. It had a reputation as a vacation destination, known for its spas and schools. A recently published Vas County guidebook called *Kőszeg a Treasure Chest of History and Natural Beauty*, says nothing about the town's synagogue, ghetto, labor service camps, mass graves, and memorials, or the Soviet occupation, the Border Guard training center of the Cold War period, and the closed border itself. Others have noted the prevalence of right-wing conservative political and social views. Parish priest László Székely commented in his diary in 1944 about the attraction to Hungarian-style Nazism: "Arrow Cross supporters are numerous, maybe more in our city than elsewhere."[1] The majority of the most prosperous residents were Christians, even before the deportation of the town Jews in 1944.

1 Székely quoted in Horváth Ferenc and L. Kiss Csaba, *Végjáték a határon: Kőszeg 1944–1945* (Szülőföld Könyvkiado, 2015), pp. 10–11, 16.

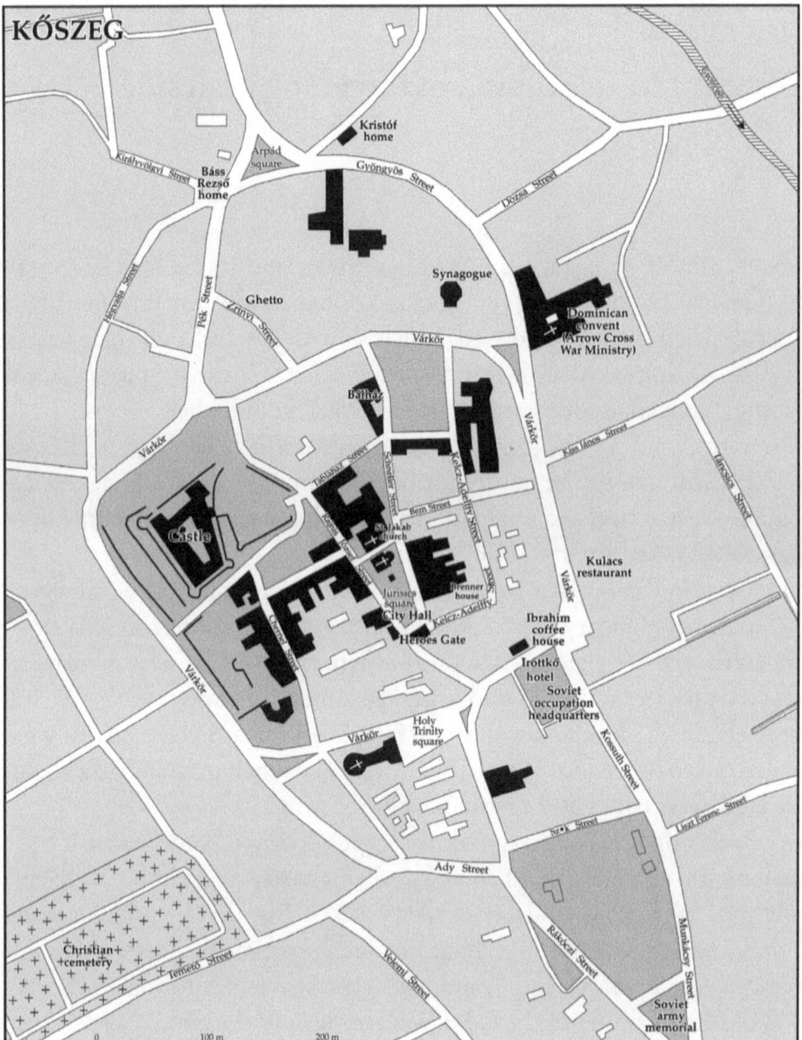


Figure 3.1 Kőszeg [Map 4].

Writer Agota Kristof (1935–2011), who was born nearby in Csikvánd in Győr-Moson-Sopron County, went to elementary school in Kőszeg. According to an interview with her brother Jenő, her family moved there in the summer of 1944, when their father became a professor in the teacher training school. The family lived at Árpád tér 12 on the north side of town. While she was aware of Kőszeg's murderous past, she never lost her fondness for the community, which she considered the most beautiful in the world. But the physical setting was not everything. She left in the wake of the 1956 revolution with her husband (and former history teacher) and their baby, settled in French-speaking Neuchâtel, Switzerland, and ultimately flourished there as a writer in French. When she died, she was buried in the Kőszeg town cemetery, on Temető Street southwest of the town center. Her grave is in the outer row on the northern edge of the cemetery.

Kristof sited much of her trilogy, *The Great Notebook*, here. Her story of twin boys surviving without conventional family support during the last days of World War II pulled few punches. The novel and the acclaimed 2013 film version called *The Notebook* drew from her experience. One powerful scene, which she recalled from her childhood, shows bedraggled Jewish slave laborers being marched past her home. The Kristof family's domestic servant reaches out of the window and offers a piece of bread to a starving man. He reaches for the bread, but the girl pulls it back and shuts the window. In both the novel and the film, the twins exact a bloody retribution for the servant girl's viciousness. It must be noted that there is no known family connection between Agota Kristof and a far more famous British crime writer with a similar name.

The Jewish cemetery lies beyond the Christian cemetery near the southwestern edge of the city. My visit in April 2017 reminded me of an earlier excursion to Csepreg in Győr-Moson-Sopron County. An Australian acquaintance and I asked a store clerk for directions to the Jewish burial site. She said it was behind the *rendes temető*, the normal Christian cemetery. So it was in Kőszeg, well beyond the normal cemetery and not even contiguous, on the corner of Károly Mihaly. The gate is locked, and the key is available from the office at the Christian cemetery. The grounds are overwhelmed with trees, ivy, and moss. There are individual Holocaust memorials inside and a monument that commemorates the Jewish community. It is the only place in town where the names of those who were killed are listed, and it is safely out of sight and out of mind, unlike the memorials to soldiers killed in action during the same war, which are visible in the town center at Jurisics Square.

According to the city's official home page, there is no apparent connection between Kőszeg, World War II, and the systematic murder of Hungarian Jews. After World War I and the signing of the much-loathed Treaty of Trianon, Kőszeg gradually revived as a center of education and began to draw foreign visitors. Otherwise, nothing much happened until after the Second War, when development stopped and the Communists shut the border. Those who faced the daunting task of restoring a normal life to Kőszeg after the war, well knew what had transpired and would perhaps even understand why an observer might come to call Kőszeg the murder capital of the Hungarian side of the borderlands. In fact, Mayor Endre Gyöngyös, presiding at a meeting of the town's general assembly on June 15, 1945, expressed concerns about such an outcome. He reported, according to minutes of the meeting:

> "With a sad heart, I have to report that they brought to Kőszeg thousands of labor-service Jews. With a sad heart because, if not yet, then soon our city will become the center of a national scandal, because—let's speak plainly—they killed about 2,000 Jews here. These are buried here, and if the Katyn episode became an international scandal, then there will at least be a national scandal out of this."

Among themselves, city fathers blamed the slowness of rehabilitation funds for the town on influential Communist officials of Jewish origin. These government functionaries were thought to be punishing the city by blocking and constricting sources of money in retribution for the horrible things done to Jews of the city during the late war. Decimated though they had been, the Jews were still considered powerful enough to retaliate. In any case, Gyöngyös overestimated the ability of the Jewish catastrophe to cause outrage in Hungary. Tourism started to pick up in the 1970s, around the time that Kristof started to come back to town regularly, and a new age opened with the dismantling of the Iron Curtain.[2]

2 "Kőszeg története," <http://www.Koszeg.hu/Koszeg tortenelem>, accessed November 20, 2014; Ferenc and Csaba, *Végjáték a határon: Kőszeg 1944–1945*, pp. 146, 153. The Katyn episode refers to the murder in 1940 of more than 20,000 Polish officers and intellectuals in the Katyn forest and elsewhere after the Soviet occupation of eastern Poland the preceding year.

From a table at the Ibrahim coffeehouse at Fő tér [Main Square] 17, Kőszeg shows a charming face. Brutalist Communist architecture is nowhere to be seen, the square itself is off limits to vehicular traffic, and quiet prevails. Inside the Ibrahim, founded in 1988 and set in a row of picturesque storefronts, the small round tables provide an intimate setting, and the service is accommodating. There is home-made ice cream, a tasty Somlyói galuska, and Hausbrandt coffee, stronger than at the Claudia in Szombathely, where they use the same brand. Eccentric touches include the washbasin faucet shaped like a coiled cobra, head raised and hood flared, ready to strike.

Outside, under an umbrella on the square, you face across the plaza to the window of room 214, the last room on the right on the second floor of the Irottkő Hotel, Agota Kristof's favorite lodging place after the hotel opened in 1972. Once the site of the Elit Restaurant, which until 1957 served as a social club for Soviet officers of the occupation force, the Irottkő lobby displays a framed color map of Hungary in 1942 above the fireplace. The map shows Hungary at its largest in the century since the dismemberment of 1920. It includes areas Hungary took back from the Czechs (1938), Romania (1940), and Yugoslavia (1941) under agreements imposed by Germany. Tourists from Romania, and the successor states of Serbia and Slovakia may find the map provocative or merely amusing, assuming any come to town. The formal documents covering the return of northern Hungary and part of Transylvania are still called "accords" in Hungary and "diktats" by the losing states, just as the Treaty of Trianon remains a "diktat" in Hungary. Kristof said she could look out from her room to the stationery store that was featured in her novel, and in fact some old-timers say the Ibrahim occupies the very spot. It certainly offers a strategic position from which to consider the twentieth century and the city's approach to memorialization. There are important places, marked and otherwise, in every direction, within half a kilometer of the coiled snake inside the coffeehouse.

Figure 3.2 Under the awning at the Ibrahim. The room at the top right is 214.

Almost right at the eastern corner of the main square, where it bends around to the left and heads north, is the Kulacs Restaurant at Várkör number 12. The restaurant was already closed when we looked inside the door in 2014, but the symbol of the establishment, a *kulacs* or donut-shaped wine canteen, still hung over the door three years later. During the latter days of the Arrow Cross regime, Minister of Cults Kálmán Hubay, latter executed as a war criminal, liked to guzzle wine with his friends there. Postwar Communist politicians liked the place as well, and the local party organization met for dinner there two years later.

The Kulacs is best known these days as the site of an oft-told Cold War–era story regarding border enforcement. In 1967, a middle-aged man from Nográd County along the Slovak border to the northeast made his way westward, determined to escape to Austria. Under cover of darkness, he reached the barbed wire fence near Kőszeg, cut his way through, followed the patrol road through the mine field, and strode into the next town. "I did it! Everybody is my guest!" he shouted as he entered a pub at the edge of town. But he had not made it. He had cut the wire and picked his way across a training field at the border guard garrison on the north side of Kiss János Street just east of Kőszeg and walked into the Kulacs and the arms of the border guards, becoming one of the estimated 90 percent of aspiring crossers who failed to make it.

Just south of the corner formed by the eastern end of the main square, on Kossuth Street, at number 10, is the building that housed the headquarters of the Soviet military occupation. For officers assigned there, it was convenient to the Elit on the square. Nowadays, it faces the local office of the Vas County government and holds a local court. Farther south on Kossuth, after it becomes Munkácy, is the triangular park with the Soviet war memorial. The current monument, designed by Endre András Tornay, was dedicated in 1985 and is the third one on the site. The first, installed in July 1945, was replaced a year later to accommodate the names of additional combat casualties, soldiers who had been hospitalized and died after the first memorial was dedicated. The second lasted until the mid-1980s. The names of 122 soldiers killed in action in the vicinity are inscribed on the tablet embedded in the ground. Until 1989, the memorial was the site of an annual liberation day ceremony. The northern side of the triangular park with the Soviet obelisk, once the location of the Gesztenye [Chestnut] restaurant, known as the best eatery in town, is now home to the Hong Kong department store, one of the Chinese retail businesses that have appeared in towns throughout the region.

Munkácsy merges into Rákóczi at the southern tip of the park and continues south to the train station, site of the deportation of the Jews in June 1944. The intersection is the site of a well-known photograph from the collection of Yad Vashem in Jerusalem, used in Steven Spielberg's book *The Final Days*, which accompanied the film of the same name. The picture, one of a series capturing the deportations from Kőszeg, shows gendarmes taking the town's Jews from the ghetto, down Munkácsy to Rákóczi Ferenc Street (barely visible on the left). The walk is about 1.2 kilometers (about three-quarters of a mile) through the heart of town, not much of a stroll unless you are being driven out of your hometown, with your household goods on your back. They were destined for the collection ghetto in Szombathely, and then in a few days for Auschwitz. In the foreground a man rides by on a bicycle. It is an encounter between two worlds, one approximating normality, albeit in wartime, and another far from it.[3]

3 The image is accessible at <http://talkinghouseseurope.com/wp-content/uploads/2018/01/kep-4_2_3-b.jpg>, accessed May 7, 2018. For other pictures from the series, see Tim Cole, *Traces of the Holocaust: Journeying in and out of the Ghettos* (London: Continuum, 2011), pp. 94–5.

About a quarter kilometer down the road after Munkácsy joins Rákóczi, halfway to the depot and about 50 meters to the east off Sánc Street, is Petőfi Square, now dominated by a football field. There is a bread factory on the west side, on the former site of city outbuildings that once housed slave laborers. More prominent on the west side of Rákóczi is the former Huszár garrison. From the beginning of World War II, the complex served as headquarters for the huge Third Hungarian Army General Purpose Labor Service Battalion command group and cadre. The yellow main building stretches between Gábor Áron and Rohonci Streets. Rechnitz is across the border about 20 kilometers (12 miles) away and was the massacre site discussed in chapter 2 above. As the murder capitals of their respective sides of the border, Rechnitz and Kőszeg might be considered the twin cities of the region.

Figure 3.3 The main building of the garrison from Rákóczi Street, on a postcard published in 1936.

Kőszeg was an important labor service center throughout World War II. The labor service [*Munkaszolgalat*] had been established on May 5, 1939, as part of the Hungarian army. Jewish men, from that date banned from regular military service, as well as Romani, members of Christian pacifist sects, and political enemies, were conscripted as laborers. They served without uniforms or weapons, often exposed to the most severe hardships and greatest risks. Nine battalions were distributed throughout Hungary, each divided at full strength into four 250-man companies and in turn into sections. On December 2, 1940, the Jewish labor service battalion of 600 arrived in Kőszeg and was put on road construction. There were five subsequent mass augmentations. In fact, many thousands of labor service men worked or passed through the town before the start of fortification construction in the late autumn of 1944, as the town became the intake center for the Third Military Region as well as administrative headquarters for the battalion. Conscripts lived in the garrison itself, and under extremely primitive conditions in wooden barracks, some built as vacation facilities for employees of the state railroad MAV, and others in barracks in the Hámori woods. They were used to cut trees, repair roads, and build tank obstacles and firing positions. On July 5, 1944, the formation moved from the city itself and remained scattered in nearby camps.

The Third Battalion was a huge organization that controlled thousands of Jewish slave laborers, both men and women. Initially, Jewish men taken for labor service were assembled at the Rákóczi Street barracks for transport elsewhere. Late in the war, when construction started on the East Wall fortifications that the Germans planned for the entire border of their empire, Kőszeg was inundated with these workers, and slaves assigned to the battalion were distributed to several locations in and around Kőszeg, where they were kept under primitive conditions. These included the grounds of two brick factories on the southeast side of the city, a brewery to the north, and the Gulner mill along Gyöngyos Creek southeast of town. But the center of the operation remained the Rákóczi Street garrison.

Back at the corner of the main square and Kossuth, where the Várkör or ring road starts its loop around the historic town, and directly across from the Kulacs site at number 27 is the former location of Organization Todt. The building had been the home of Jewish merchant Hugo Kopfstein. Named for its founder, Fritz Todt, this agency managed engineering and construction projects for the Third Reich. Its presence in Kőszeg, unmarked today, indicates the importance of the town in the distribution of slave labor for construction of the East Wall defenses roughly along the border between Hungary and Austria, which was then part of the Reich. The building now houses a dental office and a "National Tobacco Store," part of a chain of identical shops operated under franchises granted by the government. The shops monopolize tobacco sales, and sell alcoholic beverages, coffee, sundries, and newspapers. Intended to combat tax fraud, they also hearken back to the state capitalism of the Communist years and reflect the centralizing tendencies of the current government.

Behind the shop, at number 6 on parallel Kelcz-Adelffy, the Brenner House, owned by the Roman Catholic Church, housed some of the slave laborers deployed along the border, although most of them were kept at locations outside of the city. The Church still owns the building, in which I made a presentation to a local group, the *polgári kaszino* [citizens' club], in the autumn of 2017. I had been invited to talk about my experiences in the Pentagon during the terrorist attack of September 2001. I was not accustomed to making presentations with a crucifix on the wall behind my back in a building that had once been used as a resting place for Jewish slaves, but the talk went well, once I discovered that my interpreter was not up to the task, and I had to do it in Hungarian.

Back on Várkör, the road goes north about 250 meters from the Kulacs and the Todt sites before it bends to the left toward three sites relevant to the destruction of the Jewish community. At the bend, the street that continues straight north is called Gyöngyös and leads to Árpád Square, the location of the Kristof residence (number 12) and the home of veterinarian Resző Bass (number 13, but diagonally across the square from the Kristof home), leader of the Jewish community until he was murdered at Auschwitz. The first Kőszeg stumble stone installed by Gunter Demnig is in front of the house. Since 2011, the location has been the site of an annual May 11 memorial observance of the ghettoization.

As the Várkör turns westward toward the synagogue and the ghetto, it passes the Dominican convent and school. This became the home of the Arrow Cross ministry of war after the government fled the Red Army's

Figure 3.4 The Brenner House and the historical marker. It is all about the architecture and the music school.

advance toward Budapest. Right after the bend to the west, on the north side of the street, is the synagogue, which was built in 1858–9. Fülöp Schey (1798–1881), a local entrepreneur (Kőszeg Broadcloth and Tweed Factory Association) and supplier to the Imperial Army, who headed the Jewish community during 1870–4 and became personal banker to Archduke Albrecht, financed the construction. Emperor Franz Joseph elevated Schey to the nobility, making him the first Jewish Hungarian so honored.

The synagogue, inactive after the deportation, came under state ownership and city custodianship in 1970. After 25 years, the complex, which included a ritual bath and a rabbi's house on the right along the path from the gate to the temple, the synagogue itself at the end of the path, and the schoolroom and teacher's house on the left, fell into private hands and is now only visible through a locked gate. When we first visited the site, it was possible to read something about the compound on a computer-printed sheet inside a window of the school building, but the rectangular space with four screw holes at the corners, clearly at one time the location of a memorial tablet, was empty. The tablet had been removed and only its outline remained. Since then, the memorial has been replaced twice. Clearly, affixing a memorial to a wall does not assure its permanence.

Across the street from the synagogue and a little farther to the west, past the Balház on the corner of Schneller István Street where the Arrow Cross held its Christmas 1944 celebration, Zrinyi Miklós Street branches north to Pék [Baker] Street and Árpád Square, the location of the Bass and Kristof homes. Zrinyi number 8 became the ghetto where Jews were held until their deportation. This community was not particularly large, numbering 95people in 1944. Originally the street was named Tyuk [Hen] Street because the poultry market was located there. In 1896, the city council renamed it in memory of Fülöp Schey, recognizing Schey's role in town development. The house had been occupied by the Schey family from the third quarter of the eighteenth century, was attacked by anti-Semites during an 1848 rampage, then became an orphans' boarding school in 1912. Later it was sold to the Deutsch family. The property included the Deutsch residence and the warehouse of the Futura grain company.

In the spring of 1944, the mayor designated the property, which included the Deutsch home and the grain warehouse, as the ghetto for Jews in the Irottkő district of Vas County. By that time, the anti-Jewish laws prohibited Jewish commercial activity, so the Deutsch family only occupied the home, while the new Christian owners ran the Futura firm. The courtyard and wings of the house were already surrounded by a continuous brick wall of adequate height; the only wall construction necessary was across the Schey Street facade, built two meters high and one half-meter thick. The compound's single gate faced Schey Street. The Jews were taken there on May 10 and 11. Doctors warned on May 25 of potential epidemics in the crowded ghetto, especially typhus. Fearing the spread to the general population, the Interior Ministry sent serum with which 107 were inoculated. On June 12, men fit for labor service were removed from the ghetto; six days later the remaining Jews were marched to the train station and shipped to Szombathely. They were deported by train to Auschwitz on July 4. After the Jews were removed, so was the Schey name, and the street got its current name.

A marble memorial tablet installed in April 1970 to the left of the massive double-door entrance gate, makes it clear that something terrible happened there. The tablet says, "In memory of the victims of Nazism who in 1944–5 lived in our city and died." It does not mention that the victims were Jewish or that there were Hungarians among the Nazis who persecuted them: left unsaid is that the site was a ghetto, that it had been selected by the mayor, and that Hungarian police had taken the Jews there. Even that watered-down text turned out to be too much for some people. The plaque has been repeatedly scrubbed as if by an eraser, defacing the text so it is extremely hard to read. This is not easy to do with marble and is clearly no accident. Like the disappearing wall plaque at the synagogue, the condition of the marker reminds us that affixing a memorial to a wall does not guarantee permanence.

It remained unreadable through the spring of 2017. At that time, the compound inside the gate contained small public housing units, and laundry hung from informal drying racks in the courtyard. Two women who lived there at the time seemed satisfied by the residences. One was particularly pleased that she had her own bathroom with a tub in it. She didn't know what the tablet at the entrance said—it was after all hard to read—but she thought it had something to do with Jews. Surprisingly the marker has since been cleaned. In the spring of 2018, we were surprised to find that the tablet was clearly legible. All that is now required is that it actually tell the story of what happened to whom and who carried out the project.

Figure 3.5 Can you read this?

This style of memorialization, which did not name the victims while purporting to commemorate their tragedy, can be seen elsewhere in Kőszeg and in the country at large. It can be seen east of town at the (slave) labor service memorial on the east side of Route 87 just south of Kórház (hospital) Street, provided that you can find the memorial to begin with. In fact, this "soft-core Holocaust denial," as Deborah Lipstadt called it, is not particularly remarkable in Hungary. Almost 50 years after installation of the ghetto tablet, however, it made the leap to the United States. The presidential proclamation marking International Holocaust Remembrance Day, issued annually since 2006 on the date of the Allied liberation of Auschwitz (January 27), for the first time neglected to mention that Jews comprised by far the most persistently pursued and the largest category of victims, or to note the pervasive anti-Semitism that led to the catastrophe.[4]

From the ghetto site, the western side of the Várkör leads back to the main square, the Heart of Jesus Roman Catholic Church, and the Ibrahim. But before going back for another coffee or maybe something stronger, it is worthwhile to turn north onto József Rájnis Street and go through the Heroes Gate to Jurisics Square. The left (west) side of the gate, facing a tablet in memory of the defenders of the town during the Turkish assault, bears a panel with the names of nearly 240 Hungarian soldiers who were killed during World War I. Another text commemorates the Kőszeg citizens who died in World War II, military and civilian, whether in combat or in bombing raids, worked to death and starved or as a result of deportation and murder, in the country and elsewhere, without reference to how or why they fell. This common practice in Hungary obscures the differences between the deaths of armed uniformed soldiers and noncombatants of all kinds, including those deported to their deaths because they were Jewish or Romani. Soldiers killed in action during the war are named on another tablet, on a side wall of St. Jakab Roman Catholic Church, farther inside the square.

The big attraction though is the city hall at number 8 just inside the arch on the left (west). The building is on a site thought to be the location

4 *Washington Post*, January 28, 2017. The quoted phrase is from the *Post* editorial of January 31, 2017.

of the oldest city hall in the country. The frescoes go back to the early seventeenth century, and blend with the gaudy Biedermeier appearance that dates from about 1820. Two works in the courtyard are by local sculptor Endre András Tornay, designer of the Soviet war memorial in front of the Chinese department store.

In the first week of June 1919, Dr. József Halász, who had changed his name from Hirschler, a World War I veteran and a functionary in the Hungarian Soviet Republic, was beaten in front of the entrance, then imprisoned in the cellar along with other supporters of the Kún government. The counterrevolutionary crowd screamed for him and the others to be thrown from the building's windows so they could work their way with the prisoners, but soldiers from the cavalry garrison saved them, shooting some political opponents while doing so. Miklós Éberling Nagy, leader of the local rightists, fled westward to Austria.

Tensions festered after the signing of the Trianon Treaty. The presence of members of the international commission marking the border, along with security forces that protected them, helped restore calm, but the situation remained uneasy. Halász was ultimately arrested, tried, and convicted of murder. After one year in prison, he was deported to the Soviet Union. Kőszeg remained a center of legitimist sentiment, hoping for a Habsburg restoration, and troops had to be called out after the Hungarian army beat back supporters of Charles IV at Budaörs in October 1921. Finally, Admiral Horthy, the head of state, came to Kőszeg in December 1922 and appeared before the city council. Only then did calm return to the city.

Miklós Éberling Nagy returned. By 1933, with his right-wing sympathies evolving into unabashed support of Hitler and the Third Reich, he was appointed by the local council as mayor of the city. After Hungary abrogated a treaty of friendship with Yugoslavia and joined the Germans in a 1941 invasion, the government in Budapest appointed Éberling Nagy mayor in newly occupied Novi Sad, Ujvidék to the Hungarians. He presided over the city during the massacre of Serbs and Jews in January 1942. After the war he fled again, was captured, and brought back. The Tito government executed him as a war criminal.

Fittingly for a town that qualifies as the murder capital of the Hungarian side, at least six other future war criminals spoke at city hall during the war.

These included Prime Minister Béla Imredy (1939) and three cabinet ministers in 1944, Ándor Jaross (Interior), Minister of War Károly Beregfy, and Foreign Minister Gábor Kemény. Ferenc Szálasi himself in 1942, two years before he became head of state, and his deputy minister, Jenő Szöllősi, in 1945 rounded out the group. A seventh, Endre László in the Ministry of the Interior, oversaw the execution of anti-Jewish decrees and directed the police and gendarmes in ghettoization and deportation. When he attended a 1944 church service in the village of Bozsok southwest of town and the priest prayed for peace, László leaped to his feet and shouted that the prayer should be for victory. And Kálmán Hubay, who entertained his cronies with wine at the Kulacs, was another who hitched his star to the Nazi cause and was later executed.

This survey of the marked and unmarked sites inside the city does not provide a complete picture of the twentieth-century catastrophe. Some of the major sites are outside of town, beyond the train station to the south or Árpád Square to the north. Two of them, the 1956 memorial and the Trianon Cross to the north are easy to find. The Trianon Cross towers over the city from a little more than a kilometer beyond Árpád Square. The cross is visible for miles on the other side of the border, which is so near that the whole area was in the prohibited zone during the Cold War. This is probably why the cross was not dismantled by the Communist regime.

The border fence that kept visitors from approaching the Trianon monument, could be useful as a garden fence. When they rolled up the fence in 1989, they also opened access to the gardens that abutted the border. One woman's hens took the newly available option to depart and left her without eggs. She wrote the authorities and asked them to please reestablish the Iron Curtain.

The route to the Trianon monument, and it is a monument—anything that stands eight meters tall on a hilltop is nothing less—leads up Sziget út to a fork where Meskó út goes off to the right and Kálvária utca goes to the left. Meskó út, which becomes Kethelyi út before merging into Route 87, leads directly toward the old brewery, visible across 87 to the north. The brewery was one of the dilapidated places used as nighttime resting places for Jewish slave laborers. Just beyond the fork with Meskó, after a tiny triangular park divides it from Kálvária, the latter becomes a pedestrian trail, eroded by runoff from the top of the hill, and winds its way up past sheltered sculptures along the right side marking the stations of the cross toward the Kálvária church. Before the first station is reached, there is the entrance on the left to the bunker dug into the hillside where the crown of Szent István was stored for 10 days at the end of World War II by its Arrow Cross guardians. The Szálasi government was then in its final days before fleeing to its congenial home in what was left of Nazi Germany. Entrance to the bunker is possible, but it is not clear what the hours of accessibility are. The entrance fee was 300 forints in 2015, just over one dollar at that time. The tiny chapels illustrating the stations of the cross along the 400-meter trail to the church were the work of stone mason Georg Schweitzer in 1763. The path leads generally northwestward into the once inaccessible border area. During those bad old days, innocent mushroom gatherers who forgot themselves would quickly find themselves looking at the hooves of a horse, then up at the border guard in the saddle.

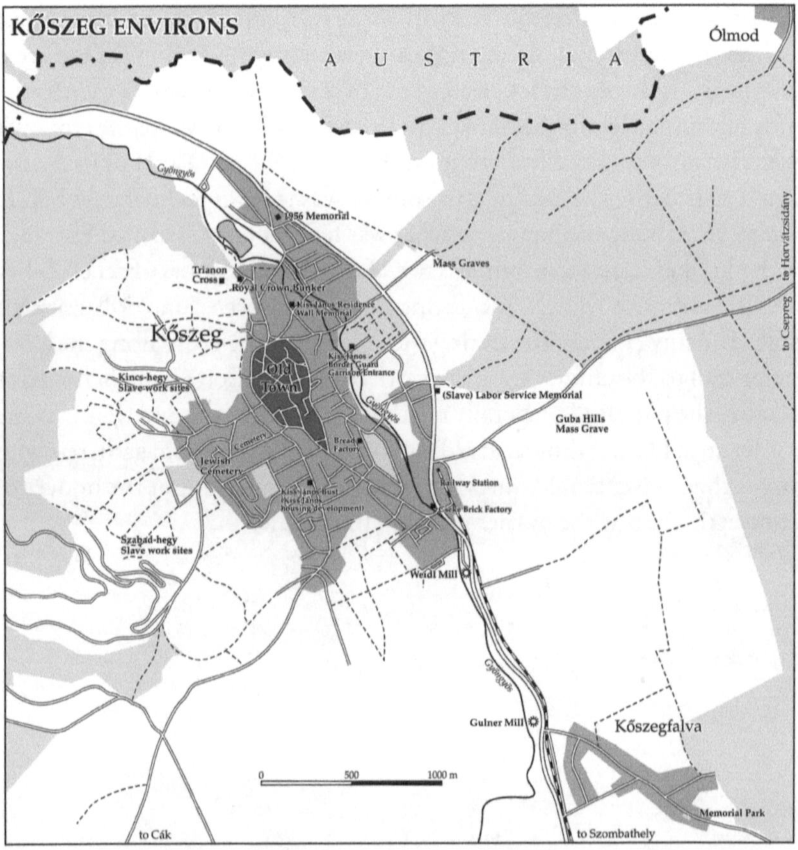


Figure 3.6 Kőszeg environs [Map 5].

The Kálvária church, formally named the Glorification of the Holy Cross Kálvária Church, was designed in the 1890s by Ludwig Schöne, the architect of the synagogue in Szombathely. There has been a Roman Catholic religious structure on the top of the hill since at least 1715, when a plague monument was erected, followed a few years later by a chapel. The hill is the highest in the immediate area, 20 meters above the site of the Trianon Cross. As the old adage goes, the army and the church habitually got the best real estate.

Beyond the church the path forks at a sign indicating a protected natural area, a "Tajvédelmi Körzet." The right side leads to the Trianon Cross, no more than 200 meters ahead. The cross was first intended to commemorate the 400th anniversary of the Turkish siege that started in 1532, but Endre Gyöngyös, then the deputy town clerk, suggested dedicating it instead to the memory of the universally loathed Treaty of Trianon and placing it where it could be seen from territories severed from Hungary and assigned to Austria. The monument was emplaced in its current location in 1936 but cut off from visitors when the Communists created the militarized border strip. It has been accessible since 1989 and was renovated in 1993. The base of the cross includes a tablet in memory of the "martyr" Miklós Nagy, who was mayor when the cross was erected and later hanged as a war criminal.

The Austrians responded with a cross of their own. They erected a monument to the Treaty of Saint Germain, the part of the post–World War I settlement that created the small Republic of Austria out of the remnants of the Empire, installing it right at the border, on a higher hill, where the chestnuts are said to be plentiful in the autumn, and in view of the Hungarian cross. The structure itself is not nearly as tall and is hidden during the warm months by a canopy of trees, but it is a reminder that the Austrians too considered themselves victims, deprived of their glorious stature at the end of the war. As the bullet holes on the Austrian side of the Trianon Cross suggest, individual Austrians may not have been particularly impressed with the case for Hungarian victimization.

It may be possible to visit the cross in about half an hour, walking briskly up the hill from the bunker where the crown was briefly hidden to the monument itself and back. But the wildflowers are many, the view into the valleys on the Austrian side is beautiful, and the historical circumstances leave something to ponder. So the visitor should allow time to look around and ponder what is represented both explicitly and implicitly.

The 1956 memorial is easier to reach. It is on Route 87, just before the border crossing at Rattersdorf, and designed by Endre András Tornay. The sculpture stands near the location of the first advance into the territory of the Third Reich by Soviet forces in the spring of 1945, northward across the border toward Klostermarienburg. The Soviets returned in November

1956. Their tanks covered the Rattersdorf crossing from the Hungarian side as they staunched the outward flow of refugees. Brigadier Nikolaus Horvath of the Austrian army was part of a four-man jeep patrol at the border when the T-34s approached from the Kőszeg side:

> Soviet soldiers sprang out of the tanks and drove the disarmed Hungarians towards the interior of the country. They watched us, the T-34s heading for cover and spinning their turrets. Then it was night. Just behind the Hungarian border you heard loud men's voices, children's whines, dogs barking, flares rose high, short bursts of gunfire. Presumably they caught refugees. I was filled with anger—not being able to help.[5]

Visitors who approach the 1956 memorial via Meskó Street up from Sziget and follow it as it bends to the left into Kéthelyi út go right past Bajcsy-Zsilinsky Street, named after the best known of the few overt opponents of the pro-Nazi authoritarian regimes of World War II, Endre Bajcsy-Zsilinsky. Retired Lieutenant General János Kiss, the leading military *resistant*, lived at number 18 on the street that bears Bacsy-Zsilinsky's name, until the Arrow Cross hanged him at Kőhida prison outside Sopron in 1945. Kiss had been a judge on the court that had convicted the senior perpetrators of the Ujvidék [Novi Sad] massacre in January 1942, four of whom had been released on their own recognizance before sentencing and then fled the country. They returned with the Germans in 1944, got their revenge on Kiss, and fled at the end of the war. Ultimately, they were brought back, tried, convicted, and executed. There is an appropriate plaque on the front wall of Kiss's former home. Kiss is also remembered at the border guard garrison that bears his name, at a housing development south of downtown with a bust statue at Velemi Street 34, and with an imposing crypt at the cemetery.

The village of Velem, about seven kilometers southwest of town, has important sites from the last days of the Arrow Cross regime. The Stirling villa on Rákóczi Street, at the intersection with Petőfi, near the top of the hill

5 Quoted in Tamara Scheer and Erwin A. Schmidl, "Der Einsatz des Bundesheeres im Spatherbst 1956 zum Schutz der Grenze," in Wolfgang Etschmann, Tamara Scheer, and Erwin A. Schmidl, eds., *An Der Grenze: Der erste des Einrückungstermin des Bundesheeres und der Einsatz während der Ungarnkrise 1956* (Graz: Vehling Verlag GmbH, 2006), p. 160.

and across the street from the town hall, was the regime's last headquarters. Behind the villa, the bunker in the hillside held the holy crown during the Arrow Cross's presence there. The bunker has a wooden historical marker as well as wreaths and flowers in front of it. The villa has nothing, although in 2014 a poster indicating it was a stop on the Iron Curtain Trail still adorned an outside wall by the door. A city employee occupies an apartment in the otherwise empty villa, and the grounds are used for an annual autumn chestnut festival, as well as for meetings of Hungarian wood carvers.

South and east of Kőszeg, numerous places have connections with the use of slave laborers in and around the town. The most noteworthy memorial, not clearly visible from the road and without any signage indicating its presence, is at the site of the Szabó Construction Materials Company. During World War II, Jewish slave laborers were kept here, at what was a brick factory. The monument is east of town and just to the left (east) off Route 87, behind two large bushy pine trees. If you find the monument, you will see that it refers to 2,400 *Hungarian* victims of fascism, once again obscuring the fact that these slaves were murdered because they were not considered Hungarians but Jews. Originally, when the city and the surviving anti-fascists erected the monument in 1985, the text read "To the memory of the victims of the war and fascism, 1939–45." It did not mention that the Hungarian slave-laborer victims were Jewish or that the fascist executioners probably included Hungarians.

The Anti-Fascist Association represented the survivors among the young left-wing opponents of the wartime regime, as well as a national myth about an active resistance. A minor irritant at best to the dominant pro-German consensus, opposition figures had included the poet János László Nemeth, as well as the Bajcsy-Zsilinsky and local hero János Kiss.[6] This marker briefly survived the visit of historian Mária Schmidt, later director of the short-lived House of Terror Museum in Budapest, who expressed her

6 Lieutenant Colonel Alfred Trenker, who commanded the Gestapo element in Budapest, brushed off the resistance as practically irrelevant. As noted by historian Krisztián Ungváry, Trenker thought that "for Germans a year in Hungary was less dangerous than a day in Yugoslavia." Krisztián Ungváry, *The Siege of Budapest: 100 Days in World War II*, trans. Ladislaus Löb (New Haven: Yale University Press, 2005), p. 305.

outrage in the newspaper *Magyar Nemzet*. The result was a compromise that adhered to the taboo against mentioning that the victims were Jewish but acknowledged that they were Hungarian. Those who knew about this episode could recognize what was being commemorated here, but no one else would learn much about the identity of perpetrators and victims. The original memorial stone was replaced in 1989, with a text that referred to the death of 2,000 slave laborers at the hands of fascist executioners but still refrained from mentioning Jews or Hungarian perpetrators.[7]

After the war, mass graves were found east of town on Guba-hegy, beyond the brick yards and mill where slave laborers had been kept. The pits contained the remains of at least 1,000 people, and the total after the exhumations of 1947 was estimated at about 2,500 killed. The victims were exhumed and buried in Budapest's Rákoskeresztúr cemetery. With so many of those associated with fortificiation construction brutally deprived of life and health, the project at Kőszeg amounted to annihilation through work.

Pál Bács, who as a 16-year-old spent the winter digging tank traps in the rocky terrain around the border town of Bucsu about 20 kilometers south of Kőszeg, remembered being taken to "the Kőszeg transit camp" in late February 1945. He was held for a month before being moved to Möschendorf deeper in Austria, and from there began the three-week forced trek to Mauthausen. He claimed to have witnessed the use at the brickyard of an impromptu gas chamber, created by sealing the cracks in the walls of a barrack on the brick factory grounds, to kill nearly 100 of the sickest and most debilitated slave laborers. He also identified the spot on which the monument to the 2,400 was later erected as having been a mass grave from which the bodies had been exhumed for reburial after the war. This gas

7 The original marker is reminiscent of what happened after the 1946 pogrom in Kunmadaras in the eastern part of the country and reflects the overall efforts of Hungary when it became part of the Soviet empire to avoid acknowledgment of specific anti-Jewish outrages. In this case, the People's Tribunal managed to portray the outbreak of anti-Jewish violence that led to the death of three Jewish Hungarians as a resurgence of fascism aimed at the emerging people's democracy—without mentioning that the victims were Jewish. See Peter Ápor, "The Lost Deportations and the Lost People of Kunmadaras: A Pogrom in Hungary, 1946," *Hungarian Historical Review* 2 (2013), pp. 566–604..

chamber was said to be the brainchild of an SS noncommissioned officer named Bauer and thought to be unique in Hungary. Despite this testimony, serious questions emerged about whether such a murder facility existed in Kőszeg. The book *Végjáték a határon: Kőszeg 1944–1945* [*Endgame on the Border*] carefully lays out the case against successful deployment of a temporary gas chamber in a leaky frame building without temperature, humidity, and air pressure controls. The logistical difficulties of gassing, the authors argue, overwhelmingly favored the tried-and-true methods of exposure, beating, shooting, and starvation. The recollections of numerous other postwar witnesses did not support Bács's testimony, either in court or elsewhere. No one ever questioned the murderous brutality toward the Jews, but no one supported the claim that a gas chamber was employed.

In any case, three memorial places (the ghetto, the synagogue, and the 1985 memorial) near each other all commemorate the same catastrophe in one way or another, but none mention that what was being noted was a crime against *Jewish* Hungarians, perpetrated substantially by other Hungarians. This approach linked efforts to obscure the centrality of Jewishness to the victims of this crime and to conceal the role of Hungarians in committing it. It can be distilled down to the conclusion that the Jews were not victims, and the Hungarians were not perpetrators. This approach is visible all over Hungary, but at Kőszeg it takes a remarkably coherent and spatially compressed form.

The Jews murdered in Kőszeg never received recognition as individuals or as Jews, unlike the Hungarian soldiers who died in forlorn causes in two world wars and even the soldiers of the much-despised Soviet Union. The Jews remain filed in the category of unnamed and undifferentiated Hungarian martyrs, as asserted on the plaque at the base of the memorial along Route 87. The fascists labeled as perpetrators of this crime are not identified as Hungarians, although many of them were. So, the perpetrators' Hungarianness is now denied. The Jews, on the other hand, while they were alive were not recognized as Hungarians and were singled out as Jews, to be robbed, deported, and worked to death or murdered. In death they have been subsumed under the broad category of Hungarian martyrs and are no longer Jews. A third iteration, dedicated in March 2020 along with a memorial trail that commemorated the slave laborers and connected Route 87 to a mass grave and two defensive outposts they dug in the hills east of town, was revised to indicated that Arrow Cross members were among the Germans responsible for the brutalization and killing. Still the tablet identified the victims as Hungarians rather than Jews. Thus, remembering and forgetting remain incorporated in the same acts of memorialization. A Hungarian sense of the absurd is conspicuously absent from this sorry story.

Route 87 south from the slave-laborer memorial goes past the train station toward Szombathely, parallel to Gyöngyös Creek a few meters to the west. Just outside Kőszeg on the right, it goes past the Alpokalja restaurant on the unmarked site of the former Weidl mill, a place where slave laborers were kept during 1944–5. A kilometer farther south, it reaches the Gulner Mill. There 87 bends to the right. The road to the left leads to Kőszegfalva, a tidy village settled mainly by ethnic Germans. On main Kőszegfalva utca (formerly Fó utca), opposite number 81 and near the far (southeast) end of the street, there is a small park, with three memorials, in order northwest to southeast. The first commemorates the removal of ethnic Germans under the aegis of the victorious Allies in 1946. The middle one is a Christian memorial to all victims of war, again the generic lumping together of soldiers, civilian victims of air raids, and Jews deliberately deported to be killed. The last of the three is dedicated to Hungarian soldiers killed in action during World War II. Slave laborers were also housed in the village, but there is no mark of their presence.

In September 2014, Irene and I trespassed onto the Gulner Mill property with Lajos and Éva Simon. We thought it was uninhabited and wanted to see the site where sources indicate that Jewish slave laborers had been housed. We stepped around wads of soiled toilet paper that marked the bathroom breaks of long-distance truckers. We scanned the dilapidated buildings, from the left where the creek-side millhouse stood, to the grain warehouse and residence in front of us, then the stable on the right, and finally noticed a car parked in front of the door. A few seconds later, much to our surprise, a woman came out and asked us to explain ourselves. She was Hungarian but she also spoke English. We overcame our embarrassment and explained our interest. She called her husband, who also appeared and turned out to be British. Paul and Hajni Tinsley graciously welcomed us and showed us the steps they had taken to renovate the property. From this strange beginning a friendship evolved, and the six of us get together regularly whenever Irene and I return to Hungary.

We ate lunch at the mill on April 22, 2015. This was the main event of a day of research and visiting with friends, and not just for the company and the food, as enjoyable as both were. The scale of the atrocity committed at the Gulner mill does not come close to what happened at the death camps or even at the nearby Kreuzstadl. The unfortunate people who were kept here, were more often worked or starved to death than systematically murdered. Neither the Tinsleys nor the Simons knew this part of the mill's history when Irene and I met them, but we all did by the time we sat down to lunch on that Wednesday. Nobody at the table said anything about it, and I am not privy to the thoughts of our friends, but I was uneasy, sitting comfortably in this warm, pleasantly appointed home, among congenial people, and eating a fine meal while facing a window through which I could see the stables where slave laborers had been stashed rather than housed. That the slave laborers had been Jewish and that they suffered in the same catastrophe that consumed parts of my family sharpened the discomfort. Similar sensations intrude at receptions for new art shows at the former Somorja synagogue in present-day Slovakia, the temple where my father's parents worshipped until they left for Vác during World War I on a journey that ended at Auschwitz for my grandfather and in Washington for my father. There too the bitter history disturbs the comforts of friends around well-stocked tables, an emphatic reminder that the past is far from past.

Paul Tinsley sent me a copy of what appears to be an official historical report on the mill. The bilingual "Documentation to the No. 8 building Szombathelyi Road (Gulner Mill) story," as it is called, was filed in the county land office in 2008. It is accompanied by a land office map, showing the layout of the structures and the course of the stream. The text covers the history of the mill from its establishment in 1810 to 1973, when a tour company wanted to restore the building as a visitors' attraction but lacked the money to do it. Rich in detail about design, construction, and use, and even naming the man who might have resided there as a servant with the Gulners in 1944, the document is singularly unenlightening about the role of the mill during the war:

> In 1942 some of the rooms of the buildings, as they were out of use, it had been proposed to make use of on behalf of the town for accommodation for Serbian workers. In 1944 according to the details of the national census, 2 owners Mária and Theresa Gulner, as well as a man called Florian Neuwirth (he was said to be a servant), lived in the dwellings.[8]

In 1947, there was an attempt to restart production. Stephen Hende, who had earlier leased another mill, jointly with miller John Holczer, invested 10,000 forints in the property. They renovated the building and put the machines in working order. The report notes the possible use of the buildings to house Serbian workers. This could have been a reference to Jewish Hungarian slave laborers marched up from the mines at Bór. Beyond that there is no reference to the use of the complex to house Jewish slaves. This is about par for the course.

8 "Documentation to the No 8 building Szombathelyi Road Koszeg (Gulner Mill) story," a report prepared in both Hungarian and English and preserved in the Vas County Archives, Szombathely. The report is undated but was prepared c. 2008 in preparation for the purchase of the mill property by Paul and Hajni Tinsley.

CHAPTER 4

# Oberwart: Jews, Romani, and murder

The town is in a valley, between the railroad embankment to the northeast and the Pinka River to the southwest. It is situated 38 kilometers (about 24 miles) west of Szombathely, via Route 63 (Austria) and Route 89 (Hungary). Oberwart (Felsőőr in Hungarian) has about 7,500 residents, a little more than double the number who lived there at the end of World War I. Sites in the compact downtown reflect the treatment of the Jewish and Romani minorities and include a well-tended Soviet military cemetery south of town. The graveyard is next to the hospital and bordered by Freudgasse on the south, Roentgen gasse to the north, Billrothgasse on the east, and the Reform church's cemetery on the west. All together there are sites related to four waves of population movement as well as identified perpetrator sites of the Nazi regime and the scene of the brutal murder of four Romani men in 1995.

Wiener Strasse is the main street, and the Konditorei Schranz at number 11 offers a centrally located spot for viewing the town and considering its past. The Schranz is a bustling, friendly place, and the espresso is Meinl, whose advertising boasts that it has inspired poets since 1862. Oberwart's important points reflecting the twentieth century extend a short distance in both directions along Wiener and just off it on side streets. This cheerful coffeehouse with its Jugendstil interior of honey-toned wood is well situated for a meditation on the recent past.

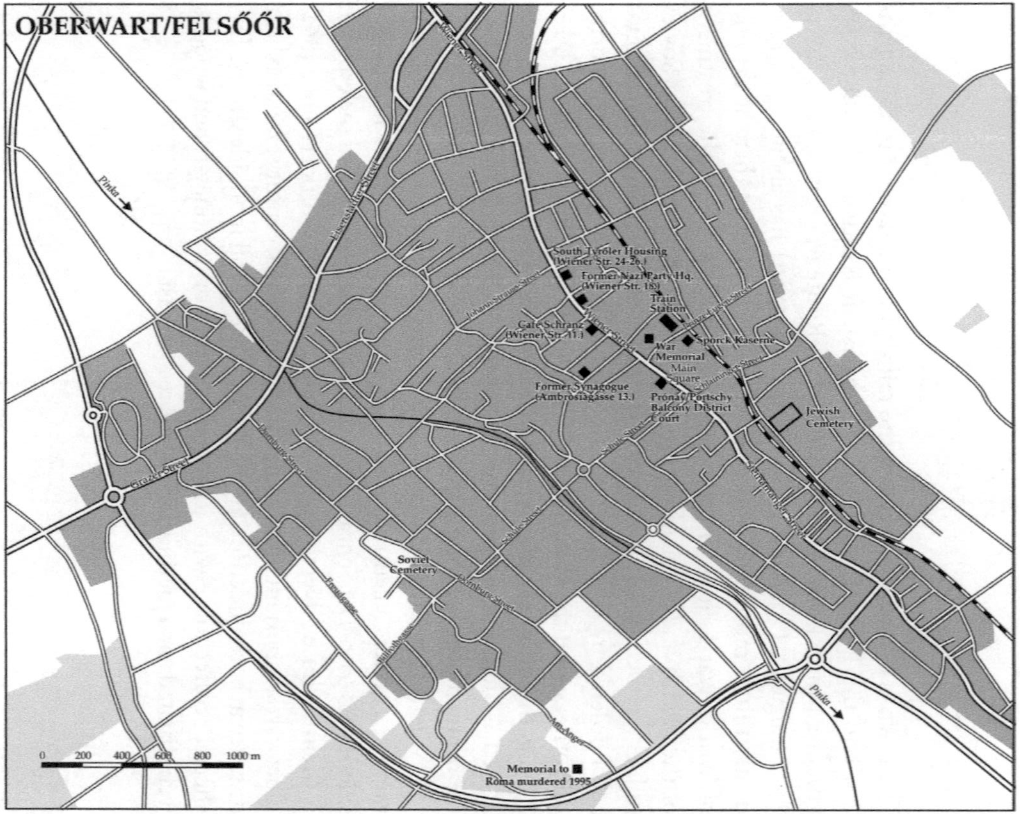


Figure 4.1 Oberwart/Felsőőr [Map 6].

Figure 4.2 Inside the Schranz.

About 250 meters east from the Schranz, after Wiener Strasse becomes Hauptstrasse or Hauptplatz, is the court building that for a month in 1921 was the capital of the ephemeral entity known in Hungarian as the Lajtabánság [Leitha Principality]. In September, Pál Prónáy and his band of Hungarian irredentists drove off two companies of Austrian Volkswehr, captured the town, stitched together a flag, and on October 4 declared an independent country. Like *caudillos* and aspiring dictators everywhere, Prónáy chose a balcony for his declaration, in this case over the main entrance of the district court building, facing city hall across the street. Along with the proclamation came assertion of a desire to remain loyal Hungarian citizens. Local judges and officials, along with a clerical delegation signed a declaration to that effect and affixed the town seal. There were celebratory speeches from the balcony, a blessing of flags, and a parade. Although some administrative services got started, a newspaper was printed, and postage stamps were issued, the regime was never completely formed, ministries went unstaffed, and the Hungarian government prudently withheld support. One-time foreign minister Miklós Bánffy considered the enterprise childish nonsense and opined that Prónáy's "new self-appointed status had clearly gone to [his] head and [he] was behaving as if he was a legitimate ruler."[1] In any case, the whole thing lasted only a few days. A month afterward, all traces of the Prónáy usurpation were gone, and the settlement reverted to Austrian control.

The principality lasted long enough to provide early examples of two hallmarks of the twentieth century in the borderland, large-scale population movements and systematic theft. Those who did not belong, according to the Hungarian irredentists who established the Lajtabánság, were weeded out, put in sealed railroad carriages, and sent away. The sacred mission of redemption could not be put at risk. Warehouses were established for confiscated public property, providing quantities of arms and supplies unimagined by the threadbare rebels at the start of their uprising.

The balcony again became the focal point of political turmoil in February and March 1938. The largest pro-Nazi demonstration in Burgenland during the days before formal inauguration of the Nazi regime took place here on February 27. An estimated 8,000 people, including Hungarians on horseback, attended the festivities, which started in the early afternoon with singing, the waving of Nazi flags, and endless columns

1 Miklós Bánffy, *The Phoenix Land: The Memoirs of Count Miklós Bánffy*, trans. Patrick Thursfield and Katalin Banffy-Jelen (London: Arcadia Books, 2003), p. 254.

converging on the town. Portschy and his friend and propagandist Hans Goger spoke from the balcony. With this display of local support for the Hitler regime, organizer Tobias Portschy got out in front of Interior Minister Arthur Seyss-inquart, the Nazi point man in Austria. The tail wagged the dog.

As the Anschluss approached, local Nazis became bolder and more celebratory. During March 11–14 three huge public gatherings rocked the town. On March 11, the day Portschy proclaimed Nazi rule in Burgenland (see chapter 8), the largest demonstration was still in Oberwart, where bands played, the Horst Wessel song rang out, and 14,000 celebrants crowded the town and the square. The next evening, around 3,700 came out to celebrate the "liberation of German-Austria." Again, speeches boomed from the balcony, where the mayor announced that the main square was now Adolf Hitler-Platz. The festivities ended with a torchlight parade through town in a western direction on Allhauer Strasse, now Route 50. On March 14 came the final dramatic act of the transition, as the military garrison assembled on newly named Hitlerplatz and swore an oath of loyalty to the führer and chancellor.[2]

Between the balcony and the Schranz but across Wiener Strasse, the *Kulturpark* bounded by Prinz-Eugen Strasse and Bahnhofstrasse contains two memorials. One is a conventional memorial to the bloodletting of two world wars, listing names of local soldiers who died "for the homeland," including 16 men with the surname Zámbó that they shared with Jimmy Zámbó, a famous Hungarian pop star of the late twentieth century and a kind of Central European Tom Jones. The other memorial, installed in 1988, commemorates Jews, Romani, political opponents of the Nazi regime (two locals were executed), and those killed in the Nazi euthanasia program called Aktion T4. Oberwart apparently had no direct role in the

2 Norbert Pingitzer, *Der Anschluss 1938 Burgenland* (Schwarzach: Heimat-Verlag, 2018), contains 27 images from the commemorative album Portschy assembled as a gift for German Minister of the Interior Hans Frank. The album, found by American occupying forces at the end of the war, was among documents transferred to the Library of Congress in Washington after the war. The images show Oberwart during its turn as center stage for the emergence of the Nazi regime in Burgenland.

program, but the hospital on Spitalgasse toward the eastern end of town was used for forced sterlilizations and racial examinations, according to the RE.F.U.G.I.U.S. brochure "Oberwart Path of Commemoration and Education," which illuminates and gives equal weight to the Romani and Jewish catrastrophes with brief text, pictures, and a sketch map that notes a few key sites. The booklet is available along with the other tourist brochures in the city hall across the street from the Prónáy-Portschy site.[3]

The memorial to multiple categories of victims—Romani, Jews, political opponents, and targets of the euthanasia program—more or less reflects the widely accepted style that subsumed all fatalities into a single category. The site also marks the spot of a bit of guerilla theater, an effort by some bold young artists to erect a monument specifically to the Romani killed during the war. In 1980, the group installed the tablet as part of "Aktion Ziguenerdenkmal," or Operation Gypsy Memorial. The black wooden panel, surrounded by four pillars and crowned with barbed wire, was intended to commemorate the more than 300 local Romani murdered in concentration camps and bore the cross-shaped inscription: "dead, dead, carried off, murdered, dead, dead, dead." The positioning in front of the military memorial

Tot
Tot
Verschleppt
Ermordet
Tot
Tot
Tot

with its list of men who died in the service of the regime that had been responsible was no accident. The installation was widely resented, vandalized the first night, and removed by the artists after the city threatened

3 The brochure is published by RE.F.U.G.I.U.S., Rechnitzer Fluchtlings Und Gedenk Initiative Stiftung, A-7400 Oberwart, Raingasse 9b. Also see <www.refugius.at>.

to make them pay for taking it away.[4] Later, in 1988, a memorial was installed, but it was broadened to commemorate murdered Jews, political opponents, and euthanized citizens and put on the same spot in front of the military memorial.

The site just east of Prinz-Eugen and the memorial park is singular in content and format. Immediately in front of the District Commission on the site of a store once owned by a local Jewish citizen named Benö Lőwy and later used for interrogations by the Nazi regime, is an "Infopont," a digital slideshow presentation on local Romani history shown on a screen about the size of the display of an automated teller machine. This and the RE.F.U.G.I.U.S. brochure certainly have no parallels on the Hungarian side of the border.

Across Wiener Strasse and about 150 meters down Ambrosiagasse at number 13 is the former synagogue. Part of the facade is all that remains of the original structure, which was built in 1902 and destroyed in 1938. The memorial tablet was installed in the 1990s, and, like the much larger synagogue in Győr, the current building houses a music school. The rabbi resided next door at number 15. The only other institutional remnant of the Jewish community is the cemetery, adjacent to the Christian cemetery on the northeast side of town. Most of the tombstone inscriptions are in German, rather than Hebrew, reflecting the rather recent arrival of Jews in Oberwart in the 1880s.

In the other direction, northwest of the Schranz, also across Wiener Strasse and within a quarter kilometer of the coffeehouse, are two more notable places. Between Andreas-Hofer Gasse and Molkereisstrasse and divided by Neutergasse are two long two-story buildings. When we first visited Oberwart in 2014, we parked behind these buildings and walked past them toward the middle of town. We thought they looked like military barracks, probably from the interwar period. It turned out that we were seeing public housing constructed to accommodate ethnic Germans caught up in a round of mass population movement. The South Tyrolean ethnic German

4 For a still photo showing both the text and the damage by vandals, see: <http://www.waechter-oberwart.at/uploads/pics/3_3_Zigeunerdenkmal.jpg>, accessed May 8, 2018.

migration north into Austria was based on an agreement between Hitler and Benito Mussolini in 1939. German- and Ladino-speaking South Tyroleans, who had found themselves in territory awarded to Italy after World War I, could opt to stay or move to Germany or Austria, which by then was known officially as Ostmark. Around 80 percent of the more than 165,000 (about 132,000) ethnic Germans indicated a desire to leave, and about 75,000 did so. The authorities settled them in towns throughout the Ostmark.

Oberwart was the only such town in Burgenland. Construction of the dwellings, located at numbers 24 and 26, began in 1940. The land, then in the northern suburbs, had been the site of a sawmill owned by Jewish lumber merchant Samuel Schlenger. Daisy Schlenger, later the wife of financier George Soros's brother Paul, was born in Oberwart in 1935.[5] After 1938, the property once owned by her family was available for other uses.

A little nearer to the center on the corner of Liszt-Gasse, a modest building with a corner tower contains shops on the ground floor and apartments above. The almost nondescript combination of retail and residence turns out to be one of those rare structures, an identifiable perpetrator site. Like Arrow Cross sites in Hungary, Nazi Party sites in Austria are hard to identify. They almost never are marked as having some historical resonance and older residents who remember do not talk about the use to which these buildings had been put. But in the summer of 2015, I bought for the staggering sum of $244 at a Budapest auction a picture postcard that showed the Oberwart headquarters of the National Socialist Party, draped with a swastika banner. I sent an email to the mayor's office, and received a prompt and polite reply from Manfred Imre, whose German given name of Manfred and Hungarian surname of Imre indicated borderland roots. He did not know where the headquarters had been located either, but his grandfather did, and that was how I learned it was near the center of the town, at Wiener Strasse 18.

The building occupies the northwest corner of Wiener and Liszt-Gasse. A row of three shops occupies the ground floor, from left to right

5 Starting in 1997, philanthropists Paul and Daisy Soros created a program of fellowships that invested in the graduate education of promising immigrants and children of immigrants in the United States. The program is stills active as of this writing. The foundation's website is <https://www.pdsoros.org>.

as viewed from the street a tobacconist-sundry shop, Italy Fashion, and the Wolf bakery and café. The Wolf had a few tables, all vacant, and it might have made a perfect spot from which to consider the twentieth-century evils around us, something like the Győr McDonald's on the Arrow Cross site or Heiling Eis in Rechnitz. However, we saw no sign of restrooms through the plate glass window and went to the Schranz across the street.

The overall appearance of the building is almost unchanged from the World War II period. The only visible alteration is the removal of the dormers shown in the postcard. Irene took pictures from across Wiener Strasse, while I walked around the building. When she finished, we and our Hungarian friends Erika Szenftner and Ernő Tukovics talked on the corner, with an enlarged image from the postcard in our hands and our gaze moving between the image and the building. Just then a slender, brown-skinned young man, perhaps in his thirties, with an earring in his right ear, a silver disc about the size of a dime with a black stone, perhaps an opal, in the center, approached us about our interest in the building. He spoke to us in German but switched to English when we asked whether he spoke it. He said he lived there and pointed to the corner window on the second floor. We showed him the picture, with the Nazi banner. His jaw dropped, abruptly, and his eyes got big. He said he had family members who had been incarcerated at Mauthausen, and his grandfather had been at Auschwitz.

Figure 4.3 The district court building, with the Prónáy/Portschy balcony over the front entrance.

I asked him whether he was Jewish. I thought he was Romani, but I didn't know how to ask him that because I didn't know the proper term to use. Some might say this shows an excessive concern for political correctness, but I prefer to see it as an effort to avoid insulting the young man. How would he respond to "Roma," "Zigeuner," or "Gypsy"? He said he was indeed "Roma," and went on to string together all the other terms just in case I did not understand what Roma was. When I said that I was Jewish and Hungarian in origin and that my grandfather had been murdered at Auschwitz, he added that his grandfather had been murdered there as well. I introduced myself and gave him my card. He said his name was Oliver. I invited him to send me an email and offered to reply with a copy of the picture postcard with the building on it. I also suggested that perhaps we could talk more that way. Then we parted ways. He never took up my invitation to communicate, and I regret that I was not more assertive about wanting to remain in contact.

At this point some observations about the nature of the Holocaust might be in order. Jews and Romani were both despised, and the majority community had no qualms concerning their presumed right to dispose of what they considered to be a problem, as they saw fit. Certainly, Tobias Portschy, a native of nearby Unterschützen and deputy head of the regional government during the Nazi years, loathed both groups, and a panel at the Kreuzstadl memorial outside Rechnitz calls him "one of the intellectual fathers and ideologues behind the persecution of the Roma and Sinti people." He was not alone in his loathings. The citizens of Oberwart, whether German or Hungarian in background, who celebrated the Anschluss in a public pageant, decked out in folk costumes and waving banners adorned with swastikas, shared his views. In fact, Hungarian residents so avidly supported the Nazis that Portschy could not obey instructions from Berlin to exclude them from the local party organization.

Before the Anschluss, the focus was on the Gypsies. On January 15, 1933, the so-called Gypsy conference [*Zigeunerkonferenz*] took place in Oberwart. A representative of the Burgenland state government joined delegates of the Christian Socialist and Social Democratic parties as well as the Rural Federation [*Landbund*], local government officials, and the head of the gendarmerie to discuss what to do with the Gypsies, who were labeled as a foreign body that constantly threatened the majority population and civilized nations in general. Conference proposals included deportation to unsettled Pacific islands and even castration, and the meeting ended with a call for passage of anti-Gypsy laws. The town had 138 Jews among its residents at the time, but the focus was on the Gypsies, who numbered 332 by 1939. In November 1941, the Oberwart railroad station was the point of origin for one of the five Gypsy transports from Burgenland to Litzmannstadt [Lodz], Poland, a way station to the death camps. By that time all local Jews had fled or been removed to Vienna.

Both groups suffered greatly at the hands of Nazi and collaborationist regimes during the period of the war. Yet there were differences in how their catastrophes evolved. Nazis and their collaborators feared and envied Jews and thought somehow that Jews controlled vast resources on an international scale through nefarious means. Romani on the other hand were dismissed as contemptible and lacking worthwhile attributes.[6] There is a difference and if you want to understand it, consider whether you have ever seen any indication of establishment of an administrative and logistical infrastructure to secure, organize, and dispose of Romani property. This contrast may account for the German willingness to let Hungary devise its own solutions to problems that they thought the Romani represented, rather than compel the Hungarians to implement the systematic destruction of the Romani people. With the Jews of course there was only a single final solution, their destruction throughout the Third Reich, its dependencies, and its allies. Overall, the Romani survival rate through Nazi-dominated Europe outside of the Reich was considerably higher than that of Jews.

In Austria, the number murdered was much higher, roughly three-fourths of the 11,000 Romani residents in the country and 90 percent in Burgenland. Because of these distinctions, it could be said that the Jewish and Romani experiences, as devastating as both were, were qualitatively different. In effect there was a Romani holocaust in the territory of the Third Reich itself, but there was no consistently applied policy of systematic murder in allied and otherwise associated territories. Overall, the Romani catastrophe fell short of such an outcome. As István Deák observed, they were "perceived as undermining law and order" but not "uniformly under a Nazi death sentence," but it was a catatrophe nevertheless.[7] However, standing on Wiener Strasse, talking to Oliver, whose grandfather, like mine, had been murdered in the Auschwitz death factory, it didn't seem that these distinctions made much difference. Or as Christopher Isherwood is said to have put it, responding to a man who pointed out that more Jews were murdered than homosexuals, "What are you, in real estate?"[8]

6 On the differences and similarities, see László Karsai, *A cigánykérdés Magyarországon 1919–1945: Út a cigány holocausthoz* (Budapest: Cserépfalvi Könyvkiadó, 1992).

7 István Deák, *Europe on Trial: The Story of Collaboration, Resistance, and Retribution during World War II* (Boulder, CO: Westview Press, 2015), p. 2.

8 Quoted in Ian Buruma, *The Wages of Guilt: Memories of War in Germany and Japan* (New York: NYRB Books, 1994, 2015), p. 299. On the differences in motivation for the murderous loathing of the Jews and other groups despised by the Nazis, see David Cesarani, *Final Solution: The Fate of Jews 1933–1949* (New York: St. Martin's

The enlightenment suggested by the Infopont and the historical brochure were yet to come to Oberwart when anti-Romani savagery showed its face in 1995. On the night of February 4–5, 1995, four Romani men traveled near the cluster of Romani dwellings about 100 meters north of the modern embankment of the 63A motorway that skirts Oberwart on its western and southern sides. They came across a sign declaring "Roma zurüch nach Indien," or "Roma back to India." When they tried to remove it, they triggered a bomb that killed all four, Peter Sarközi (age 27), Josef Simon (age 40), and the brothers Erwin (age 18) and Karl Horváth (age 22). When the authorities found murderer Franz Fuchs after a routine traffic stop in 1997, he tried to blow himself up, failed, and lost both hands in the attempt. Shortly after he was sentenced to life in prison in March 1999, he was found hanged in his cell. The prison doctor declared his death a suicide. How he managed to hang himself without hands is hard to comprehend.

The bomb attack at Oberwart was the first racially motivated assassination in Austria since 1945. At the state funeral on February 11, 1995, Austrian president Dr. Thomas Klestil delivered the official eulogy. Members of the federal government, the National Assembly, the provincial government, and the provincial assembly attended as did thousands of mourning friends and sympathisers. Moreover, the murder had the unintended consequence of creating "new solidarities berween Jews and Romani, who had previously found little ground for dialogue."[9] The victims were buried at the cemetery in Oberwart.

In January 2000, the memorial commemorating the four victims was erected at the site of the attack. The monument on Am Anger before it passes under the highway, has two parts. At what appears to be the actual site of the explosion on Am Anger, there is a religious memorial, with a crucifix, flowers at the base, and the names of the four in gilt letters. The more monumental installation across the street has a central column, with stylized representations of the four men at the corners of the slab on which the whole thing rests. Reinhard Vitus Gombots designed the memorial

Press, 2016), e-book, pp. 123, 295, 382. Also see Ari Joskowicz, *Rain of Ash: Roma, Jews, and the Holocaust* (Princeton: Princeton University Press, 2023).

9 Joskowicz, *Rain of Ash*, p. 198.

under the management of the Romani Association of Oberwart with public funding. The corner figures, facing outward in four different directions, are made of marble with some polished surfaces and some rough. The sign explaining the crime is in three languages—Romani, German, and English. The site was well maintained; no one else was there when we visited in 2016. Just a little beyond the memorial, the road passes under 63A and opens up to a dazzling vista of golden rape fields on the other side.

Figure 4.4 Wiener Strasse 18, during the Third Reich. The building housed party headquarters for both the district and the town.

Figures 4.5 and 4.6 The two memorials to the 1995 murder, across the street from each other.

So the Romani are treated with respect and the Jews are long gone. Now Oberwart faces issues raised by migration from the Middle East and Africa. In September 2015, temporary lodging for people coming west through Hungary was arranged for an estimated 200–500 people on the local exposition grounds on the southeastern side of town, not far from the hospital and memorial to the 1995 murders. This action may have been partly necessitated by the closure and sale of the Sporck kaserne at Prinz Eugen Strasse 6 to a state-supported consortium after the army vacated the premises at the end of 2013. Apparently, the sale was intended to prevent the building's use to house refugees so near the town center. The kaserne dated from Habsburg times and was once the headquarters of a *Jägerbattaillon* [hunter battalion]. The site is across the street from the northeast corner of the memorial park and faces the tax collector's office.

In the spring of 2016 about 90 refugees remained, staying with local families. They are not permitted to take jobs and depend on public assistance. Their children go to local schools. Meanwhile their applications for asylum are being adjudicated. So they are in limbo, waiting for permission to stay or to be sent back to their country of origin. We saw brown-skinned young men who did not appear to be Romani and women with headscarves, the latter coming out of a building on HauptStrasse known as "the Forum," between the Schranz and the Prónáy/Portschy balcony. There a Protestant church has created a meeting place for refugees who live in Oberwart. Local citizens also go there and meet refugees. The outcome of this encounter is yet to be determined.

CHAPTER 5

# Sopron: Archetypal border town

More than any other borderland city, Sopron bears traces of the turmoil and horrors of the bygone century. All of the outrages of the twentieth century, among them war, border and regime change, lynching, slave labor, deportations, and mass murder, left traces here, as did a catalyzing event of the end of the Cold War. Hegyeshalom-Nickelsdorf was the quintessential border crossing of the Cold War, Győr the largest border-area city, and Kőszeg and Rechnitz the murder capitals, but Sopron is the archetype with the broadest range of involvement and reminders of the period. Two events set Sopron apart. The first, in December 1921, was the referendum that resulted in Sopron remaining in Hungary instead of becoming the capital of Burgenland as initially determined. The second came in August 1989, when the city had an outsize role in the collapse of the Iron Curtain and the Soviet empire as the site of the pan-European picnic at Sopronpuszta. It also had the largest ethnic German population that faced removal after the war and thus became a major deportation site twice within two years, the Jews in 1944 to their deaths in Poland and the ethnic Germans in 1946 to zones of Germany occupied by the Western Allies. So Sopron is a paradigmatic town, the embodiment of the twentieth century in the borderlands, with important sites throughout, on its periphery, and in nearby communities. These fall into all three museum categories—marked and on display, ignored and in storage, and demolished and deaccessioned.

The Pannonia Hotel on the ring road around the medieval town provides a prime spot to think about the recent past, for its own historical resonance and its location near significant twentieth-century sites. It is just outside the walled city at Várkerület 75. Next door at number 84 once stood the business of a Jewish coffee merchant, who did business as Brüder Breuer and underwrote a 200,000-crown war loan during World War I. The thoroughfare was once known as Lenin Avenue, and the hotel is cited in

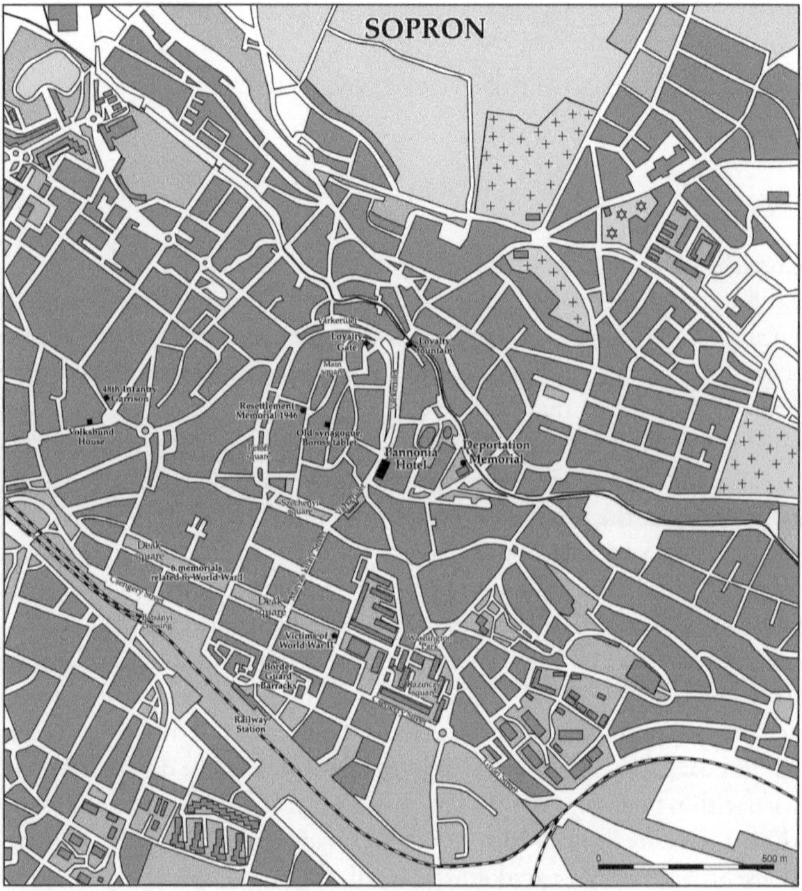


Figure 5.1 Sopron [Map 7].

novels as well as nonfiction as unofficial headquarters of the 1921 rebels who plotted to prevent the Austrian takeover in Burgenland. Pál Prónáy, leader of the insurrection, had a room in the hotel with his wife in the autumn of 1921, and there was a kind of irredentist *Stammtisch* in the restaurant. He claimed that fellow conspirator Béla Bardocs came up with the name Lajtabánság for the territory they hoped to wrest from the Austrians while at the Pannonia for meetings where they plotted the uprising.

If you go to the Pannonia coffeehouse, to the left inside the main entrance, be sure to look around the public areas to the right as well. The hotel, which opened in the 1890s, still has splendid furnishings. Modest historical exhibits along the hallway on the south side show that management is aware of the hotel's past importance. Jews as well as anti-Semitic irredentists once used the Pannonia for gatherings. In 1928 and again in 1932, the orthodox Israelite youth of Sopron had their Purim celebration in the elegant glass hall. During the 1930s, the Women's Charity Association of the Jewish Community of Sopron annually held its dress ball at the Pannonia.

The hotel hosted two commemorations of the 1989 Pan-European picnic (see chapter 10 below). The first, attended by Archduke Otto von Habsburg, took place in 2004. Ten years later, in August–October 2014, the hotel showed a twenty-fifth anniversary exhibition, sponsored by the Pan-European Picnic '89 Foundation and called "With Hungary's Help …." The exhibit, largely of photographs that are also on display at Sopronpuszta, was available to schools throughout Hungary after closing in Sopron. It recalled a recent time when Hungary was at the forefront of a movement to open borders.

Reminders of the Jewish catastrophe are nearby. East of the hotel, about 200 meters behind it, the deportation memorial stands in the park in front of the synagogue on Paprét Street. Like the Szombathely memorial created by Gábor Veres, the Paprét memorial by László Kutas uses coats on hooks as the central design element. In the center of the old city, also about 200 meters away, are the medieval synagogue and a small Jewish museum at the adjacent ritual baths. A wall plaque marks the home of 11-year-old Liana Boross, one of more than 1,800 Jewish Sopronians deported and murdered in 1944. Like the Demnig stumble stones, the Boross memorial represents a trend away from the emphasis on numbers toward a focus on individual Jewish lives and an effort to impart a sense that something is missing.[1] These identified sites are all on Új utca [New Street], one of the oldest roads in the center of the walled town.

To the west on parallel Templom Street, a monument in front of the Lutheran church commemorates the deportation of ethnic Germans in 1946. This sad episode, part vengeance and reprisal, and part opportunity to steal, formed part of a massive postwar sorting out in which 14 to 15 million Germans took flight or were expelled or removed from homes outside Germany and returned there. A substantial number, but not all, had staunchly supported Hitler and the Third Reich, and in Hungary there was a postwar tendency to scapegoat them as responsible for the alliance with Hitler. Remarkably, it is still not known exactly how many people were removed. Estimates range between 6,600 and 8,900, and those sent away tended to have shown either strong ties to the Third Reich, expressed often by membership in the Volksbund, or to have been the most prosperous, or often both.

The removal was profoundly different from the Jewish deportation. The main difference involved the divergence in destinations, the earlier group to be murdered at Nazi death camps and the latter to new lives in the Allied sectors of Germany right before the Communist regime erected and solidified the Iron Curtain. This contrast is so great as to transcend even ironic comparison. When the Evangelical community, through its John Wesley Theological College, and with the cooperation of the GYSEV railroad, launched a campaign to install plaques at Hungarian railroad stations including Sopron on the sixtieth anniversary of the deportations of 1944, no mention was made of 1946.[2]

1 Three recent exhibits in trans-Danubia, at Pápa, Szombathely, and Sopron, illustrate this trend. Benjamin Novak, "'Our Forgotten Neighbors' tells story of Pápa's lost Jewish families," January 15, 2014, <http://budapestbeacon. com/politics/our-forgotten-neighbors-tells-story-of-papas-lost-jewish-families/>, downloaded November 14, 2014; Kelbert Kriszina, *Szemből Szemben: Képek az elhurcolt Szombathelyi zsidóság történetéből* (Szombathely: Savaria Megyei Hátókörű Városi Múzeum, 2014); Tárkanyi Sándor and Tarkányi Eszter, *Faces, Fates, Victims: Chapters from the History of the Jewry of Sopron*, trans. Koltai Bálint, Szakonyi Janka, and Tárkányi Eszter (Sopron: Hungarian-Israeli Fellowship of Sopron, 2014).

2 A third massive removal of Hungarians to the Soviet Union as slave laborers, took place around the same time. It was different from the two others discussed here in

Both groups were systematically stripped of their property, the second time more efficiently than the first, and this might ordinarily be considered a sufficiently heinous crime if it had not been overshadowed in the case of the Jews by the mass murder that followed it. In any case, the major difference between the Jews and the Germans came down to the fact that the Germans were esteemed as well as hard-working and prosperous, so they were not forced to sew the black letter "A" for *áruló* [traitor] on their clothing, as some of the more vengeful among their erstwhile countrymen urged, or as thoroughly purged and as brutally treated during the removal and after. As the case of Győr in 1944 shows (chapter 9 below), stealing real estate, home furnishings, crops, and personal property was a major administrative and logistical process and involved citizens and sites that were never marked as historically important. In Sopron, locations involved in the process included city hall, police stations, a basement warehouse southeast of the old city on Lehár Ferenc utca that was owned by the Orsolyita [Ursuline] order, a detention camp at the Forty-Eighth Infantry garrison on the north side of Táncsics utca just west of Selmeci, and the two train stations from which the removals took place, both the GYSEV station and the now-closed Déli [southern] depot.[3] The theft left a paper trail too, with receipts for confiscated property filed in the mayor's office with copies to the representative of the national government. Deputy city clerk Dr. Jänos Mollay implemented the system under the direction of the economic office in city hall.

---

that it was random and opportunistic and did not target a specific religious or ethnic group. Instead, the Red Army randomly swept people off the streets and removed them. Some managed to return. See Krisztián Ungváry, *The Siege of Budapest: 100 Days in World War II*, trans. Ladislaus Löb (New Haven: Yale University Press, 2005), pp. 344–8, for a discussion of the dragnets and deportations in the capital city.

3 Győr-Sopron-Ebenfürti Vasut, once a separate railroad but now incorporated into the MAV, or Hungarian State Railroad system. For both the historical and the contemporaneous context to the German removal, see Alfred J. Rieber, "Repressive Population Transfers in Central, Eastern, and South-Eastern Europe: A Historical Overview," *Journal of Communist Studies and Transition Politics*, 16, no. 1 (2000), pp. 1–27.

Earlier, the garrison of the Forty-Eighth had played a role in the tumultuous period of the Western Hungarian uprising and the attempt of Charles IV to regain the Hungarian throne. After he returned to Hungary in the autumn of 1921, he went to Sopron and sought to rouse the troops. He stayed in a room at the garrison, where Prónáy's men organized their attacks on the Austrian army at nearby towns, until he and his forces boarded a train for Budapest. They made it as far as Budaörs where the army blocked his way. This was the end of the line, and he was packed off to exile on a British ship. He died on the island of Madeira the following year.

The garrison was the scene of a remarkable rescue at the end of the World War II. Three hundred fifty Jewish slave laborers were driven into the complex on March 30, 1945, and held overnight in anticipation of moving them westward to Mauthausen or a roadside death on the way. Tibor Almásy, an air defense lieutenant, was in charge, while his superiors joined the westward flight from the Red Army. Lieutenant Almásy dressed his charges in Hungarian army uniforms and posted some of them as guards around the garrison. He told anyone who asked that there were no Jews at the installation, only troops designated to defend the city, and for good measure put out signs warning people away because of an outbreak of typhus among his charges. The men marched out in formation on the evening of March 31, among them Oszkár Füredi, who designed the first monument to the Jewish labor service men and slaves who were killed at Balf, that was destroyed by vandals within two years of its erection in 1968. The group wound up in a Russian prisoner-of-war camp at Székesfehérvár. Most of them were released on June 12. Almásy fled to Canada after the 1956 revolution and was later recognized by Israel as a righteous gentile. In 1993, a memorial tablet was installed regarding his successful rescue.

Figure 5.2 The entrance to the garrison on Táncsics Street during the days of the Empire.

The Volksbund House, or *Deutsche Haus* at Kossuth utca 9, on the south side of the corner of Táncsics, was the headquarters of the local Volksbund and in postwar Hungarian eyes the epicenter of ethnic German disloyalty during the war. Its location was conveniently near the detention camp in the garrison on Táncsics. Those who carried out the systematic expropriation and removal occasionally helped themselves from the Orsolyita cellar and other storage sites. Generally, there seems to have been no appreciation of the irony involved in the Hungarian government's self-proclaimed role as representing all Magyars abroad while acceding to the condemnation by the victorious allies of ethnic Germans in Hungary as traitors and participating in their removal. Hungary under Viktor Orbán again claims that protective role, offering passports and voting rights to Magyars in neighboring states.

Pondering these events might cause a visitor at the Pannonia to crave something stronger than a coffee. But a little restraint should be exercised. There is more nearby to be seen. To the north, inside the old town, the main square is full of historical remnants, including a small section of the Roman Amber Road, connecting the Baltic Sea and the Adriatic. Between city hall, from which the removal of both the Jews and the Germans was managed, and the city museum, stands the Loyalty Gate, designed by sculptor Zsigmond Kisfaludy-Stróbl and architect Rudolf Hitisch and completed in 1928. The gate leads northward from the old city, through the fire tower from which nineteenth-century watchmen warned against fires, approaching enemies, or attempts to bring wines from outside the region into town. The allegorical tableau celebrates repudiation of the transfer of the city to the Austrians by two-thirds of the voters in Sopron and eight surrounding towns in the referendum of 1921 and the subsequent designation of the city by the parliament in 1922 as *civitas fidelissima*, the most loyal city. The referendum followed a stormy period in which Hungarian troops marched out of the city, the Prónáy-led rebellion proved an irritant to all with its tactical successes, and a conference was held in Venice at which the Allies agreed to the referendum in Sopron and vicinity. The vote brought the only substantial revision of the Trianon provisions and a minor consolation to the embittered Hungarians. The scene carved into the stone above the gateway, on a ledge atop the helmeted head of a Hungarian soldier, celebrates the referendum. At its center, Hungaria wears the holy crown of St. Stephen while holding the city coat of arms in her right hand and the emblem of Hungary in her left. She collects onto herself loyal Hungarians of all religions and both Magyar and German backgrounds. For these patriots of Sopron, Jewish and German as well as Magyar, the expulsions of 1944 and 1946 remained in the unforeseeable future.

To the left of the Loyalty Gate the history museum displays its excellent and well-organized collections. Singular among the objects is the *Vas Honvéd*, or Iron Defender of the Homeland, a slightly larger-than-life wooden carving of a Hungarian soldier of World War I, with the heads of iron nails pounded into every item of its uniform, leaving only its wooden face, hands, and neck exposed. The carving was a fundraising device, not a memorial. Throughout the Habsburg Empire, the authorities placed these wooden figures, which resembled cigar-store Indians and anticipated more recent lawn ornaments sculpted with chain saws, in public places, to raise money for widows, orphans, and crippled veterans. Patriots could make a donation and hammer a symbolic nail into the soldier, solidifying and strengthening him and the war effort. The more prominent the place on the carving, the more money the privilege cost. The most conspicuous places, such as cartridge belts, even bore the names of leading citizen-donors. Only in rare cases did these figures survive the war, and those few that did remain have become unintended memorials of the war.

Figure 5.3 The *Vas Honvéd* [Iron Defender of the Homeland] in the Sopron Museum.

Sopron's designation as the most loyal city is celebrated elsewhere nearby. Through the gate, over the dry moat, and on the ring road just to the right is the Loyalty Fountain, the work of E. Tamás Soltra. Dedicated in 2003, it features three upright figures representing the years 1277, when Sopron attained the rank of a free royal town; 1921, the year of the uprising and the referendum in which Sopron voted to remain in Hungary; and 1989, the year the Iron Curtain came down. The text surrounding the base refers to the Republic of Hungary, although Hungary no longer calls itself a republic. The fountain sits on the site of a monument to Soviet liberation in 1945, one memorial deaccessioned and another put in its place. Other celebrations of 1921 are on the east end of Széchenyi Square just south of the city center, and in front of the main building of the University of Western Hungary southwest of the center of the city and across the tracks from the Déli station. The latter is another Soltra creation.

The newest monument to the tumultuous year is near the parking lot for the Károly Kíláto, an observation point named not for the last Habsburg king but for Károly Romwalter, a local friend of nature. The tower is 23 meters tall and atop a 398-meter hill, just north of the television tower south of Sopron. It gives an excellent view into Austria. However, it is not the tower but the statue in a clearing by the parking lot that draws irredentists and other hypernationalists to the spot. The lure is the flower- and ribbon-bedecked representation of Pál Prónáy, armed, alert, and resembling a Tatar warrior. The popularity of the monument is a measure of the lingering bitterness over the Trianon settlement. The avoidance of recognition of the lure of the monument in the popular press, on the other hand, is a measure of the embarrassment that Prónáy generates. The county paper and its recent guide to the top tourist attractions write extensively about the overlook but ignore the statue.

Two blocks south of Széchenyi Square, toward the GYSEV train station, Mátyás Király crosses Déák Ferenc Square, a long, narrow public space that runs from southeast to northwest about 1.2 kilometers. Starting with the World War II memorial east of Mátyás Király, there are seven memorials to wartime bloodletting among the park benches and playgrounds. As is often the case in Hungary these days, and most visibly in the contentious monument on Szabadság Square in Budapest, the World War II memorial does not differentiate between types of victims. Designed by Mihály Pál and completed in 1993 of two three-meter-tall blocks of Fertőrákos limestone topped by bas-reliefs, the sculpture remembers soldiers killed in action, civilians killed during bombing attacks, Jews and others deported to their deaths, and finally the Germans removed after the war. Although the Jews were deported and murdered because of their faith, they are remembered with other civilian casualties. Like the deported Jews of Kőszeg, they have been granted posthumous status as Hungarians and are now Sopronians.

The bas-relief shows standard Christian images, the Virgin on the left and the pietà on the right. This is extraordinary for a memorial sculpture that includes thousands of deported Jews among its subject matter. Use of mainstream Christian imagery to commemorate the deportation and murder of Sopron's Jews can only be comprehended as an effort to obscure the centrality of Jewish victimhood. The other six memorials recall the butchery of World War I.

Chronologically the other six fall into two groups of three. One set was erected in the 1930s, before the distractions of the next war and restrictions later imposed by the Communist regime that curbed memorialization. The second group was installed starting in the 1990s when Communist constraints were lifted.

Two Déák Square installations were deaccessioned over the years. One commemorated 32-year-old printer and Communist Party activist Sándor Kellner, who either died or was killed on his way to prison at Sopronköhida in 1919. It was erected in 1951 and removed after the 1956 revolution. The other, a 1970 installation honoring the Soviet liberation in 1945, was taken down after 1989.

Figure 5.4 The Kellner memorial, from a picture postcard.

Away from Déák Square, other World War I memorials include a commemoration of the locally recruited Eighteenth Infantry Regiment. It stands south of the city, a short and beautiful walk through the woods from the parking lot at the end of Ciklámen Avenue. It is modeled on another monument to the Eighteenth that is at the site of the bloody battle of August 8–20, 1917, at Ojtozi Creek in Kovaszna County, Romania. There, imperial and German forces slugged it out with Russian and Romanian units in the same mindless way so often depicted on the Western Front. Yet another World War I monument, a tablet with the names of former students who served, is in the main building on the University of Western Hungary's main campus, which was built during the days of the Empire as a military school.

Nearby, in the lush, wooded area in front of the Forestry Building, south of the main building, is the 1956 memorial, installed on the uprising's fiftieth anniversary. The sculpture is approachable by the main entrance to the campus on Bajcsy-Zsilinsky Street, which runs north-south. This work by E. Tamás Soltra, an allegory representing the struggle of humanity to achieve a noble existence, is much more appealing visually in person than in pictures. The university setting is appropriate for two reasons. Students played a major role in the revolution. Also the Sopron provisional revolutionary council had its headquarters across the street from the north side of the campus on Ady Endre Avenue at number 10. The building, once called a Children and Youth Center, still houses children's programs. It remains part of the university and is typical of 1950s construction.

During early Cold War days, trains from Austria did not stop at Sopron. They went from one corner of Burgenland to another, accompanied through Hungary by armed guards and with locked windows and doors. So Sopronians with relatives who had been banished in 1946 would wait for trains to slow down at the Batsányi Street crossing of the curved track west of the GYSEV station. There they could glimpse each other, wave a greeting, and maybe hold aloft new grandchildren, as the train crossed Hungary between the Austrian towns of Deutschkreutz and Mattersburg without stopping at Sopron itself. Not far from Batsányi, two blocks east on Csengery, the big square and otherwise nondescript building on the southeastern corner was a border-guard barracks during the Cold War.

The GYSEV station saw more than locked trains going through without stopping. In late 1944 and 1945, the station was the focus of at least three massive Allied bombing attacks. After the war, the ethnic Germans were put on trains for Germany at this and the Déli terminal. Toward the end of the Cold War, when travel slowly liberalized, the GYSEV station split into two, one domestic and another international, sharing a building yet separate, with passport control installed on the international side for those traveling to Austria. After the fall of the Iron Curtain and the emergence of a wave of migration from Africa, Asia, and the Middle East, it became the end of the line for small groups of dark-skinned men speaking unknown languages and awaiting westbound trains, as the border guards swooped down and took them away. Only the Jewish deportation is commemorated here by the plaque installed by the Evangelicals, and that expulsion took place from the Déli station, which still stands but is now a disco with no trace of its role in that episode.

Outside the city limits, the small towns and border crossings a few kilometers away bear traces and reminders of practically the whole range of twentieth-century upheavals. These include the post–World War I lynchings and rebellions, the exploitation and murder of slave laborers, political executions, the removal of ethnic Germans, the Cold War, the 1956 revolution, and 1989. More or less clockwise from the southwest, here are the most important places.

## Sopronbánfalva [Wanndorf]

The military cemetery contains graves of about 2,000 World War I soldiers of the Habsburg Empire and 600 Germans from World War II. László Molnár, Hungary's premier fighter pilot ace, credited with 25 kills before he was shot down on August 7, 1944, is buried here. When the Germans and their Hungarian allies withdrew at the end of March 1945, they left more than 500 bodies behind, mainly Jewish slaves.

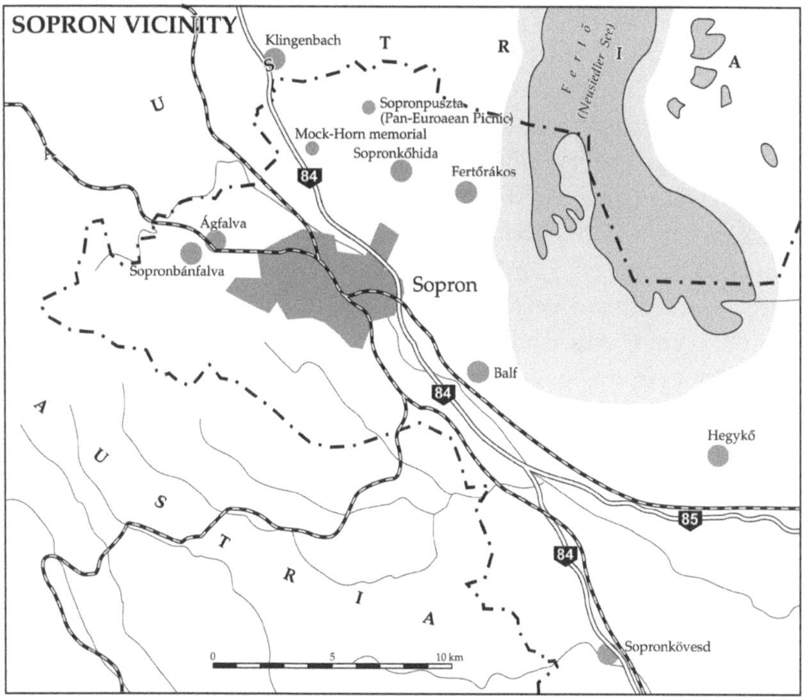


Figure 5.5 Sopron vicinity [Map 8].

# Ágfalva [Agerndorf]

The first two skirmishes of the 1921 insurrection took place here. During the first, on August 28, 1921, a 13-year-old boy from Kecskemet named László Baracsi was the only fatality. The second, on September 7–8, left four dead and led to the Venice conference and the Sopron referendum. Baracsi became known as the first martyr to the irredentist cause, though it is not clear whether he was killed by a bullet fired by an Austrian gendarme or a Hungarian insurgent. He is buried in the cemetery at Ágfalva.

In addition to the outsize grave marker, there is a monument in the village center across the street from the St. George Roman Catholic Church. His "sacrifice" is still celebrated at the loyalty monument at Harka south of Sopron, and at the Prónáy statue on the Károly hill.[4]

The village's largely ethnic German population supported Hungary's World War II alliance with Germany. When local parish priest József Várga expressed opposition to the alliance, Volksbund youth beat him to death. He died at the age of 52 on November 18, 1942. The German firm Robert Bosch moved into town in the summer of 1944, part of the effort to disperse war industry after Allied bombing started. The company's home page skips over activities from the 1942 death of the owner to 1951. Also, in 1944 hundreds of Jewish slave laborers were sent here for East Wall construction, with 1,200 estimated in town during December 1944. At the end of the war, 882 of their corpses were exhumed from a mass grave across the street from the main cemetery entrance. After they were removed to Budapest, no physical reminder of their sojourn at Ágfalva remained. Among them was the uncle of American architect and historian András Koerner, a Jewish journalist named Ferenc Doros, who had covered the 1936 Olympics and worked for a German language paper covering Budapest. He died at the Ágfalva labor camp in February 1945. In contrast, a German *Heimat* museum at 8–9 Hegy Street on the southwest edge of town commemorates the life and removal of the German community. There are also memorials to the German removal at the main square and to the Sopron referendum at Patak Street 50.

4 András Böhm, director of the Heimat Museum, agrees with historian Mária Ormos that it is not clear that Baracsi was killed by Austrian fire. Like Ormos says, there is no explanation for what on earth he was doing in Ágfalva on that day. Neither the memorial nor the grave mentions that he was 13 years old. See Mária Ormos, *Civitas Fidelissima: Népszavazás Sopronban 1921* (Győr: Gordiusz, 1990), pp. 113, 118–19.

## Klingenbach [Kelénpatak]

On June 27, 1989, foreign ministers Alois Mock of Austria and Gyula Horn of Hungary posed for a picture here, cutting the barbed wire fence that had separated their countries for about 40 years. Crossing was still illegal, but much of the actual wire had already been rolled up, and they had to search for a segment of uncut fence. The resultant photo became emblematic of the end of the Iron Curtain. The site has a memorial to their moment, in the hills off to the right of Route 84, the Bécsi (Viennese) út, on the way to the border at Klingenbach. Turn into the Arcus Étterem [Restaurant] parking lot, then walk up the dirt path angling up to the right at about 45 degrees from the main road. At the top there is a turn to the left and soon the memorial with two park benches. When we visited, there were no signs indicating the presence of the memorial, either at the top of the hill or on the main road. This could be because the memorial was just installed or because Horn was a socialist. The memorial is rectangular stone, with marble tablets affixed. Twenty-five years after the wire cutting, a commemoration brought together the foreign ministers of Austria, Hungary, and Slovakia to celebrate this milestone, on the cusp of a new wave of fence-building, this time by the Hungarians.

## Sopronpuszta

The memorial park at the border on the road to Morbisch [Fertőmeggyes] celebrates the Pan-European picnic of August 19, 1989. Hundreds of people, mainly East Germans, crossed the border illegally into Austria and did not return. A border guard detachment assigned to the event was prepared only to stamp passports for a few dignitaries planning a ceremonial and symbolic crossing. Their commander, Lieutenant Colonel Árpád Bella, became a hero of the affair, ordering his men to stand down and not resist the wave of crossers that developed. The picnic came to be seen as a catalytic event in the collapse of the Berlin Wall, as East

Germans saw a way to circumvent barriers by traveling to Hungary via Czechoslovakia and then to Austria to reach West Germany. The best of the multiple monuments, certainly from a symbolic perspective, is the open door in a frame, open toward Austria and the West, donated by the Hungarian guild of stone masons and producers of artificial stone and dedicated on the 15th anniversary of the picnic.[5]

The centerpiece is the massive, dramatic, and perhaps overwrought sculpture group by Miklós Melocco, who also created the moving statue of Miklós Radnoti on the old Vienna road outside of Győr. This one, of citizens emerging into sunlight from totalitarian darkness, has been compared to commuters coming out of a subway station. The park contains a guard tower and tablets along a border walking trail with detailed information on the working of the Cold War border control system. In 2015, the year that Hungary deployed a razor wire barrier across its southern border, the park became officially designated a European Heritage Site.

5 For a history of the memorial park since its 1989 inception, see Erwin A. Schmidl, “Eine Grenze und viele Denkmäler,” in Stefan Karner and Philipp Lesiak, eds., *Der erste Stein aus der Berliner Mauer: Das paneuropäische Picknick 1989* (Graz: Verein zur Förderung der Forschung von Folgen nach Konflikten und Kriegen, 2019), pp. 145–72. On the picnic itself, see Mathew Longo, *The Picnic: A Dream of Freedom and the Collapse of the Iron Curtain* (New York: Norton, 2023).

Figure 5.6 The open door at Sopronpuszta.

## Sopronkőhida

This is perhaps the most infamous Hungarian prison outside of Budapest, the site of political executions carried out by the wartime government allied with Germany and later by the Communist regime. Budapest architect Gyula Wagner designed the facility, which opened in 1886. The 11 wartime opponents executed there included parliamentarian Endre Bajcsy-Zsilinsky and left-wing poet László János Nemeth from Győr. Early in 1945, prisoners included four former prime ministers at the same time, all in the former hospital building, Dezső Pattantyús-Ábrahám, Móric Eszterházy, Miklós Kállay, and Géza Lakatos.

Cardinal József Mindszenty, who was born József Pehm in Csehimindszent, a village in southern Vas County, and later became the prince primate of Hungary and the international face of Hungarian resistance to Communism, was held at the prison from November 27, 1944, until the end of March 1945. He is commemorated at his birthplace with a tablet by the church and a bust in the park next door. After World War II, he openly opposed new measures including land distribution, declaration of the republic, and the prosecution of war criminals. In conrast, he did not speak out against the dispossession and murder of the Jews and the emergence of a postwar wave of anti-Semitism, including blood libels and pogroms.[6]

The prison is north-northwest of Sopron, via the Pozsonyi Road and the Pesti-Barnabas Road toward Kőhida, two kilometers before Fertőrákos. Commemorative plaques on the prison wall face the street. Eight 1956

6 Maté Gárdonyi, "Veszprémi püspöki rendeletek a zsidótörvények árnyékában," pp. 126–36, and Zoltán Paksy, "A veszkorszak Zalaegerszegen," pp. 273–87, in Judit Molnár, ed. *Nagypolitikától a Hétköznapokig: A Magyar Holokauszt 70 Év Távlatából* (Balassi Kiadó, 2016); Braham, *The Politics of Genocide*, vol. II, p. 1048–9; Paul A. Hanebrink, *In Defense of Christian Hungary: Religion, Nationalism, and Antisemitism 1890–1944* (Ithaca: Cornell University Press, 2006), pp. 156, 228; László Karsai, *Szálasi Ferenc: Politikai életrajz* (Budapest: Balassi kiado, 2016), p. 334; Jenő Hejjas, *A Nyugat/Magyarországi Felkelés: Kecskemetiek az 1921. Évi Nyugat-Magyarországi Harcokban* (Budapest: Magyar Häz, 2006), p. 106.

revolutionaries, including three leaders of the Győr uprising (Gábor Földes, Árpád Tihanyi, and István Török), were hanged here and buried in an unmarked field reachable by turning west onto the country road just north of the prison. A tablet on the burial ground lists those buried there as well as Attila Szigethy. However, his death resulted from a fall from a hospital window in Győr. The field and the graves are now marked.

## Fertőrákos [Kroisbach]

The town is on the road from SopronKőhida, just inside the border on the southwest end of Fertö tó, the lake that the Austrians call Neusiedler See. A borderguard garrison stood on the west side of the road. The buildings are a shambles now, but you can still see the tower from which guards scanned the marshy grasslands leading to the lake for unauthorized traffic. Since 2009 Imre Csapó, a retired borderguard noncommissioned officer, has maintained an Iron Curtain museum in the town at Fő utca 242, with free admission. He offers modestly priced local red wines from his own cellar.

Hundreds of slave laborers toiled at Fertőrákos, along with Italian prisoners of war and convicts from Kőhida, quarrying limestone and digging stone, gravel, and sand for construction. Stone was quarried by hand, and guards amused themselves by singling out Jews for target practice. Survivor István Dobi called Fertőrákos the most brutal workplace in Hungary. The workforce in February 1945 included two companies of the military labor service, along with 2,150 Hungarian soldiers, 347 SA and SS men, 144 employees of the Todt organization, and 1,200 to 1,400 slave laborers. The camp was hastily abandoned, starting on March 27, 1945. When the march to Mauthausen started, about 400 dead were left behind, including literary scholar György Tamássi. Two hundred forty were exhumed in November 1946 and buried in Budapest; 163 others remained unidentified. Hardly any trace remains of bunkers, trenches, and other barriers, but hand-tool cuts in quarry walls remain visible.

## Balf

The town is southeast of Sopron, on the Balfi road, which runs parallel to and east of Route 84. At the site of a mass grave stands a 1992 monument to Jewish slave laborers murdered in winter of 1945.[7] Among them was Antal Szerb, one of the leading lights of Hungarian literature in the twentieth century, whose prodigious *History of World Literature* remains useful. László Kutas designed the monument, which replaced the original 1968 memorial, that was destroyed by vandals soon afterward. The Gestapo, the Nazi Party, and the SS all had headquarters at the thermal baths building in town. The slave camp housed between 1,800 and 2,000 men and women in barns, sheds, and stables behind residences, all of them frequently wet from seeping groundwater. Those who arrived on forced marches in the worst shape were taken to Ilonamajor, now an equestrian center near Hidegség, and killed there. Every day the dead were hauled on ladders from the Balf hovels to the church hill [local name Kirchner] where a burial place had been designated outside the cemetery fence. Some locals, among them bath manager Ernő Wosinski and his family, responded to the plight of the prisoners with compassion and risked their lives to sneak food to them.

## Sopronkövesd

A memorial in this village 16 kilometers southeast of Sopron along Route 84 commemorates the lynching on June 7, 1919, of two men from Ágfalva, 50-year-old railroad lineman Mátyás Schmidt and his 23-year-old son, also named Mátyás. The pretext for the hanging by Red Guardists under Tibor Szamuely came down to the failure of the elder Schmidt to stop

7 For images of this memorial, see <https://www.kozterkep.hu/~/14832/ Nemzeti_ irodalmi_tortenelmi_ emlekhely_Sopron_Balf_2008.html/photos>.

striking workers from tearing up tracks. His son brought him a hot meal before the hanging, and they tried to force him to participate in the killing of his father. He refused and they hanged him as well. He was one of eight Schmidt children and one of two who had served in the World War. The monument is at the site of the lynching in front of the town hall on Kossuth Lajos Street and is the work of local sculptor Zoltán Kottrik, who also designed the Iron Curtain memorial just southeast of the village near the chapel dedicated to Saint László.

Figure 5.7 The monument commemorating the lynching in Sopronkövesd.

CHAPTER 6

# Eisenstadt: Mass graves and museums

Eisenstadt [Kismárton in Hungarian] had the oldest continuous Jewish community in Austria. It was also the site of the fabulous court of the Eszterhazy family and the home of court musician Josef Haydn. The town is 50 kilometers from Vienna, 20 from Sopron, and is a district administrative center as well as the capital city of Burgenland. The major twentieth-century sites are arrayed from west to east rather than radiating outward from the center because of the dominant central location of the massive Eszterhazy estate and grounds. The Restaurant Henrici, comfortable and welcoming on Eszterhazyplatz south of the castle, is well located about a half kilometer from the Jewish sites on the western side and a kilometer from the easternmost sites. The coffee is good, but a Golser pils from the Pannonia Brauerei is even better. The bright fresh beer is made in Gols, the site of the first of a series of mass National Socialist demonstrations in Burgenland during the February 1938 run-up to the Anschluss.

East of Henrici there are four sites of twentieth-century importance. These places are all accessible by walking east on either the pedestrian HauptStrasse or the parallel Haydngasse just to the north, which skirts the Eszterhazy palace grounds. On earlier visits we had walked HauptStrasse, which has numerous coffeehouses and the tourist information center at city hall, but in May 2018 we chose Haydngasse. Josef Haydn spent much of his life here, and the city highlights his presence from the moment you enter. Like the sign along Route 50 says, "Haydnstadt, Eisenstadt." The city guide notes that some of the buildings on the street that bears his name were lost during the bombings of 1944, choosing to describe the bombing as part of the liberation of Austria rather than the defeat of the Third Reich, of which Austria was a willing participant. The bomb damage appears to have been on the westernmost part of the street, where some of the buildings appear new even though they harmonize with the rest of the architecture. Number 2 at the west end on the south side has a plaque that notes it was

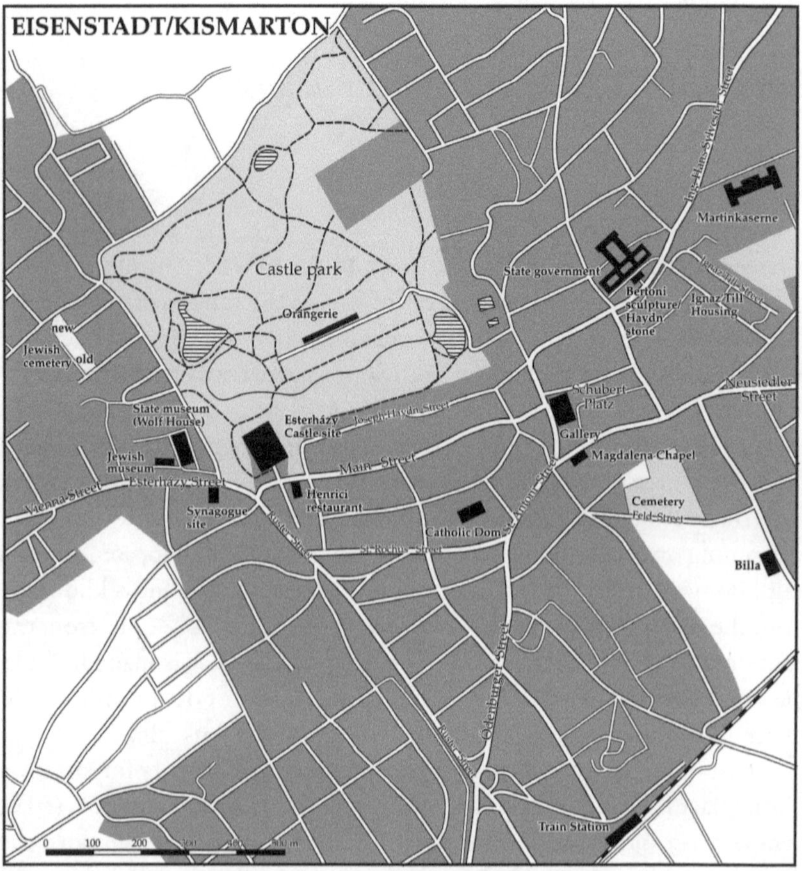


Figure 6.1 Eisenstadt/Kismarton [Map 9].

built in 1955–6, while the Augustine cloister at number 3 across the street and a bit farther east dates from the late seventeenth century. Number 11 houses the city library and we wandered in to have a look. On the second floor, in a glass-encased seminar room, a teacher conducted a German language class with about 20 young adult students, almost all brown-skinned, including a woman wearing a headscarf.

The students in this class were not the only people in town from elsewhere. The young bespectacled man at the cash register in the museum was Hungarian and commuted from Nagycenk near Sopron across the Hungarian border. The waitress at Gasthaus Kis where we ate lunch had emigrated from Hungary 22 years earlier. She came from Salgótarján. The waitress at Henrici, who had come from Szekszárd, also in Hungary, had been educated as a teacher and had resided in Eisenstadt for two years.

To the east of the library, number 19 is the Haydn home, and number 21 is the Haydn Museum. The entrance to the Schloss Park, where the Austrian army's Thirteenth Infantry band gave a celebratory concert at the time of the Anschluss, is after number 29, just before the Diocese Museum. Haydn lived in the house at 19 with his wife, Mária Anna Theresia, during his 12 years as music director at the Eszterházy court. For Haydn fans, the museum is a good place to learn about his life and for guidance regarding other Haydn sites in the city.[1] At the end of Haydngasse and a block to the south at Franz Schubert Platz 6, the Landesgalerie, the spacious new state art gallery, complete with an auditorium, cinema, and flexible walls, emphasizes contemporary painting. There is no admission charge.[2]

Another block south is the Magdalena chapel. Built in 1764–5 with money from a bequest left by Haydn's neighbor Magdalena Frumwalden, the chapel has old-world origins. But the attraction is the line of 14 tablets on the eastern exterior wall along Neusiedler Strasse (Route 50). From left to right, the first two commemorate the military dead of both World Wars. The next 12 list all 563 of them alphabetically, the 131 from World War I followed by the 432 from World War II.

1 Information on hours, entrance fees, and exhibits may be found at <https://haydnhaus.at/besucherinfo/>.

2 Hours and exhibit information may be found at <https://landesgalerie-burgenland.at/ besucherinfo/>.

From the church, the Landhaus, as the government center is called, is 200 meters to the east and 100 meters north (left) on Burgerspitallgassse. The building has been occupied continuously since its completion in 1930. Until that time the state operated out of the Martin kaserne, the military garrison built during 1853–5 and located about 250 meters farther up the road to the east and across the street. The kaserne remains an active military base. The housing development nearby on Ignaz Till Strasse, between Ing. Hans-Sylvester Strasse at the northwest end and Golbeszelle Strasse to the southeast, was built at the same time as the state office building and initially occupied by state employees. Till was a social democratic politician who tried to stave off Nazi control of Burgenland in the spring of 1938 by organizing an anti-Hitler coalition that included the workers' movement. At war's end he was liberated from Dachau but died before the year was out. The dwellings on the street that bears his name were damaged during the war and restored in the late 1950s. They are a striking case of town planning. In terms of their importance to the character and appearance of the town, they resemble the Oberwart residential area developed for settlement of Germans from the South Tyrol at the end of the 1930s (chapter 4).

Figure 6.2 The Ignaz Till dwellings today.

Till's efforts were bound to fail given the powerful local National Socialist wave led by Tobias Portschy (see chapter 2 above). On March 11, 1938, the Nazi Party in Vienna sent out the order for mass demonstrations. Portschy and his comrades were ready. Standing in front of 8,000 followers, atop the Haydn memorial stone in front of the Landhaus, he demanded that the state government yield power to him, then led a torchlight procession to underscore Nazi power and success. With the Nazi leadership behind him, he and his followers took over the building and drove out the old administration. On the day after this show of force, the actual occupation started, and the plaza where Portschy had stood became Adolf Hitler Platz. Three days later, the former leadership was moved from house arrest to the detention camp at Kaisersteinbruch (see chapter 10 below) and then into the hands of the Gestapo.

Now the 1991 bronze and steel column "70 Years of Burgenland" by Wander Bertoni dominates the plaza in front of the main entrance to the government building. Bertoni came to Austria at the age of 18 in 1943 as a slave laborer. He stayed, studied at the Academy of Fine Arts in Vienna, worked on the postwar restoration of Vienna monuments including the plague column on the Graben, and achieved fame in his adopted country as a sculptor. There are more of his works at an outdoor museum at Winden am See. That town was the southern terminus of the road from Kaisersteinbruch built by Russian prisoners of war during World War I and known as the RussenStrasse (see chapter 8).

The plaza now bears the name "Europa Platz," and the Bertoni column reflects a profoundly different vision from the Haydn stone and Hitler Platz. The stainless steel column emerges from and soars above the carnage and rubble of the past, visible in the body parts and blocks of stone heaped below it. Recognizing past catastrophes and especially the times of Bertoni's arrival as a conscripted worker, the column rises optimistically upward, reflecting his own emergence from forced labor to become a recognized artist.

Despite the change in tone represented by the Bertoni column, the Landhaus still symbolizes Portschy's display of Nazi power. It remained the seat of government during Nazi rule, although the state of Burgenland was abolished in October 1938. Burgenland was then divided between Lower Austria to the north and Styria to the south. Eisenstadt was reduced to the capital of a district [*Kreis*] in Lower Austria for the duration of the war, and

Portschy wound up as deputy *Gauleiter* of Styria with its capital in Graz. The Landhaus contained the offices of the local police, the gendarmerie, and the Gestapo, as well as the *Volkstumstelle*, which coordinated activities of national groups, including ethnic Germans outside of the Reich, such as pro-Berlin *Volksbund* activists across the Hungarian border in Sopron. The office that managed construction of the local section of the East Wall in 1944–5, one of nine such offices, also occupied space in the building, as did most branches of the district administration.[3] Perhaps interest in the progress of this lunatic enterprise is what caused Heinrich Himmler to visit the city on March 28, 1945, to survey conditions.

This concentration of government offices directly representing the Third Reich indicates a major difference between the Austrian and Hungarian sides of the border. In Hungary, offices were distributed throughout the cities. For example, in Győr, after the start of the German occupation on March 19, 1944, the Wehrmacht had its headquarters in Bisinger Park, the Gestapo was on Bajcsy-Zsilinsky, and the goons of the Arrow Cross National Accountability Office operated from Liszt Ferenc Street.[4] In Eisenstadt, agencies associated with the regime were clustered in the Landhaus. But Hungarian and Austrian towns alike share a complete lack of public signage indicating the locations of these focal points of terror, theft, and murder.

From the Till residences, the Kaserne, and the Landhaus, the way to the western side of town goes back along the Hauptplatz. We were just starting to

3 In May 2016, I raised this question concerning the location of Nazi-era administrative organs with the helpful staff at the state museum. Judith Gollubits at the front desk called historian Dieter Szorger, whose work was very helpful in preparing this chapter. He clarified the locations over the telephone.

4 March 19, 1944, is a pivotal date in Hungarian history. Up to that point the government had managed to resist German pressure to deport its Jewish population. Prime Minister Miklós Kállay, in office since March 1942, was removed and replaced by Döme Sztöjay, who cooperated with the occupiers, as did many government officials and ordinary Hungarians. Prior to that time, except for about 15,000 Jewish refugees who were expelled into the arms of the SS in northeastern Hungary in the summer of 1941, almost all Jews in Hungary survived in systematically straitened circumstances. See Ignác Romsics, *Hungary in the Twentieth Century*, trans. Tim Wilkinson (Budapest: Corvina Osiris), pp. 209–12; Braham, *Politics*, I, pp. 199–207.

slouch in that general direction on our 2016 visit, after leaving our car parked on the eastern side of town, when we happened to pass the Billa supermarket on Krautgartenweg. It is impossible to get herring in dill cream sauce in Győr, a town ten times the size of Eisenstadt, so I headed for the entrance to the grocery store. I got my fish and a fresh batch of Ritter Sport chocolate bars, but I also got the chance to talk briefly with a young African man at the front door selling *Augustin*, a street tabloid sold by the unemployed.

When I asked the price of the paper and he answered in English, I bought a copy, and asked him where he was from. He had come from Nigeria, made his way to the Mediterranean coast, and come across the sea from Libya on an inflatable raft, which he called a "balloon." The sea was so violently rough on his crossing, he said, that some of his 60 fellow passengers had to be blindfolded to keep them from going berserk. He had arrived in Austria by train, had been in the country for two and one-half years, and was not permitted to work while his request to stay was being adjudicated. Resisting the temptation to attempt a full-blown interview when he had more basic concerns, I asked him the question that mattered most to me. In Hungary, the government seeks to block the migration of dark-skinned others from outside of Europe, presenting them as an existential threat to the survival of the country's white Christian character. I asked him what countries he had crossed on his way into Austria. He said he did not know. He could have come up from Italy via Slovenia, from Turkey through former Yugoslavia, or along some other route that I cannot even imagine, but the plain fact was that none of these countries, Hungary included, were on his radar. He did not even know their names. He was heading north and west.

The walk through the center of town to the western side offers a good opportunity to stop at Henrici and savor a Golser pils while reflecting on the visit to the Haydn stone and the former Adolf Hitler Platz. And the Haydn stone does merit some reflection. The inscription on the stone translates as "My language was universally understood throughout the world." Yet Haydn's music formed the basis for various versions of the Austrian and German national anthems, and the stone's dedication in 1932 featured German students bringing scoops of soil from different parts of Germany to place inside the stone, manifestations of nationalism rather than universality.

Near the Henrici, a few meters north across the plaza, is the entrance to the Eszterhazy palace, the most important and popular tourist destination in the city and perhaps in all of Burgenland. The palace is open daily April through October and on weekends from November through March.[5] The castle dates from the thirteenth century and was the seat of the Eszterhazy family from the eighteenth. Emperor Franz Joseph viewed the 1893 Hungarian large-scale military exercise with Kaiser William of Germany from the castle library.

The castle illuminates the life of the grandest of Hungarian noble families, but for the twentieth century its primary importance is as an example of a superb restoration and renovation after a destructive post–World War II occupation by the Russians. They used it as the headquarters of the provincial government of Burgenland and later the regional court. They trashed the castle, and only the stucco decorations, the tile stove, and windows opening on the castle chapel are original. Soviet forces destroyed 7,000 of the library's books and removed 50,000 others, leaving only the catalog and around 50 volumes.

The Eszterhazys encouraged and established a major Jewish presence in Burgenland and particularly in Eisenstadt, where their contributions still resonate nearly eighty years after the community was destroyed. The Eszterhazys had brought Jews into the region to work on their estates, starting at the end of the seventeenth century. They had gained permission for the newcomers to live, work, and establish their religious institutions in seven settlements known as the *Siebengemeinde* that belonged to the family. The interdependent relationship between the Jewish settlements and the Eszterhazys ended after the revolution of 1848, and the Jewish population merged into adjacent settlements. The Jewish community of Eisenstadt became an independent village known as Unterberg-Eisenstadt, with its own mayor, judge, and notary public, until the fateful year of 1938 and the destruction of the Jewish community of 446 members. The town that Hans Bodenheim, the Jewish narrator of Franz Werfel's incomplete novel *Cella* lovingly called his "obscure nest" and "this provincial nest," emptied fast. By Kristallnacht in November, there was property to vandalize but no Jews in this or any other Burgenland town. Few survived the war, and

5 Additional detailed information may be found at <http://Eszterházy.at/en/Eszterházypalace/index.do>.

fewer returned. "For most of the survivors," Johannes Reiss has noted, "the thought of living here again was inconceivable."[6]

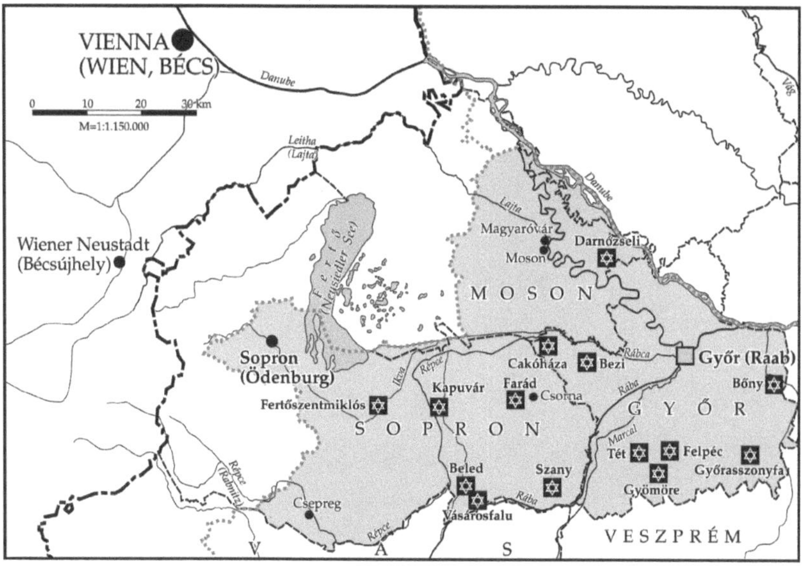


Figure 6.3 Towns in Győr-Moson-Sopron County where the only indications of a Jewish presence are cemeteries [Map 10].

Reminders of the Jewish presence and contributions to the city remain. The cemetery is of course to be expected. However, cemeteries are often the only physical reminders of once vibrant Jewish communities. This map, for example, shows 14 such communities in the adjacent Hungarian county of Győr-Moson-Sopron. The Eisenstadt cemetery, in two sections separated by Carl Moreau Strasse, includes more than the resting places of residents. The older section, closed in 1875, became the site of an effort

6 Johannes Reiss, *"… Because our love for our hometown has been drained from us …": A Walk through the Jewish History of Eisenstadt*, trans. Serge Claus (Eisenstadt: Österreichisches Jüdisches Museum, 2001), pp. 24, 26, 28, 36; Franz Werfel, *Cella oder die Überwinder*, trans. Joachim Neugroschell [*Cella, or the Survivors*] (New York: Henry Holt and Company, 1989), pp. 2, 4, originally written in 1938–9 and unfinished.

to identify the old Hebrew markers and make the information available online. The project was completed in November 2015.[7] The newer, northern one includes the remains of more than 200 slave laborers, many of whom died while building the East Wall. They were initially dumped in unmarked graves at Zurndorf [Zurány], Siegendorf [Cinfalva], Neudorf [Mosonújfalu], and Güssing [Németújvár], and have been reinterred and memorialized here.

Figure 6.4 The mass graves and memorials in the new section of the Jewish cemetery. Overall, according to a list compiled by Simon Wiesenthal in 2002, 27 mass graves contain the remains of Jewish slave laborers in Burgenland.

In Eisenstadt the cemeteries are not the only significant connections to the Jewish past. The chains that once stretched across the main street of the Jewish quarter to keep out traffic on the Sabbath remain on view, a reminder of the rigor with which local Jews observed the day of rest. Also, the Levite pitchers carved on exterior walls, for example at UnterbergStrasse

7 See the blog of the Austrian Jewish Museum, <http://www.ojm.at/blog/en/cemetery-eisenstadt-old/>, accessed May 18, 2018.

15, recall the servants of the rabbis in the ancient temple. And the synagogue site, a row house at Eszterhazy 20–22, now the location of an insurance company's office, bears a plaque attesting to its history. In 1938, it proved impossible to burn it down without destroying the adjacent buildings, so the local Nazis satisfied themselves with looting the treasures and gutting the inside. The Wehrmacht used the building as a warehouse during the war.

Figure 6.5 The entrance to the Jewish quarter. The chains are on the right, and the parking ticket vending machine is on the left.

The most significant legacies are the Jewish Museum and the Burgenland State Museum. The Jewish Museum at Unterberger 6 had been the home of banker Samson Wertheimer and had included his own private synagogue. The family of Alexander [Sándor] Wolf purchased the home in 1875. The Wolfs made their fortune as wine merchants. Sándor Wolf, who studied at the Vienna Commercial Academy and the University of Vienna, gained fame as a Judaica collector and carried out archaeological digs at Split on the Dalmatian coast before starting excavations in the vicinity of Eisenstadt in 1902. After the Nazi takeover of Germany in 1933, he fled to

Palestine and settled in Haifa. His house had once been the meeting place for writers and intellectuals, among them Hugo von Hofmannstahl, Franz Werfel, and Theodor Herzl. Alma Mahler, who dazzled a host of Central European artists, had also been there in 1929, the year she married Werfel, her third husband after Gustav Mahler and Walter Gropius.

The Burgenland Red Cross acquired the house in 1945, then turned it over to the state in the 1970s. The Austrian Jewish Museum Association opened the first Jewish museum in the country there in 1982, incorporating the former private synagogue of the Wertheimer family. The plaque dedicated to the memory of the Jewish soldiers who fell in combat during World War I, originally installed at the community house in 1934 and removed by the Nazis, has returned to public view at the museum. There are now other Jewish museums in Austria, notably the one at Dorotheergasse 11 in Vienna, but this was the first.

Figure 6.6 The entrance to the Burgenland Museum.

The Burgenland State Museum on the west side of Museumgasse between Meierhofgasse and Jerusalem Platz is practically around the corner from the Jewish Museum. The site was once the location of Sándor Wolf's private museum, based on his collections. These in turn formed much of the basis of the state collection. We have seen exhibits on shore birds, human migrations, the collapse of the Iron Curtain, Burgenland during World War I, the history of Roman Carnuntum, and most recently on the fateful year of 1938. The museum's displays have used and transcended the materials left by Sándor Wolf, and the institution remains grounded in his research, field activity, and acquisitions. Elsewhere in the border region there are small Jewish museums, in the former old-age home across Kossuth Street from the synagogue in Győr and in the building housing Szombathely's Jewish community's offices next door to the Szombathely synagogue. Nowhere in the borderlands though is the Jewish heritage as well preserved and as central to the town's cultural heritage as in Eisenstadt. So in addition to the official characterization of the city as Haydnstadt, it could also be characterized as Judenstadt, or, given what took place here in March 1938, as Portschystadt.

CHAPTER 7

# Győr: The wonders of it all

In Győr, the best spot for reflection on recent horrors is Baross 23, at McDonald's. The Hungaria coffeehouse once occupied the ground floor below the county headquarters of the Arrow Cross. At first glance, the Rába Hotel at the corner of Baross and Szent István might seem more appropriate. Built in 1903–5, it originally bore the name Royal, became the Red Star shortly after World War II, and then the Rába in 1968. As the Royal it took a direct hit in an Allied air raid of July 2, 1944, through the glass roof and basement ceiling, killing and wounding those hiding inside its bomb shelter. So the hotel has ample links with past horrors. But the location isn't as powerfully connected to the core evils of the period as the bright, cheerful, ahistorical, and very American McDonald's. It has been a fixture at Baross 23 since it opened in May 1989, a year after the chain opened its first Hungarian location in Budapest. The Győr McDonald's was the first outlet for the burger giant outside of the capital.

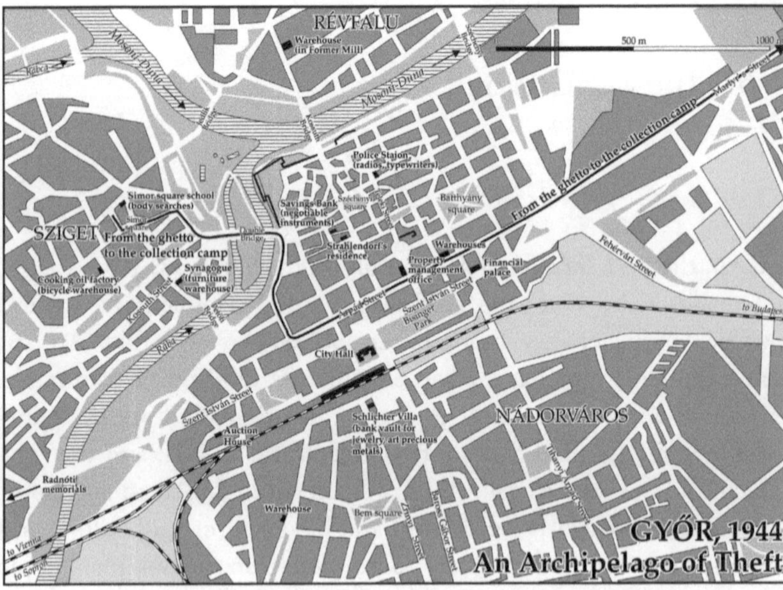


Figure 7.1 Győr, 1944, An Archipelago of Theft [Map 11].

Automatic sliding doors lead to the counter where cheerful young Hungarians dispense happy meals and shakes. At the separate McCafé counter, they also offer a respectable cappuccino or espresso and tasty pastries. This is Europe, after all, and coffee is important. But whether patrons came for the latté or the fries, they show no awareness that they are on the site of the local headquarters of the murderously anti-Semitic local variant of Nazism, the so-called Hungarist movement of the Arrow Cross. So the foray into the grim twentieth-century past in Győr starts on a site that is not on exhibit or even in storage. Its deaccessioning started during Allied bombings in 1945. It remained usable as the location of the Hungaria coffeehouse, and there was even a state-run toy store on the premises at the turn of the 1950s. In 1960, the deaccessioning was completed with demolition for a new building. Starting there, the walk around town includes locations that are marked and thus on display, albeit sometimes in an obscure or disingenuous manner, and others in storage, identifiable but unmarked. It also includes other locations that are neither marked nor recognizable.

Just across Baross at number 22, another deaccessioned site once housed the meeting place of the *Baross Szövetség*. This association of Christian artisans and businessowners, founded in Budapest in 1919, was established in Győr in 1937, and gained footholds in the reoccupied territories in the next few years. It questioned the legitimacy of Jewish craftsmen and businesspeople, and one local historian in Győr considers the group to have ardently supported the Arrow Cross. The organization lasted until 1945; the Jewish owner of the building, Nándor Lőwy, disappeared the preceding year. The building now has ground floor businesses and three stories of professional offices and residences. Its unadorned ordinariness marks it as a product of the immediate postwar period. Probably the original building fell victim to Allied bombing, making it another early case of deaccessioning.

The Rába Hotel up the street is diagonally across the intersection from city hall. The square in front of the latter building was an important site of community ceremony, such as sending troops off to war and later welcoming them back. It was also the focus of workers' protests in the tumultuous days of the Great Depression. At least once, on September 1, 1931, machine guns occupied the balconies as workers from factories east of town paraded down Szent István, then known as *Vilmos császár* [Kaiser Wilhelm] út, past the building to Petőfi tér, closely followed by mounted police. The severed right hand of King Stephen, a treasured relic kept in the cathedral at Budapest, was the focus of a worship service on the square during its 1938 tour of the country. Six years later, local authorities at city hall managed the dispossession, ghettoization, and deportation of the Jews. After the defeat in 1945, a red star above the entrance, the symbol of Communist power, dominated the facade and the square. It lasted until revolutionaries deaccessioned it in October 1956. The square was one of the three most important sites of the revolution in Győr, along with the jail to the west along Révai Street and the party headquarters, later the regional revolutionary government building at Szent István 3. From 1961 until the end of the Communist regime, monuments to the 1919 Soviet Republic and to Red Army units that took the city in the spring of 1945, flanked the entrance to city hall. Both showed larger-than-life armed fighters atop waist-high blocks of marble.

The mayor who presided there for more than a decade starting in 2006, once expressed puzzlement over continued Jewish focus on the Holocaust. At the southeast corner of Szent István and Baross, at the foot of the bridge, stands a memorial that reflects the far more widely accepted obsession with Trianon. The obligatory memorial, which dominates the corner today, shows the dismemberment of the country in maps and text. The inscription "We believe in the resurrection of Hungary" reflects a fixation more comprehensible to most Hungarians than Jewish interest in the Holocaust and reinforces the Christian nature of the sentiment suggested by the crosses.

The Trianon memorial dominates the corner today. It represents a swing in popular style unleashed throughout the country at the end of the Communist regime. The memorial has three parts, a column draped with the flag and bearing the aforementioned inscription, facing a Cross of Lorraine, and a tablet alongside a park bench. The tablet details the loss of territory and population. This ensemble was preceded by a 1971 representation of a worker, a farmer, and a student, holding high the banner of socialism. Before that, there had been a monument to Soviet war dead, from early in the occupation, when the intersecting streets had been renamed Lenin and Sztálin. The Soviet memorial was edited temporarily during the 1956 uprising by removal of the red star, a gesture of loathing for the regime that was repeated at city hall across the street and throughout the country. Then it was removed in its entirety.

The arrival of the Red Army in 1945 is now marked only in cemeteries. Most Soviet soldiers who fell in the advance into Győr are buried in the public cemetery in Nádorváros on the southern side of the city. The monument there is topped by the only red star on display in the city, except the one on the Heineken beer label, against which the Hungarian government campaigned unsuccesssfully in the spring of 2017. There is also a small military cemetery in a triangular plot west of the city at the intersection of Route 1 to Hegyeshalom and Vienna with Route 85 toward Sopron. It contains the graves of Romanian soldiers who accompanied the Red Army and fell in battle at Sopron, Veszkény, Szárföld, and Ágfalva. There are 40 individual graves and four mass graves with unidentified remains. The squat monument at the graveyard, designed by László Alexovits and installed in 1959, has seen little maintenance and seems almost intended not to draw interest. The red paint has disappeared from the star.

Figure 7.2 The only red star in town that is not on a Heineken bottle.

The 1956 revolution is commemorated near the center of the park known as Bisinger *sétány*, just east of the Trianon group. The sculture by Pal Deim, called *Golgota*, was installed in 1993. The memorial is another example of both the wave of memorialization that took place after the change in regimes and the use of Christian imagery, this time in the name, in commemorating the events of 1956. József Bisinger (1780–1843), a successful glass craftsman, left money to underwrite construction of a new city hall, finished at the turn of the twentieth century. The park, with its winding walkways, playgrounds, trees, and succession of memorials, runs eastward on the south side of Szent István, with a row of mostly residential buildings lining the southern edge. The Metropol pension at the western corner in number 2 had four rooms set aside for Jewish guests until the deportation in the spring of 1944. The elegant house at number 10 also accommodated the kosher eatery owned by Samu Schwartz, one of three restaurants that Jews were permitted to frequent in the months before ghettoization. From March 1944 occupants of the elegant bourgeois flats included the wartime German military command. By that spring, emergency shelter trenches for those surprised during a stroll by the bombers also marked the park. When the Soviets followed the Nazis, they took over the building at number 18 and renamed the park for Bulgarian party leader Georgi Dimitrov. That label was discarded in favor of the original in the wave of post-1989 renamings. Celebrations of the 1956 revolution take place every year citywide, all on October 23, but the main one occurs here, at the memorial in the park.

The earliest installation at the site of the current Trianon memorial on the western end of the park was a *Vas Honvéd*, "an iron defender of the homeland." This larger-than-life wooden soldier resembled others in cities throughout the Empire during World War I. Citizens who donated to the support of war widows and orphans pounded nails into it, transforming a permeable wooden figure into a staunch iron warrior. It stayed in place through much of the interwar period, sheltered in a six-sided gazebo. One such figure survives in the Sopron Museum (chapter 5).

VETKEZET
GYÖR. Látkép a Royal szállóval.

Figures 7.3, 7.4, and 7.5 Three iterations of the corner of Baross and Szent István, or Lenin and Stalin. The first image shows the kiosk with the Iron Warrior visible in the bottom right corner. In the next image, the Soviet war memorial is on the left. In the third one, the monument to builders of socialism is on the right. All are postcard views.

The statue site, the hotel, and city hall, at the Baross-Szent István intersection, sit at the foot of the Baross Bridge leading south over the railroad tracks. On the other side of the bridge, the Leier City Center residential-office-retail development occupies the square-block site of the former Frigyes [Friedrich] garrison, a military headquarters designed by Ignác Alpár and built in 1895–7. It bore the name of Archduke Frigyes, 1856–1936, commander of imperial armed forces from 1907. He visited the garrison in 1898 and is buried with his wife, Isabella, in Mosonmagyaróvár's Szent Gotthard Church. A 2006 statue in that town shows him seated on a bench around the side of the seventeenth-century downtown building that once belonged to the Habsburgs and is now a guesthouse. The Győr garrison, which initially housed two battalions and the regimental staff of the nineteenth K. u. K. (Kaiserlich und Königlich, or Imperial and Royal) Infantry, included warehouses, stables, billets for troops and officers, and a headquarters, all painted the customary Habsburg yellow known as

*Kaisergelb*. The central parade ground, now a park with flower gardens and fountains, sits atop an underground garage.

The garrison remained a presence during World War I, but wartime operations barely affected the city. The small army allowed by the victorious allies remained at the garrison and the expanding force at the end of the 1930s occupied it at the outset of the next war. From the start of drafting of Jewish men for manual labor in 1941, conscripts, including doctors and lawyers, were assembled, confined, and beaten there. Generally, local writers do not consider this part of garrison history worthy of mention.

The Red Army occupied the garrison in 1945, stayed for three years, then returned it to the Hungarians. Local leaders tried various civil activities: a technical college dormitory, a lumber business, even a tennis school, before the Hungarian army reoccupied the grounds. The name then changed to honor Ferenc Rákóczi (1676–1735), leader of a Hungarian rebellion against Habsburg rule at the beginning of the eighteenth century. The garrison played a prominent role in the revolution of 1956, as headquarters for Hungarian units and some state security forces, and became the site of a confrontation between rebels and soldiers stationed there. After the uprising was put down, the Russians returned and stayed until 1988. The subject of their paying rent or leaving never came up.

The Soviets left a mess, and although it remained the most substantial physical reminder of the Habsburg Empire in Győr, the authorities allowed the deterioration to continue. In 2001, the garrison was designated a historical landmark, and four years later Leier bought it and the almost adjacent Schlichter Villa. Just then, the Hungarian National Committee of the Paris-based International Council on Monuments and Sites conferred on the city of Győr, which owned both sites, its not exactly coveted Lemon award for "fifteen years of incompetent management and no hope for reuse."

By 2017, Leier had nearly completed restoration and brought the Schlichter villa back from the brink of ruin, saving Erik Pauly's splendid ceiling frescoes in the process. The villa, which dates from the same period as the garrison, sits just west of the south end of the pedestrian underpass beneath the train platforms at the railroad station. The site of outbuildings along Zrinyi Street now has retail establishments with no visible connection to the original structure. In 1944, the Schlichter became an important component of the archipelago of theft that emerged in Győr, a network of management and storage facilities that controlled, collected, and distributed various categories of property stolen from the Jews when they were stripped of their possessions, ghettoized, and deported. At the time, the villa housed the postal savings bank's secured loan branch (pawn shop) with two huge safes in which jewelry, gems, furs, and silverware were protected and managed separately from property pawned by other Hungarians. József Kóródy, who ran the facility, estimated the goods under his care to be worth many millions of pengő. The villa is now the local office of Deutsche Bahn. Some may see a bitter irony in the adaptation for use by the German railroad of a structure that played a part in the pauperization of the town's Jews before their deportation by rail to death camps. Certainly, Deutsche Bahn did not. In a more egregious example of insensitivity, the railroad announced in late 2017 its intention to name a new fast train after Anne Frank. She might be the world's best-known human being deported by train to a Nazi death camp, and the cries of outrage brought a quick change of plans.

The pedestrian underpass leads back toward downtown via the train station that from 1960 replaced the one destroyed by Allied bombs. More than 13,000 former prisoners of war came back to Hungary after World War I by way of the original station, and county *főispán* [governor or county executive] Kálmán Darányi, who stayed in office until 1928, greeted the first returning contingents there. Charles IV also detrained there in October 1921, to a serenade by a military orchestra and the salutes of an honor guard. He held audiences and asked for pledges of loyalty from the police. Darányi, a traditionalist but not a fool, knew that the *foispan* in Vas County (Béla Csiráky) had been sacked for his overly enthusiastic hospitality when the king first returned in the spring, and he was having none of that. He called in sick and took to his bed.

Immediately to the west (left) outside the main entrance of the train station, a wall plaque shows a stylized freight car and notes the role of the railroads in the deportations of 1944. It was placed by the Hungarian Evangelical Brotherhood and the John Wesley Ministerial College, along with tablets at several other railroad stations in 2004, on the sixtieth anniversary of the deportations. Tucked in the corner, the marker is not immediately visible. However, it can often be detected by following the smell of urine emanating from its semi-hidden location.

The main station entrance faces north from the station across Révai Street, through Honvéd Park to Szent István Avenue. The monument in the center, designed by Károly Csányi (the column) and Béla Markup (the turul atop the column), was dedicated to the Hungarian independence struggle of 1848–9, right at the time of the subjugation of Hungary by the Soviet Union. The jail is to the west along Révai, across the street from plaques marking the lethal encounter between revolutionaries and security forces on October 26, 1956.[1]

Figure 7.6 The center plaque names the three young people killed at the jail. The one on the right bears their likenesses.

The Révai gimnázium, or high school on the west side of the park was adapted early in the war for use as a military hospital because of its proximity to the railroad station. It also continued to function as a school through the

1 For a dramatic account of the clash at the jail (in Hungarian), see Robert Szabó, ed. "Szabó Jenő, a Hajtóműgyár Munkástanácsának titkára emlékezit 1956-ról," *Győri Tanulmányok* 28 (2006), pp. 59–71.

academic year 1942–3, when Jewish students were dismissed en masse. The building survived the wartime air raids, albeit with considerable damage. At war's end, the Russian occupiers also used it as a hospital.

When the ghetto was established in May 1944 across the Rába in the Sziget neighborhood that contained three Jewish houses of prayer, part of the Révai building became the "mixed" ghetto, where Jewish-Aryan couples were confined. Those people, numbering somewhere between 30 and 40, survived longer than people in the general ghetto. In fact, they almost made it through the war. At around nine o'clock on the night of March 26, 1945, they were taken to the Moson Duna and shot into the river, called by some locals the "moving ghetto," from the Medve Bridge, now the Széchenyi Bridge. Soviet forces arrived hours later.[2]

The Révai bears no markers to indicate its wartime use or the fate of those taken away to be killed. Nor is there a marker at the murder site, either at the bridge or along the river. All that appears to be known is the approximate number of victims. And while there are no markers for this outrage, the park in front of the school has two marble plaques embedded in the grass in front of newly planted trees, both within 20 meters of the building itself. The local natural gas company planted the first in 2009, in celebration of reaching 800,000 customers. Members of the Lions Club International placed the other one in remembrance of their international convention, held at Győr in 2015. As far as the victims of the Arrow Cross murder are concerned, they and their killers might just as well have never existed. A sense that something is missing is missing.[3]

Through the park, at its north end, Szent István (Császár Vilmos in the years leading to World War II, then Sztálin after 1948, and Tanácsköztársaság

2 The moving ghetto should not be confused with the floating ghetto. The latter name was given to boats bringing more than 3,000 Jews fleeing east from Austria in the wake of the 1938 Anschluss. The vessels tied up at places like Ásványráró, sometimes for months, before the refugees were allowed to debark.

3 The massacre of the Révai prisoners is mentioned in the text of the exhibit concerning the life of Bishop Apor Vilmos at the bishop's palace. With phrasing adapted directly from Randolph Braham's *Encyclopedia of the Holocaust* (volume I, p. 482), the exhibit identifies the site of their incarceration as *egy győri iskolaépület* [a Győr school building], without naming it.

in the 1960s, and Szent István again after 1989) runs west toward Vienna and east to Budapest.[4] Down the street to the west at number 3 stands the headquarters of the short-lived 1956 revolutionary council of western Hungary. The Attila Szigethy memorial tablet in the entryway was installed in 1992, during the initial post-Communist commemorative rush. It was put up in such haste that no one noticed until it was too late that the word "Foundation" in the name "Attila Szigethy Foundation USA," which had installed the memorial, lacked an "o". The mistake was corrected, sort of, with a tiny "o" squeezed between the "f" and the "u". The tablet reflects both Szigethy's importance as chairman of the council and the rush to memorialization.

To the right from Honvéd Park in front of the train station, Szent István goes east past city hall to the Baross corner and north on Baross toward McDonald's, for coffee and clean restrooms. As noted earlier, the coffee is respectable, although a better cup is available at the Bécsi (Viennese) in the courtyard behind the southwest corner of Baross and Arány János, the Kuglóf at Kazinczy 18, and elsewhere. These days, coffeehouses have clean restrooms for their customers, and in at least three locations public facilities are available to all for a small fee. But McDonald's, which Western tourists tend to dismiss with contempt (or furtively visit), brought the clean public restroom to post-Communist European cities. Moreover, McDonald's remains the only place open for coffee on Sunday mornings and introduced coffee to go, before Starbucks or Dunkin' Donuts showed up in the region. The chain is not often seen as having had a positive impact on European civilization, but a case can be made.

Walking back toward McDonald's from the train station, a right turn to the east on Árpád and a one-block walk to Csuczor, leads to the Béla Bartók Cultural Center. The center, the site of one of Bartók's last concerts, dates to 1904 when Mihály Bálin, a founder of the alcohol factory

4 "Street names," Deirdre Mask has observed, "are about identity, wealth, and [...] race. But most of all they are about power—the power to name, the power to shape history, the power to decide who counts, who doesn't and why." Deirdre Mask, *The Address Book: What Addresses Reveal about Identity, Race, Wealth, and Power* (New York: St. Martin's Press, 2020), p. 12.

just east of downtown on the old Buda Road, gave the city the real estate at Czuczor and Bajcsy-Zsilinsky as well as the money to build a theater on the site. Here, on March 5, 1938, Kálmán Darányi, now the prime minister, returned to Győr and presented what became known as the Győr program and sometimes the "Hungarian Five-Year Plan" for rearmament. He simultaneously promoted a law, then in the works, to reduce the Jewish economic presence and role, contending that there was a "Jewish question" that had to be resolved legally and according to plan. Darányi died in 1939 and so did not live to see where the law he promoted would lead. He does not appear to have been among the most vicious of anti-Semites, of whom there were plenty enough. He may have naively thought that limitations on the Jewish role in the society might lead to a more balanced situation. Still, the law that came soon afterward was, according to Holocaust scholar Randolph Braham, "the beginning of an avalanche of anti-Jewish measures that would end in disaster," culminating in the dispossession and deportations of 1944.[5] With these two main thrusts, a massive rearmament program and an institutional approach to solving the so-called Jewish question, Darányi sought two essentially incompatible outcomes, to curb the radical right and to curry favor with the Third Reich. Thereafter, the issue of the Jewish place in Hungarian society moved out of the realm of polemics and became a matter of political policy.

Darányi has been described as a well-intentioned man of narrow vision, modest ability, and a bureaucratic bent. During several trips to Germany after becoming prime minister, he made clear his agreement with the Germans about the need to curb Jewish influence. His Győr speech, delivered one week before the German absorbtion of Austria and, according to Jenö Lévai, with the knowledge that this was about to occur, made Hungary the first European country outside of Germany to declare its intention of resolving this issue through law. Six days after the speech, the Anschluss occurred, and the Nazi variety of anti-Semitism was at the Hungarian border. This speech set Hungary on an exterminationist course as far as the Jews were concerned and linked Hungary with Germany in a war that had disastrous long-term consequences for the entire country.

5 Braham, *Politics,* I, pp. 69, 126.

Darányi's speech may have been the most important single event of the twentieth century to take place in the city of Győr. However, local knowledge of this pivotal moment does not appear to be widespread. At a recent dinner I asked five college-educated Győri friends what they thought might be the most important event that had occurred in Győr in the past century. There was quiet, some thought, and the first response mentioned the bombing of the city by the Allies in 1944–5. The others considered this and decided, one after the other, that this was probably a good choice, that the bombings were extremely important to the city and its inhabitants. When I mentioned the Darányi policy, they acknowledged that it had wider and more profound ramifications. It was just that none of them knew that the Darányi policy had been promulgated in the city.

In Trieste, Italy, where Mussolini announced new racial laws later during the same year, the situation is different. The Italian dictator's open discussion on September 18, 1938, in the city's main square of fascist racism, and his description of his legislative plans launched a discriminatory program in much the same way as Darányi's Győr speech had done earlier in the year. The spot is marked by a historical plaque with text in Hebrew as well as Italian. Nowadays, there are still no monuments or plaques indicating that the Győr site had any importance during 1938. Moreover, the suggestion that the matter that troubled Darányi was really a "Christian question," that Jews had no questions about their legitimate status in Hungarian society but that instead the Christian majority had anxieties, doubts, and reservations that seemed in need of resolution, brings at best furrowed brows.

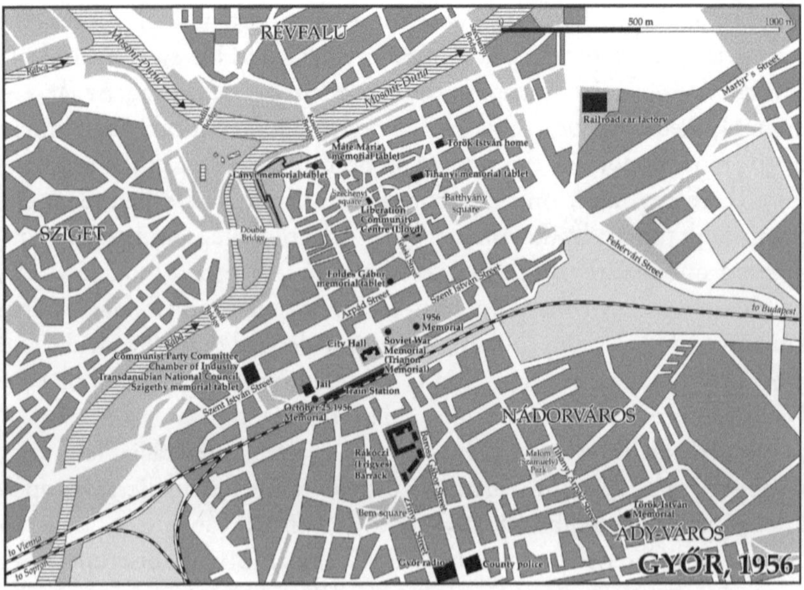


Figure 7.7 Győr 1956 [Map 12].

The year 1956 is different. The postwar theater company that performed at the cultural center returned the facility to center stage. Led by actor and director Gábor Földes, the troupe joined protests against the regime. Földes's voice boomed out the national anthem in front of party headquarters at Szent István 3 during the October 25 protests and the actors joined railroad car factory workers in opposing the Soviet presence. Party leaders hid inside their headquarters (soon to be taken over by the revolutionaries for the Trans-Danubian council), which was ringed by armored vehicles whose soldiers did not fire on demonstrators. On the 26th, the day of the shooting at the jail, a number of party men fled to Slovakia. After the Russians returned and restored the regime in early November, Földes was apprehended and hanged for his role in the uprising. He is commemorated with a marble tablet and a ceramic plaque on the south side of the Bartók center.

Diagonally across from McDonald's, at the northwest corner of the intersection of Baross and Kisfaludy Streets, is the former Matyás restaurant.

It was previously the Patio, and during the war the Sárkánylyuk [Dragon's Lair], a favorite lunch spot for Arrow Cross operatives working at Baross 23 (then called Szálasi after the Arrow Cross leader, later called Lenin, then Baross again). In 1944–5, Gyula Strahlendorf lived less than a block away in the townhouse at Kisfaludy 25, a home stolen from Jewish shoemaker Pál Neuwirth. Strahlendorf furnished his dwelling with loot from the network of warehouses bulging with Jewish property. One of the Arrow Cross's enthusiastic enforcers, he fled to Germany after the war, was brought back, convicted of involvement in more than 130 murders, and hanged. As a historic site, his former home remains in deep storage, and few are aware of his activity or his presence in the city.

Back on Baross, on the way north and on the right side at the corner of Kisfaludy, the imposing white building was built in 1905 as the first savings institution in the city. Known as the "Bank Palace," it covered an entire city block, and remains intact, with retail stores around the facade and residences above. In 1944, it became a key link in the archipelago of theft as the vault in the basement became a storage site for Jewish cash and negotiable instruments held by the city as well as the savings and investments of Christian residents. The Jewish owner of the building, Miksa Wollner, was deported in 1944. He "departed," as the local paper delicately put it, and a town tax functionary named Ferenc Földessy took over as caretaker. Only the money stayed.

Figure 7.8 The Bank Palace, on a picture postcard from 1913.

Around the next corner [Kazinczy], to the west directly facing the viewer at the end of the street, is the Carmelite Roman Catholic church. On August 17, 1938, the day that Arrow Cross leader Ferenc Szálasi received a three-year sentence for seditious activities, congregants and green-shirted Hungarists with Arrow Cross armbands prayed for his health. He was granted amnesty in 1940 and ultimately was prime minister during the last six months of the war. He was tried for war crimes and hanged in Budapest in 1946.

A little past the church on the island [Radó Sziget] in the Rába, halfway across the bridge that links Győrsziget to the center of town, is the main monument to Hungarian soldiers killed in the world wars. Like many such monuments, it was initially built after World War I, then rededicated to the fallen of both wars. Unlike most such monuments, the soldier kneels facing the river, wearing a coal-scuttle helmet and nothing else, his arms around a panther, perhaps restraining it, perhaps mounting it, or maybe just keeping warm.

Beyond it to the left and past the north end of the bridge is the former Neolog synagogue. The wartime regime used it as a warehouse for stolen furniture. Then in the spring of 1945, the courtyard became a meeting place for Jews returning from labor camps and seeking information on relatives.

Now it is home to the music program of the István Széchenyi University. It also displays paintings dating from the early years of the Communist Hungarian People's Republic and amassed by Romanian trucking entrepreneur János Vasilescu. The synagogue was recently restored with EU funds, helping bring back Jewish tourism if not Jews. The courtyard has one of the most moving Holocaust memorials I have ever seen, one that clearly indicates what is missing. The obelisk of grey marble, which is about seven feet tall, was dedicated in June 2007. György Filó and Levente Albert designed the column, which names more than 300 children under the age of 14 who were deported and murdered in 1944. Alongside their names are their ages, the years, months, and days that they lived.

Figures 7.9 (reverse), 7.10, and 7.11 Two images of the memorial to the children, followed by the Roth plaque by the door of the synagogue. The fate of the children haunted artist and memoirist Eva Quittner, who miraculously survived Auschwitz as a 13-year-old girl: "I cannot erase from my memory the fact that all the little Jewish children of Győr, without exception, were condemned to die."

The side of the column facing the front entrance has the names of Rabbi Emil Roth's children at the bottom. Eszti Roth lived seven years, two months, and two days; Gyuri Roth lived 11 years, four months, and 21 days. Roth himself had opportunities to escape the fate of his flock but declined them and went to Auschwitz with his family and the community. To the left of the front entrance, a memorial plaque honors his memory. Inside the main sanctuary, also on the wall to the left, a marble tablet commemorates the sacrifice of Jewish members of the World War I imperial forces who gave their lives for their country. The courtyard is open daily, the main building Wednesday through Sunday from 10 a.m. to 6 p.m.

Diagonally across Kossuth Street is the former Jewish old-age home. Recently renovated, it contains a small performance space in the basement, an upstairs kindergarten, and a museum of Jewish life in Győr on the ground floor. For lack of money to pay staff, the museum does not keep regular hours. Moreover, there is no information posted by the door to tell the visitor who to contact. The telephone number for the synagogue itself is 36 (06) 20 425 2660. Presumably, information is available at that number regarding the museum.

Kossuth Street goes eastward from the synagogue and it continues to undergo a process of gentrification. Still, it remains the home of a large part of the city's Romani population. Some of the townspeople, convinced that the area is dangerous, call it "Chicago" for its allegedly volatile ambiance. Friends warned Irene and me to take our walks elsewhere, but somehow we survived 15 years of occasional strolls in the neighborhood.

The center of the 1944 ghetto is nearby, to the north from the museum on Erkel Street, then left to Simor Square. Two prayerhouses that no longer exist were close by, on Híd (Bridge) and on Kígyó (Snake) Streets. Neither site is marked, and Kígyó has been cut in two by the apartment house that occupies the former location of the small temple. The school at the northernmost corner of Simor Square was the site of body cavity searches of Jewish women before the 3.2-kilometer march to the collection camp east of town on June 7 and 8.[6]

6 The women who performed these searches, among them nurses and midwives, were called *motozónők* [search women]. Historian Krisztián Ungváry discussed them in a presentation entitled "The Role of Hungarian Adminsitrative Services in Preparation for Ghettoization and Deportation," at an October 2019 conference in Győr that marked the 75th anniversary of the deportation. He noted that the position was not established on a national level but emerged independently in the gendarme districts. He sarcastically referred to *motozónők* as a *Hungaricum*, something uniquely reflective of a distinctive Hungarian culture. The term is usually reserved for such Hungarian phenomena as the csárdás dance, goulash soup, and the Túró Rudi candy bar.

On the bright sunny Sunday morning of May 5, 2013, Irene and I retraced the route from the Simor Square ghetto to the collection camp. It was an accidental counterpoint to a small (estimates ranged in the hundreds) demonstration by right-wing anti-Semites in Budapest that day. Their protests coincided with the opening of the Fourteenth Plenary Assembly of the World Jewish Congress in Budapest and received press attention in the United States. The rally purported to protest the buying up of Hungarian assets by Israelis, but we could not discern what assets exactly triggered this wave of purchases. Western banks and big box stores already dominated Hungarian commerce, and it wasn't clear to us what desirable assets remained for acquisition by the Israelis. For us, the walk through town represented a pleasant Sunday morning stroll. For the 5,000 Jews from Győr and nearby towns, forced to haul their possessions from the wretchedly crowded ghetto to the even more deplorable collection camp, the trek through Győr, past homes some of them had once owned and former neighbors watching from balconies and windows, must have been beyond horrible. Their destination was out Budai Avenue, past the alcohol factory, and along what is now called Mártírok utja [Avenue of the Martyrs], to a site now behind Lukács Sándor Technical High School unmarked and inaccessible to the public. Before the month was over, they were marched south a little more than a kilometer and packed onto box cars at the Gyárváros freight station, near the present passenger terminal on Kando Kálmán ut. From there the trains went to Auschwitz.[7]

7 Béla Vihár, ed., *Sárga Könyv: Adatok a magyar zsidóság háborús szenvedéseiből, 1941–1945* (Budapest: Hechaluc, 1945).

Figure 7.12 The facade of the technical high school. This bit of socialist realist public art from the Communist period survived the massive deaccessioning of the early 1990s.

Back at the corner of Baross and Kazinczy, and a block toward the east at Czuczor Street, Kazinczy opens onto a broad newly renovated public square named after István Széchenyi. The plaza sits atop the site of the original civil settlement of Roman Győr, known along with the accompanying military camp as Arrabona. On the south side is the Benedictine church and *gimnázium* [secondary school]. Mayor Jenő Koller, who oversaw the local dispossession and ghettoization of the Jews and even became caretaker of one of the buildings confiscated from Jewish owners, was bombed out of his city hall office on July 2, 1944, and relocated operations to the

Benedictine establishment on the square. Still, the Benedictines earned a reputation as one of the most enlightened orders in Hungary. At their mountaintop Pannonhalma monastery south of the city, they protected military deserters, Jews, and political dissidents until the end of the war. When Jewish students were expelled from other schools prior to the deportation, the Benedictines on Széchenyi Square offered places at their high school until that became impossible. Even today, at the entrance to one of their offices in Iskola Köz [School Alley], which runs between the *gimnázium* and the Liszt Ferenc Music School, they have installed an unlocked cabinet where citizens leave food, sandwiches, bread, fruit, and the like, for the destitute, who can take what they need at any hour of the day or night.

At the east end of the square, the Lloyd building is the dominant presence. It dates from around 1875 and housed the local Commercial Guild as well as a restaurant, coffeehouse, and ballroom. It was modernized in the 1930s and started its interwar political career as headquarters of the Agricultural Workers Organization. The building expanded in the 1950s and became the trade unions headquarters. The plaque on the north wall asserting the dignity of labor is an artifact of that time. The building also housed the Felszabadulás Kultúrotthon [Liberation Cultural Center] movie house, the site of a public meeting of discontented citizens on October 16, 1956, which the postrevolutionary regime identified as pivotal in the beginning of the 1956 revolution.

Earlier, the Lloyd provided a meeting place for murderous radicals of both the left and the right. Tibor Szamuely, who had gone to secondary school in Győr, spoke on the square on April 20, 1919. The Hungarian Soviet Republic was new, and blood was on his mind. He warned that it would flow copiously, calling it the steel that strengthened the fist of the proletariat. For Szamuely, this was no mere abstraction. Later in the spring, he led lynch mobs disguised as revolutionary justice in both Sopronkövesd and Csorna, where there are memorials to the victims of his work. Szamuely's name was once on a park in the Nádorváros section of town, but the park is now named Malom [Mill] and the bust statue that once stood at the center vanished in the deaccessioning of the 1990s.[8] The street bears the name of a leading figure of 1956, Árpád Tihanyi. Szamuely's name was once on the facade of the secondary school on Bem tér, four short blocks to the west of the park, along a street named Álmos for half the distance and then Dr. Petz Lajos the rest of the way. The school is now named for Gábor Baross.

Fifteen years after Szamuely's sanguinary presentation, the Lloyd and the square provided a stage for the first German-style national socialist party, which was established in Hungary during 1928. The county movement led by Count Miklós Pálffy dated from 1932, the year a large crowd greeted Prime Minister Gyula Gömbös. Gömbös denied a desire for dictatorial powers but later adopted the slogan "One party, one leader." The Győr branch of the National Socialists formed in 1933, when various tradesmen held an organizational meeting in the Catholic Circle Hall at the Lloyd. The party set up its office at the Lloyd and announced its program at a mass meeting there on June 29, 1933. Pálffy became a member of parliament on the Arrow Cross list in 1939, as right-wing groups consolidated under Ferenc Szálasi's leadership.

Enthusiasm for the new German order in the mid-1930s was not confined to the Lloyd. On May 3, 1934, a formation of 152 motorcyclists from one of Mussolini's fascist legions roared through the city on a Bologna-to-Budapest jaunt. City notables and representatives of the Austrian *Heimwehr* greeted the travelers at Bisinger Park, and after speeches and a reception, the blackshirts roared out of town on Kaiser Wilhelm Avenue, as Szent István

8 For a picture of the statue in the process of being deaccessioned, with the bust removed from the pedestal and resting on the ground, see <https://www.kozterkep.hu/~/20979/Szamuely_Tibor_Győr_1963.html/photos/237961>, accessed May 20, 2018. The process continues in the twenty-first century. When the building at Aradi vértanúk útja 20 was renovated in the second half of the second decade, the 1969 tablet identifying the building as a center for the Communist Party newspaper and recruiting efforts in 1919 disappeared. There is a photograph of the tablet in Orbánné Horváth Márta, *Győri Emlékhelyek és Köztéri Alkotások* (Győr: Gálgócsi Erzsébet Városi Könyvtár, 2006), p. 35. The tablet was once just to the left of the door to the tavern in the cellar. For images of this tablet and of many deaccessioned memorials from the Communist regimes, see Ernő Molnár, ed., *Munkásmozgalmi emlékhelyek Győr-Sopron megyében* (Győr: Győr Megyei Lapkiado Vállalat, 1986), illustration section, p. iii.

was known at the time. Then on October 3, 1936, a 31-vehicle motorcade of German auto enthusiasts arrived for a meeting with Hungarian buffs. The excitement was not just for the vehicles. They passed through an entry gate decorated with a "Heil Hitler" greeting and returned the salutation by presenting a Nazi flag during breakfast at the Royal. One local historian looked back on the parade as foreshadowing the cavalcade of German vehicles that entered the city as part of the occupying force on March 19, 1944.

The political action continued at the Lloyd. Late in August 1937, the Lloyd hosted what was called a Christian economic mass meeting, filling both meeting halls inside. The gathering generated such interest that many could not get inside and listened to the proceedings through windows open to the square. Member of Parliament Ferenc Rajnis spoke, dating the colonization of the Hungarian economy by Jews to Anselm Rothschild in 1867. An ardent supporter of the Third Reich and its racial policies as founder and editor of the wartime weekly *Magyar Futár* [*Hungarian Messenger*] as well as the daily *Esti Ujság* [*Evening News*], Rajnis represented two parties, Hungarian Life and later Hungarian Renewal, before joining Szálasi's Arrow Cross and becoming minister of cults and education. He was executed after the war.

In Győr, executions during the Arrow Cross reign of terror took place behind the Lloyd, across Teleki Street and a half block down Liszt Ferenc Street. On the north side of Liszt at number 13 the county administration building, now the county archives, became in December 1944 one of four regional offices in the western borderlands of the Nemzeti Számonkérő Szék (NSzSz), the national accountability office. This arm of the Arrow Cross, charged with securing the area behind the front lines by discovering and arresting those who did not believe in final victory, essentially sought to terrorize the population into submission. The other offices were in Sopron, Kapuvár, and Vép, five kilometers east of Szombathely. In addition to offices, the building contained three holding cells and a gallows in a small courtyard to the right rear. Visitors need passes to enter the archives but not the main courtyard, so it is possible to walk into the center and look to the right rear to the green doors that now enclose stacks of archives boxes. The first door past the stairway leads to the gallows; the next three to the cells. Boxes of papers in various stages of processing now reach toward the ceiling.

Figure 7.13 The doors to the gallows and cells.

Arrow Cross agents employed there included Gyula Strahlendorf and gendarme Lieutenant Zoltán Demeter, a veteran of a massacre of Jewish slave laborers near Debrecen when he arrived in Győr in the last weeks of 1944. An elegant and slim interrogator according to writer Miklós Gerencsér, Demeter worked for gendarme Captain Ernő Csergő, an avid torturer with a fondness for electricity.[9] Demeter transferred to Sopron in February 1945. He and a German SS lieutenant named Karl Zimmermann directed the massacre of slave laborers on Munkácsy Street by the Hegyeshalom train station three days before Soviet troops arrived.

9 Miklós Gerenscér, *Fekete Tél* (Budapest: Szepirodalmi Könyvkiado, 1973), p. 363. Demeter is listed among gendarme members who died after the revolution of 1956 in Szelei Jozsef, "Losses in Hungarian Royal Gendarmerie," 1994, <www.csendor.com/konvtar/biografia/>, accessed July 3, 2014. The list was compiled "with comradely commiseration" with the mourning families. The headnote says, "We preserve your memories with reverence."

The exterior of the building has six plaques. Two identify it as a regional tax and customs office and as the county archives. The other four refer to the historical significance of the site. On the western side one notes that Polish king Jan Sobieski visited in 1683. Another relates that Franz Liszt gave a concert there in 1840. On the south face, to the left of the entry, a ceramic image of Liszt was installed on the 200th anniversary of his birth, and another mentions that János Hunyadi, the father of the bibliophile king Matthias had been on the site in 1455, along with Saint John of Capistrano. Together, the pair led a crusade against the invading Ottoman Empire in 1456 and drove the Turks from Belgrade. There is no mention of the use of the building as headquarters of the Soviet Republic in 1919; nor is there mention of the wartime functions of the building or the NSzSz. Essentially the site remains as it was in 1944–5, but in deep storage.

A nearby site on Teleki Street should be noted before moving back to Baross and heading to the end of the street at the base of the hill dominated by the church. Toward the south on Teleki, after the theater with its geometric wall patterns designed by Hungarian-born Victor Vasarely, and between Bajcsy-Zsilinsky and Árpád there is a parking lot of recent origin. The address was 38 and the building that had been there was known as the iron workers' home, a site of cultural programs and social gatherings. During World War II, in the wake of bomb damage to city hall, it became home to the managers of city real estate, bureaucrats who allocated living quarters to families that lost their homes in the 35 Allied bombing attacks that shook the city beginning in April 1944. Real estate stolen from Jewish owners was managed there. And the two missions came together when Christians displaced by bombing attacks queued up in front of the office to apply for places to live. In the second half of May 1944, the office received some 2,400 inquiries, and lines of those requesting new places snaked along the sidewalk. After the war, the building remained standing on Teleki Street for more than 70 years, with plaques noting its connection to the iron workers but nothing else. Like the county archives building, it was clearly in storage. In 2016, this status changed. The building was demolished to make way for a residential project that remained incomplete in 2019. It has now been deaccessioned. Croatian novelist Dasa Drndic may have been right when she observed that "people forget, buildings remember," but only if they are marked. Demolition completes the erasure.[10]

Back at the northern end of Baross, Király Street goes one block to the west, and then a right turn leads uphill on the cobbled road to the bishop's palace, the cathedral and church offices and residences, a visitor center, and the remains of a chapel from around the twelfth century. It is a commonplace in Europe that the best real estate historically belonged to either the army or the Catholic Church. In this case the army came first. The hill was the site of the Roman military camp at the confluence of the Rába and the Moson Duna, an outpost on the northern frontier of the Empire. For centuries now, it has belonged to the Church, and to take advantage of its dominant location, the visitor should pay the modest fee and climb the spiral staircase to the top of the tower that is part of the museum at the palace. Outside the entrance to the tower, which is approached through a gift shop, is a full-size bronze statue of Bishop Vilmos Apor, and the entrance to a shrine-like museum is next door. There can be little question that Apor deserves our admiration and respect. He was the only one of the 19 bishops in the Hungarian archdiocese to offer moral and material support to Jews incarcerated and awaiting deportation in the collection camp east of town. Apor also tried to protect Hungarian women from assault by Soviet soldiers (there is a reason why Viennese call the Soviet liberation memorial in their city the statue of the unknown rapist), and he paid for that effort with his life. His noble behavior was exemplary just as the inactions of the other bishops provide collectively an opposite example. His remains lie in a permanent place of honor inside an alcove of the Hédervári chapel of the cathedral across the plaza from the bishop's palace.

The murder of Bishop Apor early in 1945 is one of three prominent events in Győr during 1944–5, with the Allied bombing and the deportation of the Jews.[11] The bombing started on April 13, 1944, less than a month after the

10 Dasa Drndic, *EEG*, trans. Celia Hawkesworth (New York: New Directions, 2018), p. 277.

11 In three volumes published between 2007 and 2012, photographer and historian István Nagy chronicled all of them. They are in order of appearance, *Húsvéttól húsvétig: Győr harmincöt bombazása* (Győr: Győr-Moson-Sopron Megye Győri Levéltára, 2007); *Quiritatio. Sikoly. Győri zsidő tragédia 1938–1945* (Győr: A

German occupation began. Two memorials commemorate the bombing, one behind the Arkád shopping center at the eastern end of the central city, once part of the destroyed industrial area known as Gyárváros [Factory City], and the other at a university building just north of the main campus at Áldozat utca [Victims Street 12]. The street was so named in 1948 because 61 people had perished in the basement shelter of the villa belonging to lawyer Mór Torkos during the bombing raid of November 17, 1944. Indeed, the whole city is a visual memorial to the destruction. Many streets near the center show effects of the attacks, with postwar Communist blocks next to structures dating from the Empire, indicating where buildings had survived and where they had been destroyed. There are also the underground remains of myriad bomb shelters that crisscrossed the city. Twenty-five had capacities ranging from 30 people up to 345 for the one under the Erste Bank branch at Árpád 42, just west of Teleki. This underground network has left no commemorative trace. Less than 75 years ago, trenches and shelters along with military hospitals and warehouses stuffed with Jewish property were everywhere. As Győr historian István Nagy remarked about the archipelago of theft, "As I understand it, every school gym and every warehouse space was put to use [...]. Imagine hundreds of apartments, how much furniture and how many household tools were collected."[12] Today they are invisible.

Recently museums have started to put names and faces on deported Jewish citizens. Exhibits, first in Pápa during 2012 and shortly afterward in Szombathely and Sopron, all in western Transdanubia, have pioneered in this effort. This falls short of putting names and faces on perpetrators and enablers and clarifying the specific experiences of individual citizens. The disparity between illuminating the experience of individual victims and obscuring those of individual perpetrators carries over into memorials and markers. Victim sites, not always clearly and honestly explained and vulnerable to vandalism, are nevertheless often identified. Ghettos and collection camp sites are known, not just to readers of Randolph Braham's definitive *Geographical Encyclopedia of the Holocaust in Hungary* but to residents who pay attention.

---

Győri Zsidő Hitközség, 2010); *Győr vértanú püspöke, Apor Vilmos* (Győr: Győri Egyházmegyei Levéltár, 2012). These books form a trilogy but were published separately and with separate funding.

12 Email, István Nagy to the author, February 24, 2015.

Perpetrator sites are harder to find. Usually deaccessioned or hidden in deep storage, they become apparent only to the diligent or fortunate researcher. But it can be confidently said that during 1944–5, the Gestapo had offices in every substantial town on both sides of the border, and that Hitler Youth in Austrian towns and the Hungarian equivalent, known as *Levente*, were everywhere. *Volksbund* homes nurtured German nationalism and supported the Third Reich throughout the Hungarian border communities, and toward the end of the war Arrow Cross Party *Hűség házok*, or Loyalty Houses, as the local headquarters locations were called, were also ubiquitous. Finding them is the challenge.

During the latter days of World War II, as the Arrow Cross government agencies fled Budapest to escape the oncomng Red Army, they established ministry offices in western cities. The Ministry of War in Kőszeg has already been noted (chapter 3). The Ministry of the Interior and minister Gábor Vajna settled temporarily in Szombathely at the city hall, along with three subordinate offices, including the Jewish Affairs Department under Dr. Árpád Toldy. Four other subsidiary elements found places in Sárvár, where we once asked a local historian about where Arrow Cross agencies might have set up shop. He recognized that the government had in fact had offices in town but did not know where they might have been.[13]

Significant sites on the periphery of Győr include two statues of poet Miklós Radnoti west of the city. Starting at the end of Kossuth Lajos Street, across the main road (M-1) westward from Győr, just beyond the cemetery on the left and the go-cart track on the right, there is a remnant of the old main road to Vienna, 1.75 kilometers (just over one mile) long. At its western end, facing back along the line of the road toward town, is a granite statue of Radnoti, sculpted by Miklós Melocco, who created the 1989 statuary group

13 They were as follows: the gendarmerie and police division and administrative and orderly justice division in the castle at the center of the city; the public law and citizenship division and three other offices in the town hall; the social security and health-child welfare divisions at the health office; and the party committee office and oversight directorate at Batthyány Street 35 on the west side of town. Zoltán András Kovács, *A Szálasi-Kormány Belügyministériuma—Rendvédelem, Állambiztonság, Közigazgatás A Nyilás Korszakban* (Pécs: Bölcsészdoktori Disszertácio, 2008), pp. 248–9.

at the Sopronpuszta memorial park. Radnoti stands shrouded in a blanket, his only protection against the November wind. About 100 meters before the clearing, a connecting road no more than 20 meters long links to M-1. Female sex workers, either singly or in pairs, sometimes wait here for customers, presumably among truckers who pass through rather than the upright citizens of Győr. Prostitutes have used this spot to solicit business for more than 30 years, inquiring of prospective clients, "Do you have any work for me, young sir?" Locals sometimes refer to the women as "tour guides."

The current statue is actually the second on the spot. The original, erected in 1980, lasted until the night of November 17, 2013, when a man in a black Mercedes Benz rammed it and broke it in two at the knees. The car was later found in a field in nearby Öttevény; the driver had walked away. He later turned himself in, claiming that his private act of deaccessioning had been accidental. In the darkness and fog he had mistaken the unmarked and untraveled stretch of old road for the main highway and crashed into the statue by mistake. Sculptor Melocco made an identical figure, using the original as his model, and installed it within a year. The city provided lighting and surveillance cameras. The authorities also cleared the shrubbery from around the statue, creating an even starker scene, the lone man exposed to the evils surrounding him.

From that point, on the north side of M-1 and alongside it, a westward bicycle path opened in the spring of 2013. The lightly used trail goes as far as Abda, is smooth and flat, and crosses only a few roads. Right before the bridge over the Rábca River, 2.7 kilometers (about 1.7 miles) from the start of the bike path and just before the embankment parallel to the river, a sign directs visitors to the right toward the Radnoti monument. The sign is barely large enough for motorists to read, and in any case, there are no obvious turnoffs for those who might be interested in the spot where Hungary's most highly regarded twentieth-century poet was murdered. A gravel road following the embankment is not good for road bikes. After a half kilometer, another similar sign directs the traveler to the right onto another gravel road. The memorial, on the left side just after the turn, commemorates the murder of 22 conscripts in the "labor service," the official euphemism for enslavement of Jewish men by the military. A cast bronze bust of Radnoti created by László Alexovics, has been installed on the grassy site with a separate monument naming the men shot there. A Radnoti statue also stands at the south entrance to the hospital on Zrinyi Street, north of the bus station, an ironic location considering the denial of medical treatment to Radnoti and his mates before their murder.[14]

Figure 7.14 A copy of the Alexovits Radnoti on the grounds of the hospital on Zrinyi utca.

14 On the establishment and operation of the labor service, see Braham, *The Politics of Genocide*, I, pp. 285–361.

The 35-year-old Radnoti was in a three-company contingent marched north from the mine in Bor, Serbia, on November 3, 1944. He spent his last night on the grounds of the brick factory at Pannonhalma, about 20 kilometers south of Győr. The factory is at the south end of Arany János Street, and in 1983 a statue of Radnoti by János Meszlényi was installed in a brick shelter designed to resemble a kiln. The statue was vandalized early in this century and moved to the auditorium of the Radnoti elementary school at the corner of Petőfi and Dozsa Streets, where it has been placed, as it were, in protective custody from vandals as well as thieves who scour the countryside for scrap metal. The move might ultimately serve a positive function if students are taught about the poet and his fate as well as that of the sculpture itself.

Vandalism of Jewish memorials and cemeteries in the border counties, by the way, is not unusual. There are examples in Balf, Győr, Hegyeshalom, Jánosháza, Kapuvár, Körmend, and Kőszeg. Other subjects that draw the attention of vandals are the Romani catastrophe (Szombathely) and the 1919 Communist republic (Jánosháza and Szombathely).

On either the 8th or the 9th of November 1944, he was moved through Győr in a cart with others who could march no farther. An effort to get medical care in Győr failed: no hospital would admit the slaves. They never made it to their destination of Mosonmagyraróvár because Cadet Sergeant Ándrás Tálas and four soldiers killed all 22 of them along the Rábca and dumped them into a pit. Tálas was captured in Budapest in 1947, tried, and executed. By the time he was caught he had changed his clothes, discarding his Arrow Cross uniform and becoming a member of the Communist Party.

Radnoti's renown is based on poetry published before his murder and on a stash of verse written in this most bitter time of his short life, found in his coat pocket when his body was exhumed. By the time the corpses were unearthed, seven men were not identifiable. A recent edition of the Győr-Moson-Sopron County atlas explains that Radnoti and his fellow slaves fell "victim of the fascist terrorism in the vicinity of the village." The text does not mention that the perpetrators were Hungarian.[15]

15 *Győr-Moson-Sopron Megye Atlasza*, 4th expanded edition, 2009, p. 7.

Beyond the Rábca Bridge, the bike trail crosses to the south side of M-1 before ending at Abda. Before crossing the highway, it passes a monument, about 20 meters to the right and surrounded by trees, that commemorates the appearance on the shore of the Rábca of the eighteenth-century rebel Ferenc Rákóczi. At that spot, the story goes, Rákóczi was being taken to prison when a fisherman gave him a freshly caught fish. Rákóczi tossed it back into the river, declaring the fish free and expressing the hope that he too would soon be free. The monument to Hungarian freedom was conceived in 1935 and dedicated in November 1943, four months before Germany occupied Hungary and ended the limited freedom that went with being Hitler's ally, eight months before nearly a half million Jewish Hungarians were packed off to death camps in Poland, and one year before Radnoti's life ended nearby. A sense of irony about the juxtaposition of monuments to Hungarian freedom and Hungarian slavery is not apparent.

So, armed with an idea of what happened during this terrible time and how it has been remembered, what can we say about the guided walking tour called "Seven Wonders of Győr," offered by a local company? This tour was first scheduled for July 24, 2017, in conjunction with the grand opening of the European Youth Olympics Festival, an extravaganza to the liking of Mayor Zsolt Borkai, a former Olympian. The website of the tour provider, "Gyere Győrbe" [Come to Győr], promised to highlight the most interesting sites in the city. These wonders, likened to the elements of a string of pearls, could be seen on a 90-minute walk for the equivalent of about nine dollars.[16] The operator did not reveal which marvels were to be shown, but another site reproduced two overlapping lists of Győr's most imposing sights. Both included the light show on the new Jedlik Bridge over the Moson Duna, a low-budget music-free mimicry of Walt Disney's 1940 film *Fantasia*.[17] They also agreed on the appeal of the banks of the Rába and the head reliquary of eleventh-century king Szent László in the cathedral. Other popular places included the outsize soda bottle that

16 "Gyere Győrbe," <http://www.gyereGyőrbe.hu/varosnezo-setaink/eyof>, accessed July 24, 2017.

17 More recently, music has been added to the light shows at the fountains in the river at the confluence of the Moson Duna and the Rába, and on the square across Szent István from city hall.

splashed water into a pool at the intersection of Jedlik and Apáca near the Kossuth Bridge across the Moson Duna, and the painting of the weeping Virgin in the cathedral, first reported in the eighteenth century by a priest of Irish origin.[18] Of the sites mentioned in this chapter, only the synagogue made it onto one of the lists.

18 Both the life mask and the portrait of the Madonna were temporarily in the diocese's museum near the bishop's palace during spring 2018 renovations.

CHAPTER 8

# Bruck an der Leitha: The multicultural border town

No town in the borderlands reflected the multicultural nature of the Habsburg Empire better than Bruck an der Leitha. The settlement straddling the Leitha River [Lajta in Hungarian] was Bruck in Cisleithania on the Austrian side and Királyhida [King's Bridge] in Transleithania on the Hungarian, and they were often written as Bruck-Királyhida. Jaroslav Hašek, who served there in the Ninety-First Infantry Regiment during World War I and later wrote *The Good Soldier Svejk*, would have agreed that the parts were connected. He shrugged off any distinction between the two sides of the river and saw the whole place as a giant whorehouse. But the point is that he did it in Czech, while Stefan Zweig in his novel *Beware of Pity*, Josef Roth in his 1919 essay "Bruck and Királyhida," and Thomas Bernhard in *Old Masters*, his 1985 rant about Austrian society and culture, wrote about Bruck in German. Miklós Bánffy, a postwar foreign minister of Hungary, told anecdotes about the place in his memoir, *Phoenix Land*, in Magyar. Bosnian soldiers of an elite battalion at the huge garrison on the Hungarian side added to the mix, underscoring the complex character of the small town tied together by a hyphen, with the river bridged by a narrow lane that had once been part of the Roman Amber Road.

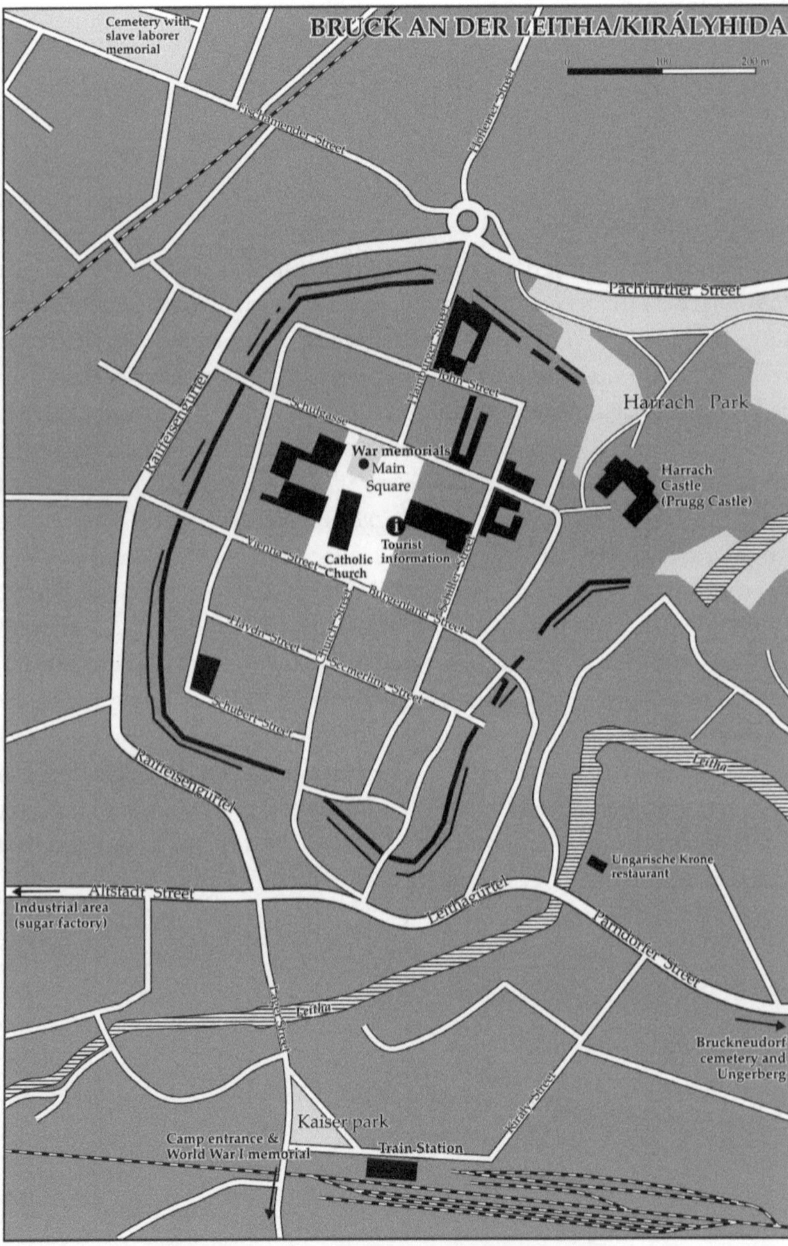


Figure 8.1 Bruck an der Leitha-Királyhida [Map 13].

Figure 8.2 The "hyphen," that is, the bridge connecting Bruck and Királyhida. Even the postcards were bilingual.

Like Rechnitz and Oberwart to the south, the best place to start to get a feel for the recent history of Bruck is at its center, on the main square. The white Roman Catholic church dominates the southern half of the square, but the northern portion is green, with benches and a remarkable arrangement of war memorials. Closest to the church but facing north, the Red Army memorial honors Soviet soldiers killed in battle during the Russian push toward and through the town in the spring of 1945. The monument is topped by the obligatory red star and lists the names of fallen soldiers. The left panel proclaims in Russian and without ironical intent "Eternal glory to heroes of the Red Army killed while fighting German Nazis for freedom and independence of the people of Europe." The right panel adds, "For happiness of all nations, you gave your lives far from your native Soviet land. Glory to you! Brave Russian soldiers! You fell honorably. Rest in Peace. You will never be forgotten by our people."

Ella Davletshina translated the Russian text for me in 2015. Irene and I had invited Ella, a documentary filmmaker from Novosibirsk in Siberia, on an excursion to Bruck primarily to see this memorial and its extraordinary setting. We relaxed on a park bench by the monument, facing south to the obelisk not ten meters in front of us, honoring the sacrifice of soldiers of the Austro-Hungarian Empire who fell in the Great War of 1914–18. Just behind it, spread over a much larger space and with many more names, another monument named the local soldiers who fell in the service of the Third Reich during the second and even bloodier war of 1939–45. The northern face of this memorial carries the German inscription "In memory and warning," a message that frequently accompanies World War II memorials in Austria, according to historian Erwin Schmidl. So the main square provides a meeting point for memorials to the military dead of two great war machines that faced each other in a huge and bloody war, an arrangement rarely seen in the region, and the admonition on the Austrian World War II monument could be considered as an addendum to all three memorials, making them into a single installation that reminds the viewer of the horrific cost of every war.

I mentioned to Ella that the victorious Allies occupied Austria until 1955, the year the Republic of Austria was established. Until then, all four powers had separate occupation zones and shared control of Vienna. The Red Army zone in the eastern portion included Bruck. She took this in quietly before politely but firmly objecting. "No," she said. Soviet forces did not "occupy" the region. They "stayed." And that was that.

One substantial category of wartime casualties goes unmentioned on the square. During the last winter of World War II, Jewish slave laborers from Hungary were used on sections of the East Wall near Bruck. They were brought from the transit camp at Strasshof and billeted in barns on Fischamender Strasse and on Am Stadtgut, both on the north side of the town, under the supervision of Hitler Youth guards. Toward the end of the war, many were consolidated in a barn just east of the traffic circle at the east end of Fischamend and past the Neugebauer funeral home on Pachfuhrter. The barn remained until 2017, when it was demolished and replaced by a Billa supermarket, another case of deaccessioning a site of twentieth-century horrors. Just before the war ended, most East Wall work sites in Hungary and Austria were evacuated on foot, and sometimes by barge. Most prisoners from sites along the northern section were assembled at Királyhida, which was called Bruckneudorf after it became part of Austria in 1921, then marched north to Deutsch-Altenburg and Engerau, for barge transport to Mauthausen.

Estimates of the number of slave laborers at Bruck range from between 1,500 and 2,000 up to 3,000. On Christmas Eve in 1944, the camp commander is said to have raised his glass before the assembled Hitler Youth and pronounced the following toast: "I raise a glass in the hope that a few Jews will still die."[1] They did. The cemetery on the north side of Fischamender, across from the academic high school and commercial academy has a monument to 155 of them who succumbed to the usual causes of starvation, exposure, and overwork. Hungarian chess master Kornél Havasi, who accumulated three Olympic gold medals before his death on January 29, 1945, was among them.[2] The inscription on the memorial reads, "Remember them, Our G-d, for good with the other righteous of the world."

There are at least five places for coffee around the main square. All provide comfortable places to consider the war monuments and what they might represent as well as to admire the tree planted on the square in 1928 to mark the centennial of the death of Franz Schubert. None of these spots have any historical resonance of their own, unlike the McDonald's in Győr, the Pannonia in Sopron, or Heiling Eis in Rechnitz. One, just south of the Tourist Information Center on the east side of the square along with city hall and the public library, has the word "pizzeria" in its name. Another is a Greek restaurant, and a third is a kabob stand, so the whole effect is almost like a shopping mall food court surrounding the war memorials and the church. In any case, the weather was pleasant, so we stayed in the park and discussed the meaning of the monuments before us. Since this was not my first visit to Bruck, I also knew that it was worth our while to wait until we walked toward the river before we looked for refreshment.

1 Michael Achenbach and Dieter Szorger, "Der Einsatz ungarischer Juden am Südostwall im Bauabschnitt Niederdonau 1944/45," unpublished manuscript in author's files, pp. 50–1.

2 The list on the horizontal tablets naming the 155 forced laborers was compiled by Petra Weiss and Irmtraut Karlsson for their 2008 book *Die Toten von Bruck*.

The bridge across the Leitha is a few blocks from the southeast corner of the square, along Burgenlandgasse to Parndorf Strasse, then east to the bridge. Just across the river and to the north is the Ungarische Kröne restaurant and hotel. The bridge is on the site of the structure built by Roman legions as the Amber Road crossing of the Leitha. Coffee at the restaurant is fine (it's Meinl), but they also serve a rich, creamy garlic soup, one of the best I have tasted. The main hall and central dining room have trophy heads mounted on the wall and a pictorial history of the restaurant and town, told in postcards, documents, and photos. The Third Reich period is conspicuously missing. There are also testimonials from soldiers deployed to Bruck after the Cold War in response to the increased migration from the east.

Soldiers were of course far from new to the neighborhood. From World War I to the last battles involving the Red Army in the spring of 1945, there was a major military presence at Bruck. The military base on the southeast side of the Leitha dates back to 1867, the year of the compromise that created the dual monarchy. Much of the land was acquired from the estates of the Batthyány and Harrach families, the latter of which owned the castle inside Bruck. The castle is two blocks west of the main square at the intersection of Stefaniegasse and Schlossgasse, visible from the street but not open to visitors.

The castle figured in the Western Hungarian uprising that took Pál Prónáy to the balcony in Oberwart where he declared the ephemeral Lajtabansag in October 1921 (see chapter 4). The literature of the uprising, far more plentiful in Hungary than Austria, was mainly produced by participants and remains popular among right-wing irredentists. It shows the rebels as dashing and dedicated patriots. The Austrians come off as plodding and a little oafish. Books in this genre are often available in Hungary at hypernationalist bookstores with *turul* or *Szkítia* in their names and windows decked out in the national colors of red, white, and green. One such shop in Győr even has a sign in the window boasting of its Hungarian ownership, as if purveyors of such reading material would come from elsewhere.

Prónáy never showed up in Bruck. However, his ragtag insurgents occupied the castle grounds briefly in the second half of September 1921, when they fought their way across the Leitha bridge and into town, marking their farthest advance in the direction of Vienna. Some of the fighting between the *Rongyos Gárda*, or ragged guard, as the Hungarians styled themselves, and the Austrian Heimwehr took place on the military base that sprawled from the edge of the one-time independent town of Kaisersteinbruch eastward more than halfway to Parndorf. The wooded hill known as Spittelberg, on the grounds of the military camp and about 1.5 kilometers south of the main square in Bruck, was the key high ground for insurgent operations. In one firefight on September 21, they claimed to have surprised and driven Austrian soldiers from their barracks and taken hundreds of rifles as a result. They repeated this tactical success in mid-October, this time hijacking an engine and rolling stock to advance from Parndorf by rail. The victories did not translate into strategic success beyond the Sopron referendum, but the rebels took comfort in their victorious skirmishes in what they characterized as a clash between Hungarian Christians and Austrian atheists.

The military installation occupied territory that was part of Hungary until after the World War I peace settlement. The post, formally called Truppenübungsplatzes (TÜPL) Bruckneudorf, or Troop Training Camp Bruckneudorf, originally emphasized firearms and combat training, although it ultimately served in multiple roles. During World War I, it was the site of one of 21 prisoner-of-war camps in Hungary, seven of them in communities now in Burgenland.

Just west of the city, the main road called Altstadt (Route 10) intersects with Wilfleinsdorfer. At the intersection, Route 10 goes off to the right and almost immediately passes the industrial area that was once the site of the sugar factory owned by the Jewish entrepreneur Ferdinand Bloch-Bauer. He presided over the company from 1922 to 1938 and was married to the far more famous Adele. Gustav Klimt painted a magnificent portrait of Adele, which was stolen by the Nazis, then was declared by the postwar government part of the national patrimony and absorbed into the collection of the Belvedere Museum in Vienna. There it was displayed as "The Woman in Gold" to obscure its connection to any specific person or family and remained a star attraction until it was returned to family members 67 years after it was stolen. After Ronald Lauder bought the painting, it was displayed at the Neue Gallerie in New York, where it retained its star status. The painting became the subject of a book by

Anne-Marie O'Connor called *The Lady in Gold* (2012), then a 2015 film titled *Woman in Gold*. Along with *The Kiss*, it could be one of Klimt's two most famous paintings. Adele died in 1925; Ferdinand fled to Switzerland after the Anschluss. The authorities looted the family art collection, and the factory lurched along until the 1980s, first under a Nazi "owner," then under Soviet control, before it was returned to the family in 1957 and sold to a German industrialist. There are no markers indicating that the area might have historical connections. A few two-story buildings on the northwestern side of the site appear to date from the active days of the factory. They are visible just past the oil storage tanks, but it is difficult to connect them to photographs of the factory.[3]

The Wilfleinsdorfer road leads through Wilfleinsdorf to Kaisersteinbruch on the western edge of the vast Bruckneudorf military reservation. The town's history centers on the neighboring quarries that yield "Kaiserstone," an extremely hard and dazzlingly white building material that is popular for monumental buildings and statuary. The town's Steinmetz Museum, next to the church, focuses on this history of stone masonry, displaying tools and raw material as well as the work of Alexandru Ciutureanu (1951–2013), a Romanian-born sculptor who spent more than a decade in the town. He produced a bronze relief of the nearby World War II prisoner-of-war camp, which is affixed to an exterior wall of the St. Rokus and St. Sebastian Church at Kirchengasse 1. He also designed the sundial just behind the museum at the corner of HauptStrasse and Waldgasse and the 14 panels illustrating the Way of the Cross that line the interior walls of the church.

Besides its roots in the materials and craft of stone masonry, Kaisersteinbruch went through four separate phases as a place of detention, starting with the small World War I camp that held 3,000 Russian prisoners. They worked on local transportation projects, notably the railroad bed between Wilfleinsdorf and Kaisersteinbruch and the road from Kaisersteinbruch to Winden on the Neusiedler See. The modern route, still known locally as the RussenStrasse, follows the one they established.

3 For a picture of the factory taken the year before Bloch fled, see <https://www.bildarchivaustria.at/Preview/ 10006207.jpg>, accessed May 22, 2018.

Kaisersteinbruch then became a concentration camp in the mid-1930s, and during World War II a much larger prisoner-of-war camp known as Stalag XVII A. The POW compound, the biggest among the camps established in the borderlands in the twentieth century, sprawled all over the farmland adjacent to the town. Finally, the camp housed Hungarian refugees after the 1956 revolution.

By the time that thousands of Russian captives packed the barracks in World War II, there was no town nearby. At the start of hostilities, the Nazi authorities had forced the residents to leave, closed off the site, and prohibited civilians. As many as 75,000 captured soldiers, officers, and civilians, mostly Soviet, languished inside the camp.

The adjacent *Lagerfriedhof*, or camp cemetery is accessible. About a half kilometer west of Kaisersteinbruch, south from Aussiedlerhof as it goes toward Sommerein, the burial ground provides evidence of the international scope of the carnage, with markers for Russian, Romanian, Italian, Polish, and Yugoslav dead. The tablet by the main monument also notes American, British, French, Belgian, and Bulgarian dead, as well as ethnic German refugees "and persons of unknown nationality." But mainly the cemetery contains remains of nearly 10,000 unnamed Soviet soldiers who died as prisoners of war. Soviet soldiers of the occupying force who died while serving in the postwar occupation are named and individually interred, but by and large the cemetery remains a huge mass grave. It is also a little overgrown and full of ticks.

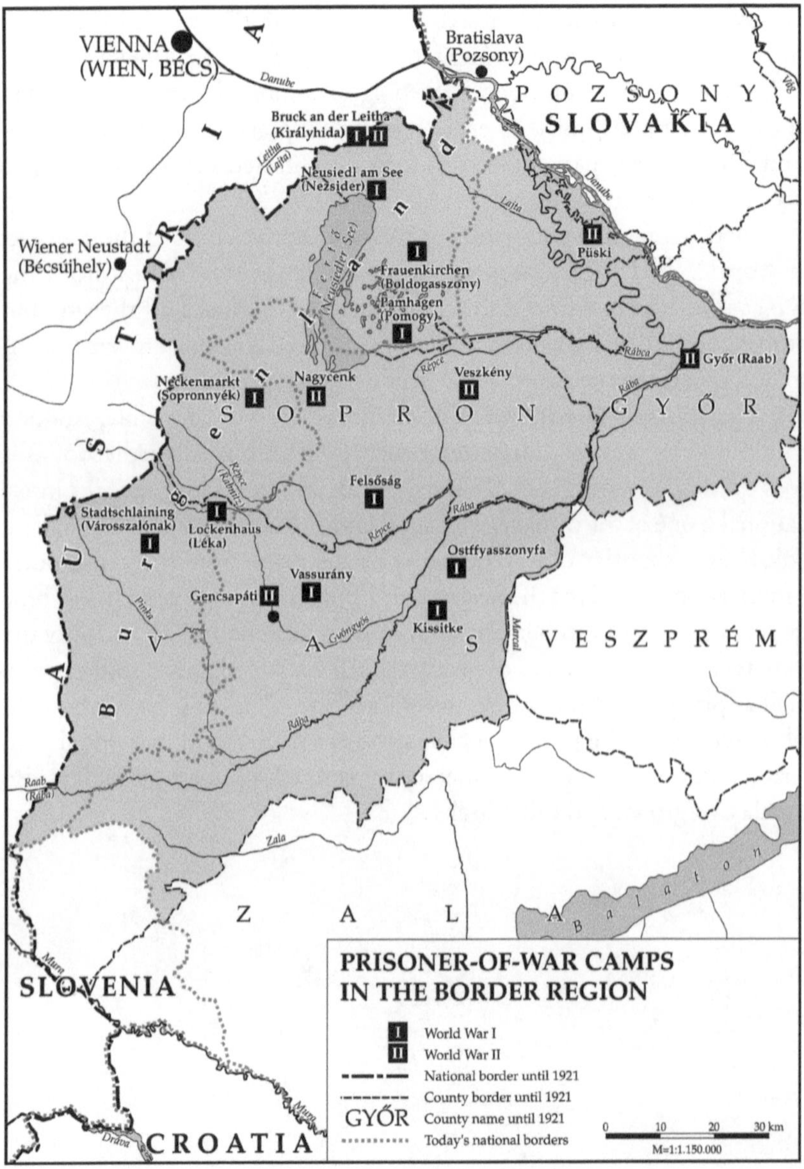


Figure 8.3 Prisoner-of-war camps in the border region [Map 14].

Prisoners from the Kaisersteinbruch lager built the 24-meter-tall World War I monument at the entrance to the main Bruck camp. It stands at the south end of LagerStrasse and was modeled on the Leipzig memorial to the Battle of the Nations during the Napoleonic Wars. Dedicated in 1917, the monument bore the coats of arms of Austria, Hungary, and the House of Habsburg-Lorraine as well as the encompassing inscription "The Fallen in the World War." The chapel inside the base of the monument was intended exclusively for masses to be said for the war dead. The design involved artists of the Austrian Museum of Art and Industry, including the prominent Secessionist designer Josef Hoffman. It now bears the coat of arms of Lower Austria instead of the Empire and remains the largest monument within the Vienna Military Command area and the third largest war memorial in Central Europe.

Also visible before the main entrance is the small memorial to Austria's only tank battalion, which was established in 1936 and absorbed into the Wehrmacht in 1938 as the Thirty-Third Battalion of the Ninth Panzer Division. Sixty-four of its 496 members returned from the war. The monument of stone quarried at the Mauthausen concentration camp was installed in 1963.

Halfway down LagerStrasse, Kaiserpark occupies a small green space on the west end of Bahnhofplatz. A bust statue of Franz Joseph, whose title after the 1867 creation of the Dual Monarchy was Emperor of Austria and King of Hungary, stands at the center. Hungarian sculptor Georg Zala created this work in 1910. It is the only memorial on modern Austrian territory that describes Franz Joseph by his title of King of Hungary and shows him in the uniform of a Hungarian general of cavalry. At the east end of Bahnhofplatz, Király Strasse comes in from the north, so the station almost seems like the conjunction of Kaiser [Emperor of Austria] and Király [King of Hungary]. However, Király Strasse is named for Josef Király, a locomotive engineer who paid with his life for his opposition to the Hitler regime. The plaque dedicated to his memory was installed on the seventieth anniversary of the Kristallnacht pogrom. Király Strasse has borne his name since 1946, when it was renamed from "Strasse des 11. Marz," the day in 1938 on which Tobias Portschy declared the arrival of National Socialism in Burgenland.

To the left and behind the "Emperor and King" is a traditional maypole. The yellow building in the background to the right is the train station. The depot and the park are in Bruckneudorf, as Királyhida is now called. The station is officially marked as Bruck-an-der-Leitha, but the authorities have put out several large signs to make sure people know they are in Bruckneudorf.

Figure 8.4 The "Emperor and King" in the Kaiserpark.

Later, in the wake of the Hungarian revolution of 1956, the Bruckneudorf post housed one of four military headquarters set up on the eastern edge of the country in response to the turmoil, as well as for temporary refugee housing. Although as many as 86 Burgenland communities housed Hungarian refugees, in schools, hotels, and private homes, Bruckneudorf and Kaisersteinbruch were the only two substantial military facilities operated for this purpose. The Austrian government and society handled this significant challenge well. Austria did not panic and certainly made no effort to keep the Hungarians from coming. As Hungarian scholar Ibolya Murber writes, "The 1956 Hungarian emigration was one of the most successful and least stressful of the post-war waves of migration in the Euro-Atlantic world."[4] Still active, Bruckneudorf is linked to the Götzendorf barracks and training ground nearby. It is used to train peacekeepers for international missions.

On Parndorfer, just east of the Leitha canal, the Bruckneudorf cemetery contains at least three memorials relating to twentieth-century wars and the remains of soldiers from seven countries, 542 from Austria and Hungary, 183 Russians, 92 Italians, 76 Serbs, 100 Romanians, and two from Montenegro. One monument memorializes this group, another remembers 106 Italian prisoners of war, and a third remembers the wartime deaths of members of the Levente [Knights or Champions], a paramilitary organization of Hungarian boys that functioned from 1921 through the war and was something like a cross between Boy Scouts and Hitler Youth. Eleven of these children from Hodmezővasarhely were killed on April 4, 1945, fighting for an already lost cause.

The Bruck post extended beyond the cemetery almost five kilometers along Route 10 nearly to Parndorf. It included on its eastern edge the Cold War outpost of Ungerberg, an artillery emplacement aimed toward Hungary. Ungerberg is now an outdoor museum, part above ground and part below. It is still maintained by the training area Bruckneudorf but operated and advertised jointly with the Heeresgeschichtes [Military History]

4 Ibolya Murber, "Az 1956-os magyar menekűltek Ausztriában: Menekűltlét és integráció," *Multunk* 3 (2016), p. 123.

Museum in Vienna since 2014. It can be reached from the east via the expressway A4 by turning off at Exit 57 and heading south two kilometers.

Signs directing visitors to Ungerberg went up along A4 in 2017. The formal title of the emplacement when it was operational was Feste Anlage Ungerberg, shortened to FAN U3. The army established it at the beginning of the 1960s as part of a barrier line between the Leitha and Neusiedler See meant to block mechanized forces from attacking Vienna. It and outposts like it were part of the Schleinzer-Wall, named for Minister of Defense Karl Schleinzer, who was in office from 1961 to 1964. Parts of the installation are 20 meters below grade and encased in two-meter-thick concrete walls, and the 40-man garrison had two 10.5 cm cannons, each mounted on a Centurion tank turret, as well as a 10.5 cm field howitzer, a machine gun, and an observer dome. The display includes two one-man bunkers called *Kugelbunkers*, of the kind manufactured by slave laborers at Potzneusiedl during World War II. Designed to be self-contained, Ungerberg had sanitary facilities, drinking water, central heating, a kitchen, two squad rooms with bunk beds, and a generator. The fall of the Iron Curtain made the outpost superfluous, and it was shut down. Most of the other outposts were removed or demilitarized. Some were sold to private owners and became wine cellars. This is the only one converted to a museum. From the parking lot by the highway, it is a short walk through the woods on a clearly marked path and worth the effort to glimpse what the Cold War looked like on the edge facing east. You can decide for yourself whether the outpost would have been a formidable first line of defense or a speed bump.

Figure 8.5 A tank at Ungerberg, dug in and facing east.

# PART II

# The Past Is Not Past

CHAPTER 9

# Reverberations of 1944

I turned one year old in June 1944, the month during which my grandfather Zsigmond Schubert was deported from his home in Vác, Hungary, and murdered at Auschwitz. Hungary was an enemy country, at war with the United States since the end of 1941. There was no communication between my family in Washington, D.C., and those in Europe. He could not have known that he had a grandson, and I never imagined until 60 years later that I would find myself living part-time in Hungary, owning an apartment in Győr, the largest town in the borderland region, among reminders of that terrible year 1944.

During the period of the war and the Holocaust, Hungarians, like almost all of Germany's allies, showed themselves to be willing accomplices and "avid expropriators."[1] In Győr, as elsewhere, elimination of the Jews accompanied by theft of their property took place in broad daylight, directed by government officials and employees in public offices. They worked in city hall, in the Financial Palace at the corner of Szent István and Gárdonyi Géza, in the real estate management office on Teleki, at the Schlichter villa and the savings bank on Baross, and in warehouses and police stations. Except for the midwives who searched the body cavities of women and girls before they were taken to the collection camp for shipment to Auschwitz, they were almost all men. Their activities generated a lot of paper, as public administration inevitably does, and István Nagy's

1 Raul Hilberg, *Perpetrators Victims Bystanders: The Jewish Catastrophe 1933–1945* (New York: HarperCollins, 1992), p. 76. For a detailed examination of the processes of theft employed by the Third Reich and its allies, see Martin Dean, *Robbing the Jews: The Confiscation of Jewish Property during the Holocaust* (New York: Cambridge University Press, 2008, 2010). David Cesarani, *Final Solution*, also looks at the various approaches to the taking of Jewish property.

book *Quiritatio* (2010) on the Jewish tragedy in Győr, includes samples of administrative documents. Some of the papers bear the titles of clerks, notaries, and counselors, occasionally accompanied by legible signatures. The virulently anti-Semitic newspaper *Győr Nemzeti Hirlap* [*Győr National Newspaper*], followed the fashion that had emerged since the second half of the 1930s with a masthead declaring itself a "Christian political daily."[2] It published legal notices of court proceedings relating to disposal of property that had belonged to Jews who "departed" from the city in the early summer of 1944, never of course to return. Such notices represented on a local level the merger of theft and murder into bogus legal procedures. The death camps, with their piles of teeth, shoes, and hair, represented the macabre apexes of the convergent theft and murder projects, but the goals and the processes they generated are visible at every administrative level.

Jewish-owned real estate represented a special administrative and logistical problem. Residential and commercial properties, along with their contents, became state property and required inventories, maintenance, and management of requests from citizens wishing to acquire the properties for themselves. With 436 Jewish-owned stores and businesses in town as well as residential properties, this was no small task, involving stocks of goods and furnishings and the real property itself. A consolidated list of Jewish real property published in the local newspaper in August 1944 included 426 separate parcels. The list, printed in sections over several issues, may be incomplete. There are no properties listed on Kossuth utca in the Győrsziget neighborhood, for example, although it was then a center of the Jewish population.

The office charged with managing real estate appears to have been established directly in response to this large-scale public acquisition of Jewish property. Certainly, no such office existed prior to the war, and Mayor Jenő Koller found himself understaffed for the mission. He called

2 *Nemzeti Ujság*, which went back at least to 1921 in Budapest and was supported by the Synod of Bishops and distributed nationally, claimed to be a "Political Christian Daily Newspaper." *Veszprémi Hirlap* made the same claim on its front page. Moshe Y. Herczl, *Christianity and the Holocaust of Hungarian Jewry*, trans. Joel Lerner (New York: New York University Press, 1993), pp. 40, 276, (note 17.) Also see Braham, *Politics*, I, pp. 55–6.

on the populace for help, inviting applicants for paid administrative auxiliary service. In a report of June 23, 1944, Koller wrote that the Royal Financial Service had started to inventory goods left in abandoned Jewish apartments, to empty out the flats, and to sort and distribute their contents to warehouses. The Jews had all been deported to Auschwitz by that time. Neither the county financial department nor his own city administration had the resources to manage what had been left behind. Just the 700 some radios now in the hands of public officials represented a substantial project. Koller hoped to lure retired civil servants and unemployed teachers to supervise and inspect the emptying of apartments. He solicited help from merchants, craftsmen, and store employees to classify property as it arrived at warehouses and to manage inventories. He hoped college students, upper secondary students, and Boy Scouts would volunteer to prepare property for packaging and shipment and to escort shipments, and he sought female students and typists to manage supplies and inventories and to keep the books of warehouses. Applicants were asked to apply to the deputy mayor's office in room 45 on the first floor of city hall. So, in addition to deploying the regular employees of the city, Mayor Koller tried to involve a wide range of citizens, male and female, young and mature, from a variety of educational levels and occupational groups. This recruitment effort did not even involve finding caretakers for the actual dwellings and buildings now available.

The nearly overwhelming responsibility was handled from city hall, until the bombing of July 2 forced relocation of the mayor's office. Thereafter, the mayor operated out of the Benedictine High School on Széchenyi Square, while important elements of the real estate office moved to the Iron Workers Home at Teleki 38. Activities at the new location included housing referrals under Dr. István Horváth, damage reporting under Dr. Sándor Szaloky, and transportation requirements under Dr. Ödön Pongrácz. The courtesy title of "Dr." did not indicate that these managers were medical professionals. It is far more likely that they were trained as lawyers. If they had concerns about the legitimacy of the mass theft of private property by the state, such scruples did not keep them from doing their jobs.

The move from city hall was accomplished even though Mayor Koller and his housing staff endured a very busy time. June had brought 460 requests for housing based specifically on bomb damage and 770 total requests for Jewish apartments. Moreover, he wrote, things were not about to get easier:

> There is quite a lot of Jewish real estate, where the required final decisions have not been handed over, or no progress has been made toward those decisions. Provisions have not been made to protect Christian residents of these buildings or groups of buildings from air attack.[3]

While operational elements moved to Teleki 38, the city maintained the financial and administrative records relating to real estate in the office of Financial Head Counselor S. K. Virág, on the first floor of the Financial Palace a couple blocks east on Szent István. A bombing raid on September 22 disrupted this arrangement. True to form, the local newspaper called it a "terror bombing." This attack damaged some records, including documentation concerning porters and janitors, the number of authorized residents per building, the precise addresses of the caretakers of buildings, and records pertaining to official administrators and trustees of specific properties. The city struggled to operate a large new bureaucracy under very trying conditions.

By then the whole project was well enough along that caretakers had been assigned to oversee the stolen real property. By mid-August, 117 caretakers had been found to look after the 426 businesses and residences that had been seized. They were charged with collecting rent from new tenants and arranging for maintenance. They also dealt with recovery after air raids—repairs, restoration, aid to victims, and reporting. The newspaper printed the list of properties in eight installments, over 11 days starting on August 13, 1944. The compilation included for each property the name of each former owner, the property address, and the name and often the occupation of the caretaker. The paper announced that the formerly Jewish houses had officially become state property. This information should have been preserved among the records in the county archives but at some point disappeared.

3 Mayor Jenő Koller, monthly (June) report to Administrative Committee, July 12, 1944, cited in Perger, p. 90.

The consolidated list of caretakers (appended herein) provides a group portrait of a major human element of the system of theft. They were respectable, mainstream professionals, mostly public officials employed by the county, the city, and local branches of national agencies, such as the office of the city clerk, the customs office, cashier's offices, and financial management offices. All but three were men. Thirty-two, or more than one in four, had "Dr." in front of their name. Horváth and Szakoly of the housing office also served on the city council as did a third caretaker, Károly Pollák. Mayor Koller too oversaw one property, and Dr. Ferenc Tomaj, who later wrote an academic article on factors involved in the reduction of the city's population, was responsible for six properties. After the war, Tomaj became director of the county archives, which also preserved city records until the end of the Communist regime.[4] It is not hard to conclude that the official list did not vanish accidentally. What had been considered a hallmark of a normal mainstream bureaucratic transaction in the summer of 1944 would shortly after the war have become evidence of the involvement of respectable professional local citizens on the kleptocratic fringe of a state-sponsored process of expropriation, deportation, and mass murder.

The caretakers' list resembles sources unearthed and analyzed by Tim Cole in his book *Traces of the Holocaust*. These included a collection of passes into and out of the Szombathely ghetto and receipts for fees paid to wagon owners who delivered Jews from their Nyireghaza homes to the ghetto. Like the list of caretakers, these collections of source materials illuminate widespread involvement of significant portions of the local population sometimes filed in the historical literature as "bystanders," which is to say they were neither direct perpetrators nor victims of the processes taking place. However, the "bystander" category is not useful. All these people—caretakers of real property, wagoneers, clerks who processed ghetto passes—were enablers, along with warehouse workers, the police, newspaper editors, and midwives who performed cavity searches. They made the system of theft and deportation work. For every victim

4 *Győr Szab. Kir. Város Cimtára* (Győr: Szép József, 1940), pp. 36–7, 53. This city directory declared itself the first such publication of its kind in Győr. The 1941 edition was the last.

there was more than a perpetrator; there were also a substantial number of enablers or "implicated individuals."[5]

Nine public employees in Győr cornered a big chunk of the fee-for-service caretaker market. They each managed at least nine properties and as many as 12, for a total of 91. Their day-job titles ranged from tax officer to state treasury senior officer, auditor, and tax office adviser. Two of the nine, Jenő Mondvay and Béla Nagy, were lawyers. Mondvay directed the Győr County central purchase tax office in the tax office of the Royal Financial Directorate, with his office in the Financial Palace, and Nagy served as a supervisory official of the city orphanage. Both managed nine properties. The city did not publicize their pay, and the local newspaper on August 16 spoke only of their "small monthly remuneration," playing down this aspect of their work. In any case, this was not pro bono work.

Another of the caretakers, city tax officer József Erdélyi, managed only two buildings, Árpád 39 and 41. These were right across the street from the cultural center, where then-Prime Minister Darányi had promulgated his plans for rearmament and settling "the Jewish question." Erdélyi's involvement with the kleptocracy probably had at least one additional side. After the Jews were ghettoized, tax officials supervised the gendarmes and women who conducted body searches for hidden valuables. These inspectors examined new inmates in family groups as they entered the ghetto, forced them to strip, and searched body cavities for hidden valuables. After confiscating everything, the tax official identified as E. J. in the newspaper, who may well have been city tax official and caretaker of two Jewish properties Erdélyi József, filled out a receipt on behalf of the treasury for whatever money, wristwatches, or jewelry had been found.

The system operated in broad daylight, with full public knowledge. The local paper, edited by ardent anti-Semite and supporter of Nazi Germany Jenő Pohárnok, had published the mayor's call for workers to help process Jewish property and the list of caretakers. His paper also recorded the negative public reaction to the use of public officers and the corresponding

5 Regarding the usage of the term "implicated individual," see Geraldine Schwarz, *Those Who Forget: My Family's Story in Nazi Europe—A Memoir, A History, A Warning* (New York: Scribner, 2017).

denial of opportunities to less well-connected citizens in parceling out caretaker positions. Pohárnok defended the selections as sound policy. Overall, the caretakers represented a core group in a broad interlocking network of people who knew about the system and benefited from it, among them lesser employees such as warehouse workers, businessmen who took over Jewish stores or acquired their stocks of goods, individuals and organizations that applied for real estate and other property, and others who took advantage of transitional times to get at Jewish homes and loot them before the city could take control.

In a city of about 50,000, more than 1,000 requests for various goods poured into city hall. Unsurprisingly, the applications for articles that ranged from baby carriages and radios to underwear and bedding have disappeared. But the registers of correspondence have survived, and István Nagy counted the requests and noted the items sought when they were mentioned. Numerous queries came from associations, firms, and government offices. Radios were in great demand, judging by requests from the gendarmes, the locomotive shop of the state railroad, and the local boating club. But the Hungarian National Bank wanted furniture, and the army, the Szent István old-age home, the freight car factory and others asked for bicycles, storage cabinets, firewood, and refrigerators. No one, it seemed, wanted to miss the opportunity to participate in this windfall. And very few in the city could conceivably claim that they did not know what was happening.

This brings us back to the law and the lawyers. A mid-1944 case before a local court in Győr at the time illustrates the legal and moral climate that legitimized this situation. Two thieves were brought before the bar for breaking into premises that had been taken from Jews but not yet officially emptied. They had stolen contents valued at 2,000 pengő, not quite $60 at the exchange rate then in effect. The theft took place on July 11, one month after the first trainloads of Győri Jews had started out for Auschwitz. In their defense, the perpetrators argued that the value of the goods involved was trivial. The judge rejected the assertion. They had stolen state property, robbing the Hungarian treasury of wealth that rightfully belonged to the government and the people. Both defendants went to jail for two years. Stealing everything from the Jews was OK; stealing a trivial portion of the same property once it had been taken by the state was a criminal offense and a moral affront. As historian Raul Hilberg observed, lawyers had to deal continuously with the "question of harmonizing peremptory measures against Jews with the law."[6] This case illustrates how easy that was.

By 1944, the lawyers of Győr had already dealt with this matter in the main, voting Jewish attorneys out of their professional organization. Neal Ascherson's observations about the staff at Auschwitz may apply to them as well. Ascherson saw those who were beyond merely brutal and stupid as

> simply boneheaded "respectable" men genuinely unable to grasp the implications of what they had been doing […]. How could men who wore clean shirts, followed football in the evening paper, and sent birthday cards to their moms plan and carry out […] this?[7]

The same might be asked about the caretakers of formerly Jewish property. They were certainly part of an entire class of people who carried out and benefited from the dispossession of the Jews before and after their deportation. They were respectable solid citizens holding responsible positions of public trust, and they were not unique. The society was laced with such enablers and beneficiaries, all eager or at least willing to exploit the Jewish catastrophe. Even where it might have been plausible to deny knowledge of the murder, it would have been impossible to ignore the dispossession that preceded it.

Austrian sculptor Alfred Hrdlicka, creator of the provocative Holocaust memorial on Albertinaplatz in Vienna, once noted that mass murder needs a mass of murderers.[8] By the same token, mass theft requires a mass of thieves. And thieves abounded. Hungary in 1944, almost resembled the Nazi equivalent of the syndicate run by Milo Minderbinder, the military entrepreneur of Joseph Heller's *Catch-22*, who pursued opportunities whether they profited friend or foe and boasted that everyone

6 Hilberg, *Perpetrators Victims Bystanders*, pp. 65–6.

7 Neal Ascherson, "How Could They?" *New York Review of Books*, 61, October 23, 2014, p. 36 of pp. 35–7.

8 Robert Singer interview, *Judische Rundshau*, 47 (November 24, 1987), p. 2, quoted by James E. Young, *The Texture of Memory: Holocaust Memorials and Meaning* (New Haven: Yale University Press, 1993), p. 110.

was a member of the syndicate, and everyone owned a share. In Győr, the most valuable items—gems, jewelry, precious metals, furs, antiques, and silverware, as well as currency and stock certificates—went into vaults at the secured loan branch of the savings bank, in the Schlichter villa across the railroad tracks from the train station. Director József Kóródy tracked this accumulation through inventory forms that differed from those used for other goods. The property went into two huge safes and added up to many millions of pengő. The clothing alone, director Kórody thought, had a value of nearly six million pengő (almost $180,000). This was a great windfall for the city treasury.

Figure 9.1 The Schlichter villa at the bus depot across the tracks from the train depot. The 2014 renovation covered bullet holes from an October 1956 firefight.

The widespread involvement of the local population in the horrible events of 1944 reverberated down through the years. Australian physician Tony Salgo, now retired, has roots in Győr. His Jewish parents survived deportation to Auschwitz and immigrated to Sydney, where Tony was born. His parents had originally returned to Hungary, but his mother refused to stay there. She did not understand how a survivor could return and live a normal life. The Holocaust, she said, connected everybody in her hometown of Győr. Tony returned to Győr several times in the decade between 2005 and 2015. He was especially drawn to the downtown building his family had owned, in which they resided before the Hungarian state stole the property. He showed no interest in claiming the building. He usually just contemplated it from the outside, although he once entered and looked at a flat that was for sale.

I know what it is like to visit such a place. In 1996, the year after my first visit to my father's birthplace in modern Slovakia, I accompanied my Hungarian cousins to Vác, on the Danube upstream from Budapest, to see where my father grew up. The prewar house and butcher shop had been owned by my grandfather and his older brother, Lipót, both of whom were murdered in 1944. The structure had evolved into a stationery store, behind which remained the stables where cattle had been kept. It is just north up the river from the triumphal arch built before a visit to the city by Empress Mária Theresa, on Dózsa György Avenue, then called Horthy Miklós Avenue, at the southeast corner of Hunyadi János Street. Plainly, Horthy was the town's main north-south thoroughfare. Irene says she felt the tension that my visit generated. Distracted by the mere fact of being where my father had spent his boyhood, I did not notice. I saw the place, took my pictures, and never went back.

The return of descendants of those deported and murdered by the Germans and their Hungarian allies and helpers does cause tensions and anxieties. These derive from concerns about claims on the property now occupied by others. They may also involve guilt about ownership of property that once belonged to people who were taken away and killed. Tony Salgo's late cousin, the literary scholar Andrew Riemer, also a resident of Sydney, described his own encounter in a memoir called *The Habsburg Café*. Andrew was born in Hungary. He and his parents did not leave until after the war, so he remembered the art deco villa of his childhood. His apparent curiosity when he appeared outside the fence generated hostility and suspicion until it became apparent that he did not seek to recover the property. The frostiness then dissolved into a sort of relieved cordiality and an invitation for a cup of coffee.

Clearly, the connections that radiate from the list and the actions that underlay it still have power, known to some and unrealized by others, and go to the core of who we think we are and who we might be. They give substance to Reiner Stach's observation in his *Kafka: The Early Years*. Stach spoke specifically of Prague but could as easily have referred to almost any city in Central Europe: "the intertwining of past and present, of death and life can make the presence of history feel downright eerie."[9]

There were other repercussions with broader implications for the future. The war left in its wake a whole generation schooled in the mechanics of authoritarian governance. People who knew how to build fences for concentration and death camps could just as easily build segments of the Iron Curtain. Those who implemented the deportation of Jews in 1944 could just as easily handle the removal of German nationals from Hungary, Czechoslovakia, and Poland shortly after the war. Those who administered the pervasive state-sponsored larceny that accompanied the mass murder of Jews during the war could just as well manage the nationalizations and other confiscations carried out by the Communists. And those who knew that such displacements meant the availability of goods and valuables understood how to take advantage. All that was required to move from serving one kleptocratic and murderous autocracy to another was a change of clothes.

Hungarian-born Jewish poet and journalist György Faludy encountered this situation as a reporter just after World War II, when he returned to Hungary after having served in the U.S. Army. He asked his chauffeur if he had been a member of the Arrow Cross, the homegrown Hungarian variant of the Nazis. "Of course, I was," he said. Faludy then asked, "And what makes you a social democrat today?" "The same thing," replied the driver, whose name was Kakus. "One must make a living." Faludy pursued the matter further, asking if Kakus believed the Nazis. Kakus smiled and acknowledged that he had, "exactly as I believe the social democrats today and the Bolsheviks tomorrow!" He had simply changed his clothes. Similarly, at the Recsk internment camp, where Faludy was imprisoned in 1949, there

9 Reiner Stach, *Kafka: The Early Years*, trans. Shelley Frisch (Princeton: Princeton University Press, 2017), p. 16.

was the example of a state security officer named Lieutenant Tóth, who "had been one of the pillars of the arrow-cross movement five years ago at Esztergom. He had joined the communist party the day the Red Army marched into Hungary."[10]

I knew nothing about the list of Győr caretakers and had not thought much about the implications for the future of the system they served when Irene and I went on a five-day tour of Istria, at the end of September 2013. Istria is a Croatian peninsula that juts south into the Adriatic east of Trieste. We went by bus with Kisalföld Volan, the local tour company, and became acquainted with Melissa Almasi on our Istrian trip, traveling with her mother and aunt, fraternal twins who were born in Győr during the war, in 1943. Like Tony Salgo, Melissa was born in Sydney. As her mother informed me more than once, she graduated number one in her class at the engineering school of the university in Sydney. Melissa's parents left Győr for Sydney, in the 1970s. They are not Jewish, and Melissa has Hungarian citizenship. Tony and I do not. I explained to Melissa, who like Tony and me is of the first generation in her family born outside of Hungary, my difficulty in bringing myself to apply for the Hungarian citizenship to which I am entitled. This is a moral problem, not a legal one. My parents were still Hungarian citizens when I was born in 1943, so I am a Hungarian citizen. All I need to do is produce the documents that show that my parents had not yet become naturalized Americans when I was born. Even though I am drawn toward Hungary enough to want to live there part-time, I can't bring myself to identify that closely with a country that rejected my family and whose current regime tends toward autocracy and shows emerging signs of the old anti-Semitism. Citizens of the country tolerated or participated

10 György Faludi, *My Happy Days in Hell*, trans. Kathleen Szasz (London: Penguin Classics, 2010), pp. 253–4, 349. At the House of Terror Museum in Budapest a few years ago, we saw an exhibit that framed the political flexibility and opportunism of the twentieth century in terms of changing clothes. A video presentation showed people entering a locker room in Arrow Cross garb, removing their uniforms and putting them in lockers, then dressing in the workers' overalls of good Communists and exiting the room. Other segments showed the same Communists or their offspring taking off their overalls at the time of the political change of around 1990 and stepping out in business suits.

in the murder of members of my family. Melissa understands that, but she is not Jewish and does not share my qualms.

Melissa speaks Hungarian far better than I do. When she showed signs as a young girl of rejecting her heritage and her language, her mother forced her to continue to learn Hungarian and use it. She and her mother both recall that Melissa hated it but nevertheless complied. When I rejected the language upon my entry into the Washington, D.C. school system, my parents did nothing that I can recall to resist my inclination. Melissa's mother, Erzsébet Mondvay Almasi, resides in Sydney; Melissa's aunt, Mária (Ria) Mondvay, still lives in Győr, on Rákóczi Street just two blocks north of Pálffy Street where we owned an apartment.

In Istria, the five of us formed a little group of our own within the tour group, taking evening walks on the forested island in Porec harbor where our resort hotel was located, and chatting on our days together. At the end of the excursion, all of us were interested in maintaining the connection we had formed. So six days after we returned, the three women came to our flat for brunch. That's when I learned that Erzsébet worked as a photographer before she left the country. I also learned that neither she nor her sister had been to university. They said they had been denied that opportunity because their family had been designated an enemy of the working class by the Communist regime. I mentioned István Nagy, my friend the photographer and local historian, and Erzsébet recalled that they had worked in the same state-owned photography concern, though he was in Csorna at the time, while she was in Győr. So I showed her some of István's books and then dialed his number on my mobile phone and handed it to her. He did not remember who she was.

Meanwhile, Tony Salgo arrived from Sydney for one of his occasional and sometimes unannounced visits. Tony is a sharp observer and an amiable companion. However, he rarely and belatedly answers emails, and this time was no exception. He just showed up and called Dezső Jakabovits, who called me. We went over to his room at the Conference Hotel and thence to the John Bull pub, where the air was filled with the German conversation of managers from the Audi factory.

As it happens, István Nagy was in the hotel that night, photographing a birthday party. The hotel is late socialist *elegante*, a style marked by broodingly dark wood and flashing white marble. I told Tony about the three women, and we agreed jointly to host a dinner. He was only staying three days, so on Sunday, I called them and István Nagy and his wife, and arranged a table for seven on Monday evening. Melissa flew back to Sydney on Monday morning. The Australians, who had never met, could establish contact; István and Erzsebet could renew a forgotten acquaintance; we could all enjoy each other's company.

I reserved a table at Szalai, the restaurant where I often share a beer with my friends in the late afternoon. The group calls itself the "library," as in "Where are you going, dear?" "Nowhere special, just to the library." The draft beer there is Pilsner Urquell, a welcome change from dreary Hungarian brews. It was a pleasant enough meal until the conversation turned political. I had seen political conversation spin out of control in a matter of seconds between friends of 60 years. Now I saw the same thing happen between people who had met barely an hour earlier. When Marika Nagy, István's wife, mentioned her left-wing leanings, Ria Mondvay immediately became indignant, angry that anyone could support politicians who were direct descendants of Communists. Sharp words were exchanged as Ria expressed her incredulity, stabbing at Marika with her finger, diagonally across the table and luckily out of physical reach. How could anyone support the political descendants of the Communists who had denied her and her sister educational opportunities and ruined her family's life? Meanwhile, István and Erzsébet found little in common in their joint occupational past, and Tony was gracious but kept his emotional distance from the Mondvay sisters. After the outburst subsided, the dinner passed without further disruption or complaints about the food. Afterward, both Ria and Marika separately expressed to me their dismay and embarrassment over what had taken place between them. I don't think apologies were exchanged between them, however.

Two weeks after that get-together, Irene and I met István and Marika Nagy for a dinner that combined a farewell visit with them before our return to the United States, and a meal at our favorite nearby restaurant, an Italian place called La Dolce Vita. The owner is from Puglia, and always manages to have fresh seafood, which his kitchen treats with respect. Over a slab of swordfish steak, something István had never eaten before, he told me of his current research, still focusing on the Jews of Győr, although his book on the deportation had appeared in 2010. At that point he alerted me to the existence of the list of caretakers. Previously I had spent some time reading the local newspaper and had become familiar with the writings and outlook of editor Pohárnok, but I had concentrated on finding places relating to the deportation early in the summer of 1944 and the establishment of the archipelago of theft—the warehouses, vaults, and offices associated with the acquisition of Jewish property. So I had stopped short of the mid-August issues, when the list started to appear in the paper. In any case, István did not have to suggest twice that I meet him the following day at his studio to look at the list.

He showed me the compilation on Thursday, October 31, 2013. He had taken down the addresses of the properties and the names of the Jewish former owners and identified the caretakers. István, true to his meticulous approach to research, had turned the string of names and addresses into a 14-page list of all the properties, and sorted the entries to produce three alphabetically organized lists, one by former owner, another by property addresses, and a third by the caretakers' names. It was my first encounter with the compilation, which I have come to call "The List." It was nothing less than a condensed statement, free of frills or distractions that might dilute its impact, of real property confiscated from the Jews of Győr before they were packed off to be murdered.

The list included the name of Dr. Jenő Mondvay, who had fathered the twin girls Erzsébet and Mária in 1943. One of the properties for which Jenő Mondvay was responsible was the commercial building at 22 Baross út, home of the anti-Semitic Baross Szövetség. The owner of the property had been Nándor Lőwy, Tony Salgo's grandfather. So Erzsébet Mondvay Almasi, the gentile from Győr who now lives in Sydney, and Tony Salgo, the Jew whose parents had fled Győr and was born in Sydney, had a connection of which neither was aware, that Erzsébet's father had been official caretaker of the property that had belonged to Tony's grandfather until it was taken from him before he in turn disappeared.

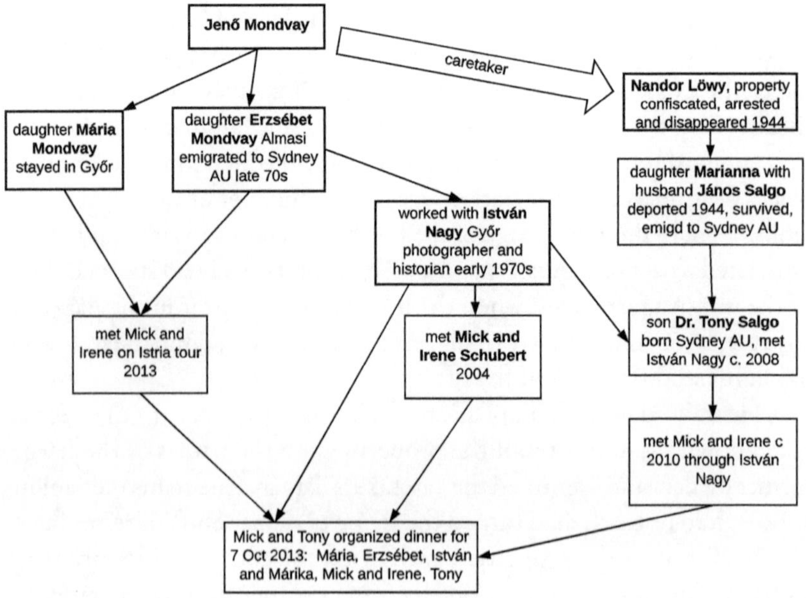


Figure 9.2 Connections with a caretaker, across generations and continents. [Chart 1].

Moreover, Ria Mondvay, Erzsébet's sister, who had flashed anger at Marika Nagy for expressing support for the leftish opposition to the current government, certainly had more in her past than parents who had been designated class enemies by the Communist regime. When her father became a manager of nine confiscated properties, he became a cog in the bureaucracy that operated the systematic despoiling and murder of the Jews of Győr. He was not a perpetrator in the conventional sense, but an enabler or at the very least, a beneficiary. Would she appreciate the irony implicit in her bitterness, that she, whose family had been stigmatized by the postwar regime, had benefited from the income generated by her father as manager of properties taken from people stigmatized by the wartime regime? Might she even (and this would be asking a lot) come to appreciate her good fortune at being merely stigmatized and perhaps therefore denied a university education as a result rather than stigmatized, pauperized, deported, and murdered?

The list also included the birthplace of Ria and her twin sister, Erzsébet, the Csillag sanitarium at Árpád 18, among the confiscated properties. The sanitarium was the modern 14-bed private hospital run by Dr. József Csillag until he too was deported in 1944. Eva Quittner, born Eva Klein, who as a teenager was the only survivor of the camps in her family and later became an artist in Sydney, remembered the facility warmly. Csillag's patients included Christians and Jews, the Klein girl, who had her tonsils removed and the Mondvay girls, who were born there. As Eva Quittner put it in her memoir, "everybody who could afford it preferred the genteel atmosphere of the Csillag sanitarium" to the public hospital.[11]

Also among the former property owners was poet and teacher Vilma Popper, who from her birth lived at Kossuth 14 at the Ujváros end of the bridge across Rado island. She owned the building at Árpád 20, next door to Csillag's clinic. At least she did until she was taken to Auschwitz to be killed. She was then eighty-seven, one of the oldest among the Jews of Győr who were murdered. Dr. Csillag was 58 when he was taken to the same camp. He survived and made it back but succumbed to tuberculosis shortly after his liberation.

11 Eva Quittner, *Pebbles of Remembrance* (Balmain, Australia: Kerr Publishing, 1993), p. 89. Stumble stones naming her parents and older brother were installed in front of the Klein residence at Ronay Street 6 in June 2019.

Figure 9.3 The plaque at Árpád 18 notes that the Csillag sanitorium operated there for 20 years. It does not mention a connection with the Jewish community of Győr. However, whenever 1944 is noted as an end date for an organization or activity, it is almost inevitable that it was shut down as part of the mass theft and murder of that year. This tablet exemplifies remembrance without revealing the reason. Only those who understand the significance of 1944 can begin to comprehend what happened.

When Erzsébet and Ria visited us for brunch in October 2013, they spoke about having been born in the sanitorium. However, they did not know where it was. After we ate, I showed them the location with the memorial tablet. They showed no particular interest when I mentioned that Dr. Csillag had been Jewish, but it was clear that they had not been aware of that fact. Moreover, they either lacked a sense of irony or, more likely, were unaware of their father's role as an enabler of the regime that confiscated Vilma Popper's property and sent her and the physician who brought them into the world to Auschwitz. Jenő Mondvay was not involved with either property as caretaker. However, he was responsible for the building on the other side of Popper's, at 22, which was owned by Dr. Lajos Rothauser and his wife, Irma, both of whom were murdered at Auschwitz, and another down the street at 32, whose owner, Kálmán Diamant, was murdered at Mauthausen in 1945 at the age of 50.

Vilma Popper was a leading figure in the educational and literary life of Győr. Her writings included a biography of Lajos Kossuth, stories for children, and translations of Hungarian novelists such as Kálmán Mikszáth into German. She spoke English, French, and German as well as Hungarian and was familiar with Latin and Greek. In addition to her translations and literary works, she taught both English and German in the academic high school for girls and was a founding member in 1908 of the Kisfaludy Literary Circle in the city.

When the Kisfaludy Literary Circle was founded, newspaper editor Jenő Pohárnok was ten years old. Born in Győr to a family that lived at Megyeház 32 (now Liszt Ferenc 32), a little east of the county office building that in 1944 housed the Arrow Cross enforcers, he also developed into a writer and taught in the laboratory secondary school of the Győr teacher's college. His oeuvre included poetry, children's novels, and an operetta celebrating the Boy Scouts. His local prominence led to his becoming the secretary of the literary circle in 1931–2. He and Popper were separated by a generation, but as writers and educators with similar interests as well as members of the same professional circle, who lived in a city of fewer than 50,000, they surely knew each other well. They were also separated by his political views. Long before the war, in 1920, he had operated an anti-Semitic newspaper called *Mire Várunk Még?* [*What are we waiting for?*]. None of the biographical articles about Pohárnok cite this experience, but the mention of it in the newspaper during his tenure as editor indicates that he was not a latecomer to journalistic anti-Semitism.[12]

12 The latest laudatory work, by local historian József Várga, is in a collection of biographical essays of teachers who worked at the school on Gardonyi Géza. The book is Gönczöl Lászlóné and Kallós Károlyné, eds., *Végtelen Pályatér: Jeles pedagógusok Győr-Moson-Sopron megyeben*, vol. 7 (Győr: "Emelj fel emlék" Alapitvány, 2016). Inside the school Pohárnok and three other former teachers are remembered for their dedication to teaching on a "Tree of Teachers" installation with gold leaves that bear their name. Várga was for many years director of the school. The fact that Pohárnok was a dedicated Nazi does not not seem to have diminished his status in Várga's eyes.

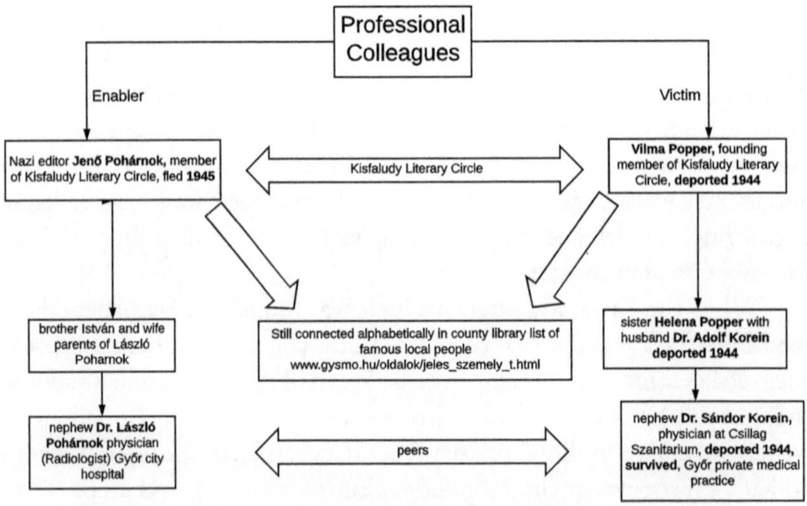


Figure 9.4 Popper and Pohárnok [Chart 2].

The daily *Győr Nemzeti Hirlap*, which Pohárnok edited from November 1941, provided a perfect venue for a rabid anti-Semite. In the same issue that included the biographical tidbit about his 1920 experience, a month after the deportation of the Jews, Pohárnok expressed his loathing for these former residents of the city in a passionate editorial. The screed was entitled "The Jews Have Gone Away but the Evil Propaganda Continues to Flow." An unwavering advocate of removal of the Jews to cleanse the Hungarian nation, the *Hirlap* did not merely follow the German line, but provided a specific Hungarian rationale for expropriation, deportation, and murder. In fact, it eagerly advocated this "solution." Pohárnok argued that the Jews got what they deserved, comparing them to rabid dogs that attack people and must be put down. He ended with a tribal declaration that could just as easily have come from a spokesman of the government of Prime Minister Viktor Orbán in 2017: "We fight for a one thousand times well-deserved better Hungarian future, a more Christian Christian and more Hungarian Hungarian homeland!"

Vilma Popper, who had been among the founders of the literary group that included Jenő Pohárnok, was among the rabid dogs taken to Auschwitz and killed. Jenő Pohárnok survived the war and fled westward with the Nazis to avoid capture by Russian forces. In Germany, he resumed his writing career in Hungarian and lived in Munich until his death in 1962. It is said in Győr that family members who remain in the city insist that the Nazis forced him to write his rants at the point of a gun. But it is on the home page of Győr-Moson-Sopron County that the erasure of his ugly past became complete and took a bizarre turn. For there they are, Pohárnok and Popper, one after the other on the list of famous local people, alphabetically joined at the hip as if they, the advocate of mass murder and one of the oldest deported Jews, belonged together.[13] There is no plaque on his birthplace to match the one at Kossuth 14.

Figure 9.5 The marker inside the gate at Kossuth 14 was placed in 1948 by Dr. Sándor Korein, the son of Vilma Popper's sister Heléna and Dr. Adolf Korein. The younger Korein was also a physician. He practiced at the Csillag sanitarium, survived deportation, although his wife and daughter did not, and resumed his practice in Győr. Pohárnok's nephew, the son of his brother István, also became a physician and practiced on the staff of the city hospital. The two doctors must have known each other, continuing the strange connection between Vilma Popper and Jenő Pohárnok into the next generation.

13 As it happens, they are once again "alphabetically joined at the hip" in the index to this volume.

Almost eighty years have passed since Popper was killed and Pohárnok fled, but the system that ensnared one and was enabled by the other remains a presence with effects both professional and personal. I have known István Nagy, through whom I met Tony Salgo, for nearly 20 years, practically since we bought our flat in Győr in 2002 and moved in two years later. We met through András and Márta Rajcsányi, who ran a real estate business. Márta showed us apartments during our short early visits to Győr, and we became friends, the four of us. How that friendship emerged or even how that transaction was completed, given my nearly complete ignorance of Hungarian at the time, are not entirely clear to me. But it became clear that they were honest and open to an acquaintance with strangers like us. We were lucky, the flat was suitable, and we bought it in May 2002.

Shortly after we moved into the apartment in September 2004, András mentioned that he and a small group of long-time friends met for a drink every weekday at 5 p.m. This was my introduction to "the library." I was the only English speaker, and the conversation flowed without much regard for my shortcomings in Hungarian. But the sessions gave me an hour's immersion in the language every day. Sometimes I could understand and contribute. Other times they left me behind. But the library represented a ready-made group of local comrades, who knew everything from where to rent a car to where to get the best Hungarian fish soup.

The rules were simple: the sessions lasted an hour, and everyone paid for his own drink. Wives were not excluded but rarely came. All the regulars were tolerant, friendly, curious about Irene and me, and knowledgeable about their city. András and another "librarian," Dezső Jakabovits, had been friends since kindergarten in the 1950s. István Nagy was part of the group. The others included a police official with a law degree, who had learned enough English as a boy in the 1970s to understand the lyrics of Beatles songs. In addition, there were two shopkeepers, a retired manager from a textile factory, and an agricultural engineer.

They had a *Stammtisch*, a regular table upstairs at the Patio restaurant. Never in my life had I been part of a group that had a *Stammtisch*, where the waiters knew my name and remembered what I drank. I loved showing up, sitting down, and having a pint placed in front of me without asking. Since those days, the Patio has closed and the group has taken to wandering a bit, to the John Bull, the now defunct Kisfaludy coffeehouse, the Palffy, Matiás, and finally the Szalai, places that achieved the status of branch libraries for a time. Departures triggered by personal disagreements as well as occasional new arrivals have altered the composition, but institutions survive personnel changes and so it was with the library, which persisted until old age and smoldering personal disagreements destroyed it.

András Rajcsányi gave me a copy of Nobel Prize recipient Imre Kertész's novel *Fatelessness*, the story of a Jewish adolescent boy who, like the writer, survived deportation to a work camp adjacent to the death factory at Auschwitz and returned home to Budapest, where his neighbors were anything but pleased to see him and wanted to know why he had come back. I heard Kertész speak once, on September 22, 2005, at the Benedictine monastery of Pannonholma. Dezső Jakabovits, the only Jewish member of the library group, invited me to join him. I had never seen a Nobel laureate, so I went. The audience was full of young seminarians. It turned out that I knew enough Hungarian to understand his reply to the question about the existence of God. Kertész said he did not know whether there was a God, but he thought it was important to behave as if there were one.

It turned out that András's father was on the list of caretakers too. A lawyer and city official like Jenő Mondvay, Lajos Rajcsányi took care of three properties confiscated from their Jewish owners, according to the list in the newspaper. This connection between Jakabovits, whose future parents survived a work camp at Auschwitz as Kertész did, came back to Győr, married in a Jewish ceremony, and had two sons, and Rajcsányi, whose father had managed property stolen from Jews sent off to Auschwitz to be killed or worked to death, was not known to either of them as far as I knew.

Because István Nagy was involved in local history and I was a historian by trade, he and I among the librarians became particularly close. He showed me sources and took me to places that were important in my research for a book that became titled *Hungarian Borderlands*, and I helped him obtain precise information on the Allied bombing of Győr through my connections among official historians in the U.S. Department of Defense, particularly Richard Davis at the U.S. Army Center of Military History.

Altogether, according to Richard Davis's list, there were 35 separate aerial attacks on the city over the last year of the war.

István's volume on the bombing was the first of the three that make up his major work. I spent parts of numerous afternoons discussing this project with him. I also accompanied him to schools and churches where I helped him set up exhibits depicting dramatic eras in Hungarian history with visual materials and objects from his own collection. Overall, he helped me far more than I could ever help him. When I first met István, he was working on the bombing volume. The bombing is still important to the people of Győr, forming the basis for a community sense of shared victimization. Irene and I sometimes went to the annual commemorations of the attacks, as István's guests, and we found the experience a little unsettling. The 2019 session was held at the Tourinform office, which shares Baross 23 with the McDonald's, but was once the site of the Arrow Cross county headquarters.

Győr had many factories. The biggest produced freight cars for the state railroad. Another manufactured engines for Messerschmitt fighter aircraft, a sort of anticipation of the dominant current position of the German automaker Audi, whose Győr factory now employs 10,000 workers and produces engines. In fact, some say this Audi factory produces more engines than any other automobile plant in the world. Győr also had a major railroad marshalling yard. Overall, it represented a legitimate and worthwhile target for bombing. There were innocent victims, to be sure. Erzsébet, Ria, and the rest of the Mondvay family were fortunately not at home when their residence was destroyed during one of the bombings.

The commemorations focus on the "innocent" victims of the city. Sometimes they feature photo exhibits, other times speeches, but they all ignore the industrial contributions of the city to the Axis war effort. They say nothing about the caretakers and the gendarmes who packed the Jews onto Auschwitz-bound trains, or those who sold groceries to the factory workers who produced the fighter engines and railroad cars, drove the buses that took them to work, maintained the railroads, and did nothing when their Jewish neighbors were marched off first to the ghetto and then to Auschwitz. Irene and I stand respectfully at these meetings, thinking quietly that Győr, now our adopted part-time home, might have got what it deserved.

Figure 9.6 The memorial to victims of the bombing is behind the Arkád shopping center, on the site of the freight car and engine factory that was a key target for bombers on the first raid of April 13, 1944. Just south of the site the water tower of the period still stands, with a bright red neon *Arkád* sign. The tower was a convenient aiming point for Allied aircraft and survived the war unscathed.

In April 2014, the city's János Xantus Museum mounted an exhibit commemorating the seventieth anniversary of the first bombings. Xantus had attended the Benedictine secondary school on Széchenyi Square, just a few steps away from the museum that now bears his name. His career included participation in the revolution of 1848, flight from Habsburg authorities to North America, and frontier service in the U.S. Army before he became the first director of the Budapest zoo. Much of his fame rests on his creative journalism, what might now be called "fake news." He sent articles back to Europe based partly on his encounters with military explorers and partly on his fantasies of personal adventures that involved Indian warriors and grizzly bears. These articles became grist for another, more famous fantast, the German novelist Karl May.

The exhibit produced by the museum in cooperation with the Military History Institute in Budapest presented a distorted picture of the terrible spring of 1944. It highlighted, albeit implicitly, a prominent characteristic of local collective memory, the decoupling of two simultaneous and critical events of the spring of 1944, the first bombing and the start of the process that led to Auschwitz. Even with a title that could have encompassed both experiences—the exhibit was called *Humans in the Midst of Inhumanity: Győr during the Time of the World Wars*—the narrative focused on the former and ignored active and enthusiastic participation in the latter, although they began and developed simultaneously as two sides of the same story.

An engrossing slide show featured the blessing of a Hungarian battalion's flag in December 1942, with wives of dignitaries in fur coats, and soldiers in German-style helmets. Behind the assembled troops and attentive civilians, you can see the office of the newspaper, but you will not learn that the editor was a rabid Nazi who fled with his German friends at the end of the war. You can also see the furniture store of Nándor Lőwy, without learning that it was stolen by the state before Lőwy disappeared. But the greatest lacuna of all, not surprisingly, concerned a matter far more significant than these details, one that is still all too commonplace in Hungary. Given the title of the exhibit, I couldn't help but think that if inhumanity was the subject of the exhibit, it might include the elimination of the city's Jews, a catastrophe that occurred simultaneously with the bombing that destroyed much of the city, made homeless many of its people, and left hundreds of dead and wounded in its wake. But I was wrong. There were no Jews in this story, just as there are almost no Jews in the city today.

The Jewish experience, inseparable from the majority experience, challenges local museums. Connecting the two means identifying perpetrators and enablers of one kind or another. A decade or so ago, in the museum at

Komarno, on the Slovak side of the divided town that is called Komárom in Hungary, Irene and I viewed an exhibit at the local museum on the post–World War II removal of ethnic Hungarians from the north side of the Danube. The central object in the display was a boxcar, the kind that has come to symbolize the shipment of Jews to death camps. As David Cesarani recently observed, "One of the most typical Holocaust memorials is a freight car mounted on a segment of rail track."[14] The freight car at the Komarno museum illuminated what might be called a kinder, gentler deportation, the transfer of Magyars to Hungary, usually about 30 to a car, for a short trip that led to life, albeit with dislocation and uncompensated loss of property that was becoming habitual in Central Europe.

At Komarno, neither the temporary exhibit nor the permanent display mentioned Jews, but there had been 2,743 Jewish people among the town's 30,858 residents in the 1941 census. I asked a staff member why the narrative did not include their story. I did not know the exact number at the time, but she and I both knew that the number was substantial. She may also have been aware that the Hungarian reoccupation of the town at the beginning of November 1938 was accompanied by a wave of vandalism that preceded the much better-known German Kristallnacht.[15] She told me that it was impossible to cover everything. On the way out, I posed the question in the guest book: where are the Jews? But nobody is being fooled here. We know where they are.

14 Cesarani, *Final Solution*, Introduction.

15 This was not unique to the recovered territory. As Cesarani noted, Kristalynacht was "an exponentially aggravated continuation of the violence that had been erupting sporadically since the start of the year." Cesarani, *Final Solution*, p. 183.

CHAPTER 10

# 1989 and the limits of change

Albertkázmérpuszta's long name belies its miniscule size. It's the kind of place former border guard István Gáll might have had in mind when he wrote his Cold War novel *Vaskor* [*Iron Age*] and created the border post of *Patkánylyuk* [Rat Hole]. The village of 400, now incorporated into the slightly bigger settlement of Várbalog, has an imposing Catholic church on the south side of Felszabadulás utca. The church is modelled on the Votive Church in Vienna, and its history is tied to the establishment and then fall of the Iron Curtain.

Archduke Friedrich financed construction, and the church opened to worshippers in 1897. A major figure in borderland history, Friedrich is also the namesake of the military garrison in Győr. He and his wife, Isabella, both born in 1856 and both of whom died in the 1930s, are interred in the cellar of the Pfarrkirche in Mosonmagyaróvár rather than the Habsburg family crypt at the Capuchin Church of Vienna. It is said that he was grateful to the Lord that at the age of 41 Isabella gave birth to a son (Albrecht) after producing eight daughters, and built the church to express his joy and thanks to God. Isabella is left out of this narrative, but she might have been thankful that she did not have to produce more children. In any case, the building is within 100 meters of the border and was inside the fenced and heavily policed border strip imposed by the People's Republic of Hungary, a veritable no-man's-land, during the Cold War. No one could approach the building or get inside, and even the bullet holes in the stained-glass windows, mementos of firefights between retreating Nazis and advancing Soviets in the spring of 1945, went unrepaired as the church decayed along with the settlement. In a project ongoing since 1996, the windows are being restored, and the church has been repaired. It is open to visitors, with the key available across the street.

Figure 10.1 The church at Albertkázmérpuszta.

Since the barbed wire was rolled up in 1989, Felszabadulás [Liberation] utca has been connected to Halbturner LandesStrasse on the other side of the border. The road leads to Halbturn [Féltorony] and a museum in a former Habsburg castle. The crossing shows no traces of the Iron Curtain or formal border controls. In fact, when the police impose spot inspections on the expressway via Hegyeshalom and traffic backs up due to searches for undocumented migrants hidden in smugglers' vehicles, the detour to

Austria via Albertkázmérpuszta only adds a few minutes to the trip. Even a quick side trip with a turn to the south before the church onto Futrinka utca to the Lapos chocolate factory does not add much time and is well worth the detour.[1] We drove into Austria that way twice and never saw another car heading west. An Austrian police cruiser does lurk behind the shrubbery more or less permanently, complete with thermal cups of coffee on the vehicle's hood. The gendarmes bestir themselves for a casual passport inspection. Overall, the change from closed to open border to today's pretty open border is emblematic of borderland developments as both countries try to control or reduce the number of undocumented cross-border migrants while retaining openness within the Schengen zone.

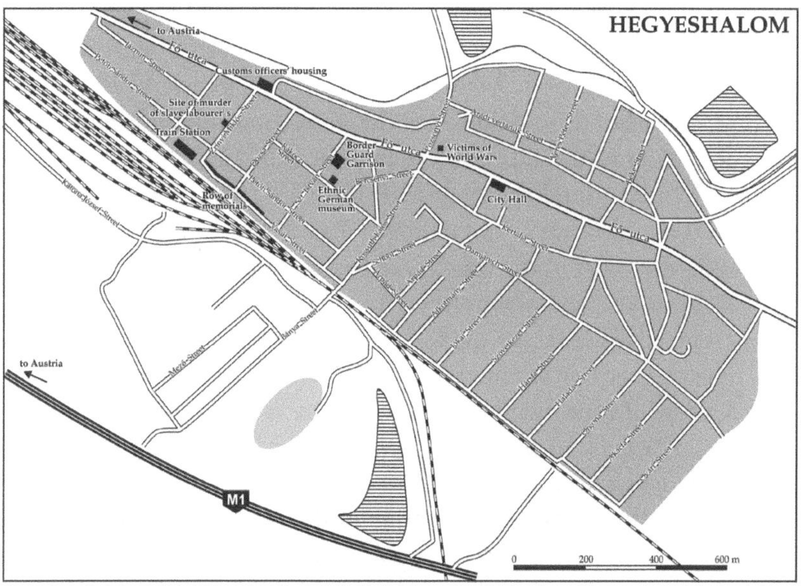


Figure 10.2 Hegyeshalom [Map 15].

1 The homepage is <www.chococard.hu>; and telephone number is 36 (06) 30 4321 251.

Hegyeshalom has been the main railroad and highway crossing between Hungary and Austria since the Trianon border was surveyed in 1922. Westbound international trains from Budapest to Vienna, Munich, and Zurich stop there, train crews change, and Austrian gendarmes walk through the cars, glance at passports, and leave the train at Bruck an der Leitha. The expressway goes just south of the train station and the town, with the decaying row of border control booths just to the right of the road, while the old main road with its border control booths is just northwest of the town. Two milestones in opening the border were celebrated at the highway border control point. On September 11, 1989, the barriers were officially lifted, and the end of the Iron Curtain was formally recognized. Then, on December 21, 2007, senior officials of Hungary, Austria, and Slovakia celebrated Hungary's entry into the Schengen group of EU countries whose citizens pass freely from one state to another, with balloons, speeches, and Beethoven's *Ode to Joy*. The marker placed at the expressway crossing just east of the old booths at the time, showing the distance to all the capital cities of the EU still stands, although it is no longer accurate since the United Kingdom voted itself out. Who knows which member will be next to either leave or be removed. At any rate, like the tiny crossing at Albertkázmérpuszta, the border is more open than not, although it is under scrutiny, particularly in the westward direction.

As a railroad center on the border, Hegyeshalom has seen many reminders of the horrible recent past. On the lawn in front of the train station there is a row of four memorials, to the deportation of ethnic Germans after World War II, to the 124 Jewish slave laborers who died or were killed while assigned to repair bomb damage at the rail yards, to victims of Communism, and to fallen Hungarian soldiers of both world wars. The Jewish memorial is the only one set horizontally in the ground. It did not start out that way, but after it was knocked down twice, it was embedded. In the town on Fó utca there is the building in which customs officers and their families were quartered. On Szent István Király utca, the disintegrating border guard garrison is also an unmarked site, in storage but well on the way to being deaccessioned. These officials were a constant and often intimidating presence during the Cold War, representatives of the fearsome bureaucracy that policed the border. My cousin's verdict on the border guards probably applied to the customs officers as well: "THEY WERE CRAP! SHIT! AGGRESSIVE THUGS."[2]

Figure 10.3 The memorial to the ethnic Germans who were removed in 1946. The severed top of the candle points westward.

There is also a museum at Rákóczi 15, devoted to the deported German community and a multipurpose memorial dedicated to the victims of both world wars, to the ethnic German removal of 1946, and to the 1956 upheaval, in front of the Catholic church at the intersection of Fó utca and Pozsonyi utca. This unusual monument consists of a massive severed head carved of white stone resting face up with eyes closed and mouth open, on a granite slab. With its allusions to several major catastrophes of the past century, it underscores the awfulness of the period. It also follows the

2 Quoted in Frank N. Schubert, *Hungarian Borderlands: From the Habsburg Empire to the Axis Alliance, the Warsaw Pact, and the European Union* (London: Continuum, 2011), p. 83.

familiar practice of not mentioning the Jewish catastrophe and subsuming it in the wider carnage that consumed soldiers and civilians. There is no marker on Munkácsy utca just northwest of the train station, where the last slave laborers were murdered days before Soviet troops arrived at the end of March 1945.

Across the border from Hegyeshalom, Nickelsdorf, with about 1,500 souls, is less than half the size of Hegyeshalom. The village has hosted an internationally recognized jazz festival known as "Konfrontationen" since 1976, and renowned musicians such as American drummer Max Roach have played at the Jazzgalerie Nickelsdorf. More importantly, while Hegyeshalom symbolized the fear and anxiety of travelers confronting Hungarian border guards on their way west during the Cold War, Nickelsdorf represented the gateway to liberty. Hegyeshalom meant dry constricted throats, clenched stomachs, and pounding hearts. Nickelsdorf meant euphoria and freedom. As one East German man fleeing by way of Hungary in 1989 said about Nickelsdorf, "How often have I caressed this name on the map."[3]

Three other border crossings (Rajka, Zsira, and Szentpéterfa, from north to southwest) illuminate the change wrought in 1989 and its limits. Rajka is about 20 kilometers up Route 150 from Mosonmagyraróvár. On the way, traces of a bygone Hungary are accessible by turning west to Paprét at Bezenye. The *kocsma* [pub] on the right just before the turnoff in 2012 is called Lesz Vigasz, or "There will be consolation," a pun on Las Vegas. The name expresses either optimism about the prosperity once expected from the opening of a grand casino just north of Hegyeshalom, bankrolled by the Hard Rock café chain owned by the Seminole Tribe of Florida, or a sarcastic pessimism that proved well founded. Anyway, turn westward on the road to Papret at Bezenye and head through Paprét, population about 300, about one kilometer down the road. The settlement includes remnants of a collective farm, and on the left side of the road a concrete socialist realist statue of a worker or farmer next to a 1950s tractor on a concrete slab. The road to a Cold War–era listening post continues to a "T" another kilometer west. Make a right (north)

3 Quoted in ibid., p. 127.

and go another kilometer. The road is concrete most of the way and in good condition, suggesting that it was meant for heavy equipment. The site is just before the road bends perhaps 30 degrees to the left, in a westerly direction, and it is off the road, on the right, a total of just over three kilometers from Route 150.

The small site has three significant structures, perhaps the only ones built. One was a three-room concrete *laktanya* [barracks], the smallest one I have ever seen. Two footpaths led to the operational elements less than 100 meters away, on and inside two low hills. About two-thirds of the way along the path to the northernmost hill are the remains of a small brick structure, perhaps a one-hole latrine. The operational sites each had a concrete-lined enclosure, cut into the hill from the east and invisible from the west. Both were big enough for a military truck and had been wired for electricity. Electric conduits led to the top of each hill, and between the two a concrete slab may have been for a generator. Radar dishes might have been installed atop the hills, and truck-mounted instruments and monitors inside the hills might have been used to read and transmit signals. The border with Austria is less than five kilometers to the west.

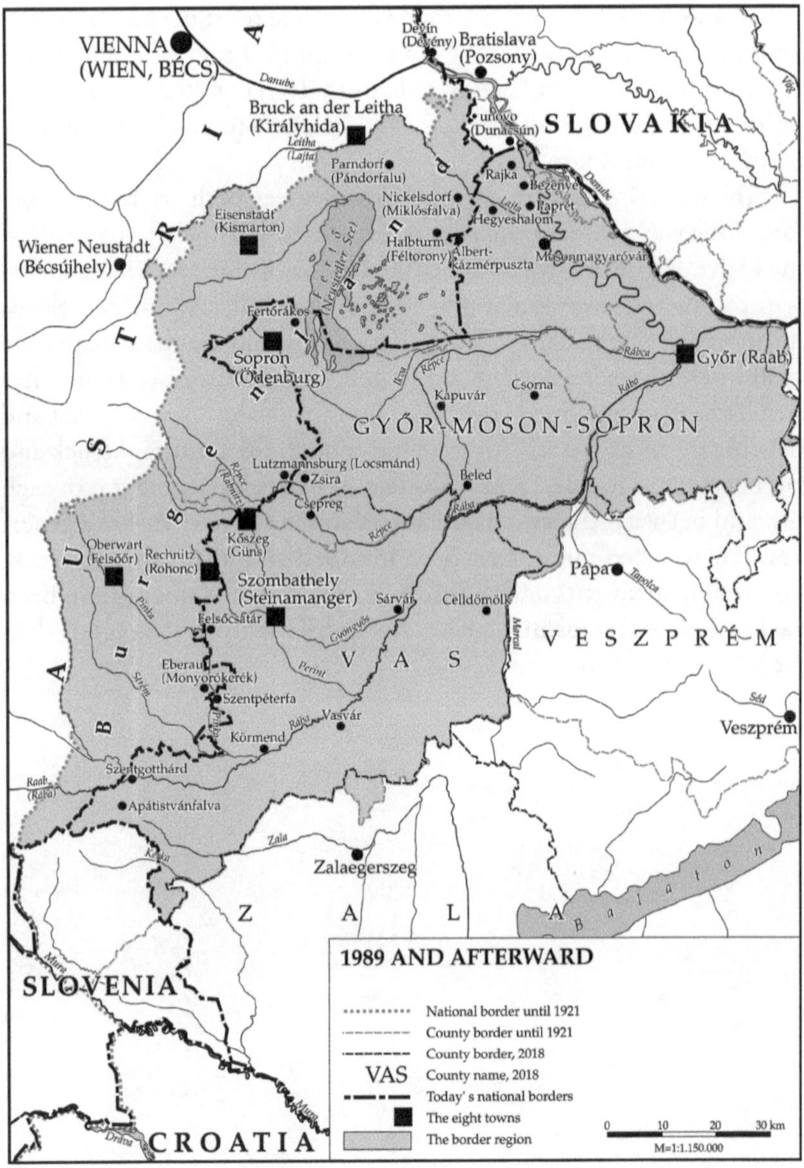


Figure 10.4 1989 and afterward [Map 16].

Rajka is six kilomters north of Bezenye on the border with Slovakia. The Austrian border is less than a kilometer to the west. Like most of the smaller crossings, it had a currency exchange office and a tourism agency but no hotel or restaurant. István Nagy and I went to Rajka in 2008, mere months after the opening. The facilities had been left unattended, and locals had taken what was movable and wrecked the rest. Nothing was usable. Windows were broken, doors and light fixtures were gone, papers and wine bottles, even a pair of women's shoes, littered the floor. But the sign still says "Rajka" and the road leads to Devin [Dévény], the fort on the bluff by the confluence of the Danube from the west and the Morava from the north. On the way, off Expressway E65, there is Petrzalka, a major 1944–5 distribution point for Jewish slave labor and a construction site for the East Wall whose northern terminus was Bratislava. There were seven small camps in Petrzalka, one of which was in the horse stalls behind the Leberfinger Inn, which still operates at the same address, Viedenska cesta 257. Mass graves with more than 500 Hungarian Jewish slaves' bodies were found in the town, and the cemetery contains a large mass grave and monument in section XII.

At Devin a monument on the east side of the confluence bears the names of those who tried and failed to swim for freedom in Austria during the Cold War. The fort itself was the entryway for new ideas from the West, according to poet Endre Ady. It was reduced by Napoleon in 1809 and remained part of the country until Trianon.

Rajka is also the gateway to Danubiana, an extravagant and little-known museum of modern art. The building and sculpture garden on an island in the Danube offer spectacular vistas up and down the big river. Dutch businessman Gerard Meulensteen founded the museum.[4] Although I lived part-time in Hungary from 2004, I learned about Danubiana from the *New York Times* in 2010 and never saw a reference to the museum in the Győr newspaper. It is little more than an hour northwest of Győr, but none of my Győri friends had heard of the museum when I mentioned it. Open borders do not necessarily mean open minds, and even in the arts, relations between Slovaks and Magyars have remained contentious.

4 The home page is <www.danubiana.sk/en>.

To the south of Hegyeshalom and Sopron and just north of the Vas County line, the crossing between Zsira and Lutzmannsburg also illuminates the great change of 1989. In 2006, just on the Lutszmannsburg (Austrian) side of the border along the south side of the road, the sculpture park Flight and Freedom opened. The park, a cooperative effort with Zsira, features the *Freiheits-Trichter* [Freedom Funnel], a steel installation by artist Karl Hiess, which leads from the narrowness of imprisonment and escape to the expanse of peace and freedom, facilitated in 1956 by the residents of Lutzmannsburg. Students from the nearby Oberpullendorf secondary school supplemented the Freedom Funnel with themes of movement to freedom. Also, a man wrapped in wire, *Der Entfesselte* [*The Enraged*], by Linda Schwarts, shows him trying to break free from the wire and reach freedom. György Kovács's 1956 sculpture complements Hiess's funnel. Thirty-one thousand people crossed at Lutzmannsburg after the 1956 revolution and were welcomed there. The inscription on the back of the Kovács sculpture is "Szerte nézett, s nem lelél Honját a hazában." The tablet identifies the source as the lyrics by Ferenc Kolcsey from one of the later, usually unsung verses of *Himnusz*, the national anthem. It translates as "Looking everywhere, he could not find his home in his homeland," appropriate enough for one fleeing after the 1956 revolution.

The crossing, well known as a pathway to freedom in the aftermath of the 1956 uprising, came to public attention again in 1989 as the site of the last death of a crosser at the hands of a border guard. On the night of August 21, 1989, two days after the Pan-European Picnic and three weeks before the formal opening of the border at Hegyeshalom, Weimar architect Kurt Werner Schulz met his unfortunate end in the Lutzmannsburg vineyards, about 30 feet inside Austria. A Hungarian border guard shot and killed the East German during a tussle after he ignored warning shots. By that time border guards had been directed not to shoot crossers. Still, the guards were armed and required to stop unauthorized crossings. During the physical struggle the guard's rifle discharged. Schulz died en route to a hospital in Hungary. A binational commission examined the matter, no charges were brought against the 18-year-old soldier, and Schulz's wife and their six-year-old son were permitted to cross. The soldier, who claimed he thought his life was in danger, went through a year of psychotherapy and his name was never released.

In 2010, when I visited the crossing, there were no visible barriers, but plainly the situation had already evolved beyond simple open borders. The road directly adjacent to the park celebrated Austrian openness and generosity in 1956, and there were no soldiers on either side of the line. But the traffic sign facing the Hungarian side, a white disc with a red circle in it, indicated that the road was closed to traffic in both directions. No corresponding sign faced into Austria. The Austrians apparently had designated the road to Hungary as a one-way street, leading from west to east, but not open in the other direction. In 2018, Google Maps directions by auto to Luztmannsburg from Zsira went south to Kőszeg and the Rattersdorf crossing, then back north, a detour of 33.1 kilometers.

The crossing farther south between Szentpéterfa in Vas County and Eberau in Burgenland is marked by one of three "Hello neighbor" commemorative benches, installed after removal of the border barricades. At Szentpéterfa, the stainless-steel slab, with its embossed heart and the letters "AT" and "HU" in the center of the bench symbolizing the open border, is next to border marker C 52, installed by the border commission in 1922, as well as a concrete post that once held up the border fence. At a December 20, 2007, celebration of the border opening, Mayor Miklós Kohuth highlighted the newfound freedom for residents to make their own travel decisions, like grown-ups. Still, for the better part of two years Mayor Kohuth kept the bench in a warehouse. The town lacked money for a permanent concrete pad to which the bench could be securely bolted, and he feared that without such a base, it would be stolen and sold for scrap. Two other benches commemorate the opening of the border, with Slovenia at Kercaszomor-Domanjsevci and with Slovakia at Aggtelek-Kecovo. Czech artist Peter Kukorelli and his Hungarian collaborator, Balázs Orlai, designed the benches.

In 2009–10, around the time the "Hello neighbor" bench was permanently installed, Eberau became the focal point of a controversy over detention centers for migrants. Austrian interior minister Mária Fekter decided to build such a facility at Eberau without consulting residents. The townspeople responded with such fury that politicians and citizens alike joined in a call for a referendum, which took place on February 21, 2010. Fekter promised to accept any outcome. A resounding majority of 90.1 percent rejected the proposal and the promise of jobs that came with it, and the facility was never built.

There is no formal impediment to crossing the border to Eberau. When taxi driver and friend István Tűttő and I got ready to leave for the north and Felsőcsatár in June 2009, Mayor Kohuth gave us directions that involved going north through Austria and going back into Hungary at an unmarked crossing. The road networks in both countries had been distorted by the irregular Trianon border and the deliberate blocking of communication during the Cold War. Remaining in Hungary would take us well out of our way before we found a route. Instead, we could go straight up from Eberau and turn back into Hungary just before Deutsch Schützen at Pornóapáti and continue north from there, cutting 20 kilometers from our trip. We followed his instructions but missed the crossing and wound up in Deutsch Schützen. There we asked around, and no one seemed to know about the crossing we sought. Kohuth had warned us that the road remained unmarked because the Austrians were not enthusiastic about seeing it used by tourists. Moreover, as we soon noticed, the GPS in the taxi did not recognize this crossing. We turned back and asked a middle-aged couple getting out of their car. They showed us where to turn. After a turn to the east, we went about 50 meters on a hard-packed dirt road and were back in Hungary. We learned that there was more to open borders than the removal of guard booths and formal barriers. "Hello neighbor" had limits that were not always obvious.

The opening of the borders and surrounding events spawned monuments, historical markers, and borderland museums. Perhaps the most important and best known was the Sopronpuszta park memorializing the Pan-European Picnic, discussed in chapter 5 above. But for an older generation, the best-known historical site in the immediate region was Andau and its storied bridge. To those who walked across the border to Austria in the wake of the 1956 revolution, Andau meant freedom and safety. It was the first Austrian settlement that many 1956 emigrants, including my 19-year-old cousin and her husband, encountered. The publication of James Michener's book *The Bridge at Andau* in 1957 made Andau the emblematic

1956 site. The bridge spanned an irrigation canal that was near the border but entirely in Austria. Nevertheless, many refugees during those short wintry days thought they were crossing the border when they went over the bridge, and Michener turned it into the focus of his story of flight, risk, and freedom. Since 1992, there has been a reconstructed bridge on the site. An observation tower and a monument to the Austrian Red Cross, all set in a commemorative park, were added in 2004. According to the Red Cross monument, 70,000 Hungarians crossed the border between Jánossomorja and Andau.

There are other important sites closer to Sopron, at Hegykő, and Fertőrákos on the southern shore of Fertő lake. Hegykő is little more than 10 kilometers east of Sopron. A 40-meter replica of the border fence at the edge of the marsh grass leading north to the lake and the border shows all three phases of the border regime, from the wood-encased mines emplaced before the 1956 revolution to the electric signal wire of the final period. As a memorial the site seeks to have it both ways. According to the mayor at the time the strip was created, the installation honors those who tried to escape and the dedicated border guards who served in the area.

Closer to Sopron a crumbling border guard garrison stands just west of the road to the border and Mörbisch. There is also an Iron Curtain museum in the middle of town. The guard post is behind a fence but the museum at Fó út 242, one of three in the borderlands focusing on the Iron Curtain and the border guard force, is open daily and without charge. The border guard as an independent agency disappeared into the national police in 2008. Former border guard Imre Csapó owns this museum. He has a wine cellar he is happy to show visitors and sells a Kékfrankos made from his grapes and those of other local growers. His museum includes a guard tower made of metal pipe instead of the usual wood, because it was designed as a lakeside observation post. One of the strengths of the museum collection is in the official periodicals published by and for the border guards during the Cold War period. He has been open since 2009.[5]

5 The telephone numbers are 36 (06) 99 355 067 and 36 (06) 30 263 9556. The home page is <www.vasfuggony-ejrmuseum.hu>.

The other two museums are in Vas County to the south. The Apátistvánfalva museum calls itself a border guard memorial site and appears to have some state support, but not enough to remain open on a regular basis. It has the most comprehensive collection, indoors and out, of the three. It also was the only one of the three with souvenirs for sale. I bought a coffee mug decorated with the insignia of the border guard during my 2008 visit and took it home to put with souvenir and presentation items given to me by a retired soldier who decorated his pub at Likócs near Győr with military memorabilia. The mug would be perfect for sipping coffee at my desk, next to the coat tree with the uniform coat of a border guard lieutenant colonel from the 1980s. But the insignia on the mug soon vanished! After three turns in the dishwasher, the logo dissolved, just like the organization that had disappeared into the police at the beginning of the year.[6]

The original borderland Iron Curtain museum, opened at Felsöcsatár in 1990, belongs to winemaker, innkeeper, and former border guard Sándor Goják. I first visited his outdoor museum in 2008 and on return visits have taken a few jugs of his country red wine home to Győr. Gojak enjoys describing his museum and sharing his experience as a border guard in the 1960s with groups that range from Slovenian tourists to Austrian historians. He also has the most provocative and thoughtful exhibit of the group. In addition to the three phases of Cold War border installations, he has recently added a fourth, depicting the border fence installed by the government of Prime Minister Viktor Orbán in 2015 to keep migrants out of Hungary. Few Hungarians acknowledge any connection between the barbed wire of the bad old days and the razor wire strung along the southern border. Gojak's display clearly links the two.[7]

6 Museum caretaker László Merkli's telephone number is 36 (06) 30 484 4347, and the website is <http://www.apatistvanfalva.hu/turizmus/hataror-emlekhely>.

7 The museum is open from 10 a.m. to 7 p.m. between March 1 and October 30. The phone number is 36 (06) 30 564 2657 or 36 (06) 30 400 3961. The home page is <www.vasfuggonymuzeum.hu and email can be sent to gojakerika@gmail.com>

Figure 10.5 Phase 4 of the Iron Curtain as shown at Felsőcsatár.

Figure 10.6 A field kitchen known as a "goulash cannon" on display at Apátistvánfalva.

There is overlap between objects on display at these three museums. All contain clothing, insignia, weapons, and other equipment, as well as photos of border patrols, document examinations, smuggling efforts, and traffic at crossings. Cumulatively they bear witness to the difficulty of crossing the border, with the array of mines, fences, and signal devices supporting a regime of travel restrictions and inspections. They also illuminate the lengths to which people went and the risks they endured to get out. All three museums are in effect real-life manifestations of the hallucinatory vision of Hungarian-Canadian writer Tamás Dobozy. His secretive and fictional Museum of Failed Escapes in the Ninth District of Budapest, featured in his short story "Sailor's Mouth," opened in 2007, right around the time the real museums started to appear in the borderlands.[8]

Borderland horrors did not vanish with the Iron Curtain. In Hungary and Austria, the present generates its own set of grim sites connected to the struggles of migrants to reach places where they might make better lives and the counterstruggles of governments seeking to keep them out. These include detention centers and the highway rest stops, train stations, and border crossings at which confrontations between migrants, smugglers, and the authorities most often occur.

They also include two roadside sites where smugglers abandoned trucks crammed with migrants and left them to suffocate and die. In Hungary, at the car park at kilometer marker 112 on Route 19 east of Győr, 18 Sri Lankans suffocated in July 1995 after a Bulgarian trafficker abandoned them in a truck trailer. Sixteen corpses were returned to Sri Lanka. Two victims, including 41-year-old Vinayaga Moorthynal, are buried in parcel 23 of the Nádorváros public cemetery. The unmarked site of the disaster outside Győrszentiván is fading from memory.

With the help of an accommodating caretaker at the cemetery, István Nagy and I found the Moorthynal grave. The broken marker lay on the ground and had already been partly covered by the grass, as the partially cleaned growth on the tablet indicated. According to cemetery records, he died of suffocation. A donor has paid to keep the marker and the letters

8 "Sailor's Mouth" can be found in the collection of Dobozy's stories entitled *Siege 13* (Minneapolis: Milkweed Editions, 2013).

on the tin tablet from disintegrating, so this record of his life and hint of his arduous journey will remain, along with the information in the cemetery data base.

Twenty years later, also in July, a sealed truck belonging to a Slovakian meat processing firm was discovered in a construction zone alongside the westbound lanes of the Austrian A4 motorway. It contained the bodies of 71 refugees. As Phil Klay wrote, "When found their bodies were so decomposed and drenched in bodily fluids that it made identification almost impossible."[9] Somehow the bodies were counted and categorized as 59 men, eight women, and four children. The unmarked site is on the north side of the highway and about 150 meters west of the Route 50 overpass at the Parndorf-Neusiedl am See exit. Hungarian authorities apprehended and convicted four suspects of several crimes, including homicide, and sentenced them to prison terms ranging from 17 to 25 years.[10]

Overall, the border opening has brought considerable change to the borderlands. The end of Communism unleashed a wave of memorialization that privileges the Trianon catastrophe and the 1956 revolution. In Holocaust commemoration, the Hungarian state and much of the population still avoid direct confrontation with the Hungarian role in the dispossession and murder of Jewish citizens.[11] Memorials in Sopron, Hegyeshalom, Kőszeg, and most notably on Szabadság Square in Budapest submerge the Holocaust in broader catastrophes to diminish or obscure its singularity. Otherwise, tablets underwritten by the Evangelical community at train

9 Phil Klay, "What Defines a Modern Warrior?" *New York Times* online, December 9, 2015, <http://www.nytimes.com/2015/12/09/opinion/what-defines-a-modern-warrior.html?emc=eta1&_r=0>, accessed December 14, 2015.

10 Sergey Pnomarev, "They Let 71 People Die in a Stifling Truck. They Got 25 Years," *New York Times* online, June 14, 2018, <https://www.nytimes.com/2018/06/14/world/europe/austria-migrants-truck.htm>.

11 Kádár Gábor, and Vági Zoltán, *A Végső Döntés: Berlin, Budapest, Birkenau 1944* (Budapest: Jaffa, 2013) confronts head-on Hungarian culpability at the top. Similarly, Tim Cole's *Traces of the Holocaust* examines in detail Hungarian involvement at the local level. Other scholarly assessments and films, such as *Fatelessness*, *Son of Saul*, and *1945*, present clear-eyed assessments of the brutality that took place. Public monuments mainly still reflect an oblique and evasive approach.

stations, Gunter Demnig's stumble stones, monuments financed by Jewish survivors and their families from outside Hungary, and the scholarship of dedicated borderland historians such as Petra Weiss in Bruck an der Leitha and István Nagy in Győr have gone a long way to illuminating what was lost and who was responsible.[12] These changes have been important, but a current of anti-Semitism (as well as of anticigányism, as anti-Romani sentiment is often called) still runs through the country that transcends memorialization of the Holocaust. In this context, it remains hard not to think about being Jewish, while the thought rarely crosses my mind when I am in the United States. At least it seldom did until President Donald Trump in January 2017 recognized International Holocaust Remembrance Day without mentioning Jews, and in August of that year could not bring himself to condemn a torchlight parade of swastika-waving thugs in Thomas Jefferson's hometown.

American Nazis were only a few years behind Hungarian fascists in coming out. In 2008 and 2009, Jobbik, the far-right political party, and its black-clad paramilitary Magyar Gárda appeared prominently in public, recruiting members and holding demonstrations. Sitting beer in hand outside a café in 2008 and watching the Magyar Gárda parade by with the red and white striped banner that had been the insignia of Hungarian Nazis in 1944, practically across the street from the Carmelite church where the citizens of Győr had prayed for the health of Arrow Cross leader Ferenc Szálasi in 1938, conjured up frightening images of Hitler's Germany. One year later, in 2009, the anti-Semitic right defiled a Budapest monument to Jews murdered and pushed into the Danube in a spasm of Arrow Cross violence in the winter of 1944–5. The monument consists of 60 pairs of cast metal shoes, representing the men, women, and children killed there. On a spring night, persons unknown filled the shoes with pigs' feet.

12 See Petra Weiss and Irmtraut Karlsson, *Die Toten von Bruck* (Berndorf, Austria: Kral-Verlag, 2008).

Figure 10.7 This placard was displayed on walls and ultility poles in Győr in the spring of 2008. The question in the center asks, "Whose children are you?" the children of Cain or the children of Árpád? The one in the blue stripe at the bottom asks, "Who doesn't belong here?"

From a personal standpoint, 2011 stands out. The Magyar Gárda, outlawed by then and existing only in secret, remained active. Fifty members reportedly appeared at Auschwitz-Birkenau in October 2011, wearing Nazi uniforms and saluting Hitler. Locally, incidents in the short span of three weeks of May 2011 reminded me that Hungary had not separated itself from its anti-Semitic past. A friend related his son's experience, coming home late from a party one night. Talking with a cabbie, he learned that all Hungarians have become slaves to the Jews. About a week later, I visited Mosonmagyraróvár to see an exhibit on the Treaty of Trianon. During a chat at the site, the porter told me his son was a major in the police, but that he once had other career aspirations. He had wanted to be a film director, but, the porter said in a matter-of-fact way, that had obviously been a nonstarter since they are a Christian family. It did not need to be said that Jews dominated the industry to the detriment of Christians. It was understood.

Meanwhile, on May 20, *Kisalföld*, the regional newspaper published in Győr, ran an article titled "Szégyen," shame in English. The short piece described something my friend Dennis Deletant, an eminent scholar of Romania, thinks could not have happened even in that benighted country. A young girl walked down the street in Mosonmagyaróvár, wearing a black polo shirt with the outline of greater (pre-Trianon) Hungary, inside of which, in sparkly glitter, was "Zsidótól vásárolni szégyen," in English, "Buying from Jews is a disgrace." This was triply disturbing, first that such shirts were marketed, then that it was acceptable to wear one in public, and third that the newspaper chose to write about it. The tone of the article suggested a possible effort at irony, but its publication raised the question of why it was considered news.

At the farmer's market that same month, Jobbik had a booth where members distributed their *Barikád* magazine, which had two explicitly anti-Jewish articles that I could see. Jobbik is, as frequently pointed out, a right-wing party of extreme views, but it is not merely a fringe phenomenon. It was then the third most popular political party in the country, with representatives in the parliament in Budapest as well as the European Parliament in Brussels. By the end of the decade, it was about even with the socialist opposition in second place .

The casual anti-Semitism represented by a Jobbik booth at the market can be found elsewhere. In October 2017, I visited my regular bicycle shop. I've known the owner for years. He is unfailingly helpful and personally hospitable. Irene and I have supped at his home, and he and his then-wife have had dinner at our flat. That day at his shop we spoke mostly about the sad state of the Hungarian economy, the flight of skilled labor westward, and the workers' action at Tesco, which netted them a 3,000 forint raise, not quite ten euros per month. He expressed his anxiety about the economic future, asking rhetorically what would happen, and suggesting that maybe the Jews would buy up everything. Taken aback, I replied that if they did, I hoped that I might pick up a small share. He cocked his head in surprise and asked if I was Jewish. I said I was. He asked if it was on my mother's side (Did he know that that was the side that determined Jewishness? Did he think Schubert could not be a Jewish name? Or maybe I didn't *look* Jewish?). I said on both sides and told him my parents left Hungary in 1939 amid rising anti-Semitism, and he replied that it was the Germans who drove the whole anti-Jewish project. I said that ultimately they did but that Hungarians laid the groundwork with a chain of anti-Jewish laws and offered plenty of help in carrying it out. That's where we left the matter. I think this was something new for him to digest, and maybe he will work this out. I don't really want to help him do it. But the whole thing about Jews, money, and avarice, waiting to pounce on poor innocent Hungary, was there.

If I wanted reminders of this view of the world while I was in Győr, I just had to leave my apartment, go downstairs and out the front door, turn right, and walk 20 meters. There, past the "Mademoiselle" wedding gown salon and next to the historical marker noting the location of a third-century Roman graveyard, was the Szkítia Könyvesbolt [Scythia Bookstore]. The chain had recently included six stores in Hungary, four of them in Budapest. By the year 2020, with book sales generally moving to the Internet, three shops remained. This one sold an array of merchandise with nostalgic, nationalist, and irredentist themes and motifs, including books, clothes, music, toys, and flags. Among the books toward the back of the store were anti-Semitic screeds with titles such as *The Jewish World Federation's Threat to Humanity* and *Conqueror of the World: The Real War Criminals* as well as David Duke's *Jewish Supremacy: The Jewish Question Through American Eyes*, all of them in Hungarian.[13]

Some scholars think anti-Semitism is losing its potency in Europe. David Marquand writes that "with all its enduring nastiness, anti-Semitism no longer has much political bite." He is certainly right that "Muslims, not

13 Gede Brothers (Tibor and Sándor), publisher of all three books as well as a Hungarian edition of *Mein Kampf*, has its office at Hollán utca 37 in Budapest, four blocks, or less than a half kilometer north of the stumble stone marking the residence of Miklos Radnoti at Pozsonyi út 1, very near the Pest end of the Margit Bridge. Both addresses are in the Újlipótváros section of the city, known as the traditional home of Jewish intellectuals. The house itself has two plaques alluding to its Jewish history, one noting that it had been the home of Sándor Blantz, who was conscripted into the labor service and killed during military operations in Russia during 1943, and the other identifying the site as having been protected by the Swiss government, whose good intentions did not keep many of the Jews of Budapest from random deaths at the hands of Arrow Cross thugs. Gede Brothers may well have deliberately chosen this site for their operations with its specific Jewish connections in mind.

Jews, are the chief targets of far-right parties."[14] But even anti-Muslim forces manage to incorporate Jews in their exclusionist worldview. Istvan Matyas Vass, a retired artist and former parliamentarian who heads a vigilante group calling itself "the Hunyadi Border-Guard Unit," claims the waves of Muslim immigrants that threaten Europe are financed and organized by Zionist Jews who want to destroy Europe. Even the Muslim threat is orchestrated by Jews.[15]

Hungarian-born American financier George Soros, who has Jewish roots, has become the poster child for anti-migrant sentiment whipped up by the Orbán government. More subtle than István Mátyás Vass of the Hunyadi guards, the government frames its opposition to migrants as opposition to the "Soros Plan" and plasters his face on buses, kiosks, and newspapers. The Hungarian neologism *sorosozni*, a verb meaning "to Soros," or to blame him for Hungary's problems, has recently come into popular usage, and the advertisements do not have to mention that Soros is Jewish. Moreover, Soros's alleged culpability has spread from Hungary to the international scene. He has been accused of everything from responsibility for poison gas attacks in Syria to meddling in American politics by surreptitiously supporting Democrats in local elections in Virginia and handpicking the students speaking out for the victims of the mass shooting in February 2017 at the Parkland, Florida, high school.

In 2017, Irene accepted a brochure urging opposition to an amorphous Soros plan in downtown Győr and asked the man passing them out to explain the plan. He paused, thought about it, and replied that he did not know its contents. He also allowed as how that was a good question. But it is clear from the anti-Jewish graffiti on government-sponsored posters opposing this alleged plan that many Hungarians think they do know, that

14 David Marquand, *The End of the West* (Princeton: Princeton University Press, 2011), p. 91.

15 Miroslava Germanova, Boryana Dzhambazova, and Helene Bienvenu,"Vigilante Patrols Where Few Migrants Set Foot," *New York Times*, Dateline Bratislava, June 10, 2016, published June 11, 2016, https://www.nytimes.com/2016/06/11/world/europe/vigilante-patrols-inparts-of-europe-where-few-migrants-set-foot.html, accessed February 26, 2024.

Soros and his plan represent an international Jewish capitalist conspiracy to subvert white Christian Hungarian nationhood.

A 2018 government campaign poster showed Soros in the center, flanked by leaders of four opposition parties, of both right and left, all holding wire cutters and poised to open the borders. A full-page newspaper ad, also sponsored by the government, showed this arch-criminal alone and declared he would bring in millions of Africans and Near Easterners. Below, a red stop sign screamed out "Stop Soros!" Some things have changed very little.

# Afterword

Consideration of the century just past calls to mind Walter Benjamin's "angel of history." Benjamin based the angel on Paul Klee's 1920 drawing *Angelus Novus*, the new angel. The angel holds its hands high and casts its wide-open eyes to the left, maybe to see what horrible event back there might be approaching. "Where we perceive a chain of events," Benjamin writes, the angel "sees one single catastrophe which keeps piling wreckage and hurls it in front of his feet."[1] In effect, the angel tells those who might have thought history to be one damn thing after another, that it was more like one *horrible* damn thing after another. From the angel's perspective, there was reason for Kurt Vonnegut's science fiction writer and alter ego Kilgore Trout to observe that "it is the *past* which scares the bejesus out of me."[2]

Neither Benjamin nor Trout was thinking specifically of the borderlands when he expressed his dismay about the past, but he could have been. Certainly, the angel of history would have felt at home here as one grim episode followed another—war, imperial dissolution, revolution and counterrevolution, more war, murder, deportation, relocation, totalitarian government and sealed borders, more revolution, and finally open borders with a migration situation marked by human misery that roils the region to this day.

Generally, communities and people on the Austrian side fared better than their Hungarian neighbors, but the region overall experienced a century of turmoil and violence. At the start of the twentieth century, the entire area was within Hungary and had a history that went far back in

1 Walter Benjamin, *Illuminations*, edited with an introduction by Hannah Arendt, trans. Harry Zohn (New York: Schocken, 1969), pp. 257–8, quoted in Susan Handelman, "Walter Benjamin and the Angel of History," *Cross Currents*, Fall 1991, p. 345.

2 Kurt Vonnegut, *Breakfast of Champions*, 1973, in Vonnegut, *Novels and Stories 1963–1973*, Sidney Offit, ed. (New York: Library of America, 2011), p. 647.

time. Organized town life emerged in the Roman province of Pannonia, albeit with interruptions. Bruck, Sopron, and Szombathely were on the Amber Road, a major trade route from the Baltic to the Adriatic. Győr was Arrabona back then and a major Danube outpost.

Hungary's bleaker experience started with the end of the Habsburg Empire and division of the region among two new post–World War I states, Austria and Hungary. It continued through 40 years of Communist rule. This difference is partly responsible for the more detailed emphasis in this narrative of the Hungarian side of the borderland. There the political and social turmoil was greater. The eastern part of Austria experienced the decade-long presence of the Red Army, but western Hungary had 40 years of Soviet rule, along with the attendant lethal border and the 1956 revolution. Economic growth of border cities was discouraged, and residents faced burdensome restrictions on their daily movement. On the Austrian side, villages that had looked to markets in Szombathely, Sopron, or Győr adapted by turning westward and forming connections to Vienna, Graz, and other cities.

Another reason for the uneven emphasis lies in the relative size of the towns. Because of how the lines of 1920 were drawn, the major cities remained on the Hungarian side, separated in many cases from their agricultural hinterlands, which had extended in all directions, including into what is now Austria. Despite stunted growth due to severance from their hinterlands by the Trianon settlement and then by the Iron Curtain, the Hungarian towns remain larger. The total population of the four Burgenland towns included here comes to about 35,000, less than Sopron alone and far less than Győr and Szombathely. Only Eisenstadt is bigger (and not by much) than Kőszeg, the smallest of the Hungarian towns. The size disparity merged with the long experience of Soviet domination to make them more complex subjects for the study of memorialization.

A third reason for the apparently unbalanced coverage is personal. I cannot escape my Hungarian background and its impact on me and my family. Breakfasting at the local farmers' market on a slab of bread and a chunk of *kolbász* from a nearby butcher, I know why I came back here. But making a presentation before a Kőszeg social club in the Brenner House, which had housed Jewish slave laborers during 1944–5, reminds me of why my parents left and what happened to those who stayed.

The most glaring similarity between the two sides of the borderland concerns the reluctance to confront forthrightly the legacy of the war and the Holocaust. Austria only slowly escaped the grip of the myth encouraged by the victorious Allies that it had been Nazism's first victim rather than a participant in the regime. Hungary, where Communist rule sustained the notion that the Germans were entirely responsible for the mass theft and murder of the World War II period, has been evasive about its own culpability. The residue of the Allied and Communist mythologies in Austria and Hungary can be seen in the equivocal approach frequently reflected by memorials that submerge the Holocaust in broader, more general events. Moreover, there is ample evidence in the borderland that remembrance changes over time and is certainly not an either/or proposition. On both sides of the border, memorialization of Jewish life and the Holocaust shows a wide range of ways in which remembrance can be turned into evasion or obfuscation.

The Romani catastrophe has been inadequately documented on both sides. Under the Nazi regime in Burgenland, the deportation of Romani and its outcome closely resembled the fate of Jewish communities. In Hungary, the government did not pursue a campaign of outright Romani destruction, but dislocations, enslavement for labor, and killing affected in varying degree 57 Romani communities in the two borderland counties. In neither country are the calamities that befell the Romani adequately represented by public monuments, which have been installed in Burgenland only at Oberwart and Lackenbach.[3] On the Hungarian side there are only the two in Szombathely.

As Magdalena Neumüller notes in her essay on memory in Rechnitz, much can be learned about a particular community or a society by examining its monuments. The number of memorials; their materials, size, and quality; their placement within the locality; their sponsors; and

3 Lackenback was used as a collection site for Roma, who were taken from there to the Chelmno death camp and murdered. Joskowicz, *Rain of Ash: Roma, Jews, and the Holocaust*, p. 101.

the timing of their installation all illuminate the feelings and interests of the population.[4] So it is that the paucity of physical reminders of the Romani catastrophe reflects the specific marginal position of the Romani throughout the region and the general complexity of the development of memorials. Memorial installations clearly do not emerge automatically to fill a need to commemorate important past episodes. They require advocates with the ability and commitment to organize, raise money, acquire real estate, engage architects and artists, generate publicity, and gain at least public acquiescence if not active support. The extant monuments show that it has been possible for the Romani and their supporters to assemble the needed resources and support, albeit on a modest scale. At the same time, with the prominent exception of RE.F.U.G.I.U.S. in Burgenland, Romani memorialization has not generated significant outside support, reflecting perhaps a general indifference to their fraught history as well as a lack of resources within their community.

In the case of the devastation of the Jewish community, philanthropic institutions and concerned citizens outside of Jewry itself have worked actively to create a visible public record and thus broaden knowledge of the disaster that befell Jewish citizens of Hungary. In this regard, the train station plaques sponsored by two Evangelical institutions, the Evangelical Brotherhood and the John Wesley Ministerial College, and the stumble stones designed by Gunter Demnig stand out. The anonymous donation by a Bruck resident of the marker at the grave of the 155 Jewish slave laborers sends the same message: the tragedy being remembered transcends that of a single racial, religious, or ethnic group. Ultimately a human calamity of huge proportions is being marked, and it should concern us all. Outside support of an effort to commemorate adequately the Romani catastrophe in the borderlands might serve to spread knowledge of what happened and present it as part of a broad human tragedy. For Jewish groups and individuals in particular, involvement in expanding efforts to mark this parallel disaster that befell the Romani might represent a step toward

4 Neumüller, "Erinnerung in Rechnitz," passim.

repairing the world and making it whole, in accordance with traditional Jewish teachings.[5] Ultimately honest efforts to understand, document, and mark all phases of the disastrous past century serve the interests of all humankind.

5 Beate and Serge Klarsfeld, renowned pursuers of former Nazis in efforts to hold them accountable and bring them to justice, also advocated for justice for Romani in Germany, for Bosnians, and for the "disappeared" in Argentina. See their *Hunting the Truth: Memoirs of Beate and Serge Klarsfeld* (New York: Farrar, Straus and Giroux, 2018).

APPENDIX

# The List: Caretakers of real property confiscated from the Jews of Győr in 1944

The importance of lists of victims, perpetrators, or enablers of the Holocaust may be apparent to some readers. Nevertheless, it bears repeating that the use of names humanizes the participants and underscores the fact that statistical aggregations are made up of distinct human beings. Naming puts the matter of involvement on a human scale, calls attention to individual people who made choices or were victims of choices made by others, rather than leaving involvement as a matter of abstract and anonymous groups, such as the number of children deported from Amsterdam, the number of Jewish chess masters who killed themselves, or the number of Latvian helpers of the SS who carried out the butcheries of 1941.[1] Anyone who has seen the heartbreaking obelisk in the courtyard at the Győr synagogue, discussed above in chapter 7, understands the importance of names. There the more than 300 deported and murdered children who are memorialized become individuals, separate innocent human beings, not just a small portion of six million.

Names are antidotes to the pervasive effort to obliterate the personhood of the victims, to strip them of their humanity and turn them literally into dust. As Jerzy Kosinski wrote about concentration camp inmates in his "Afterward," the title he gave to the preface of the 1976 edition of his novel *The Painted Bird*, "They tattoo the newcomers. Everyone gets his number. From that moment on you have lost your '*self*' and have become transformed into a number. You no longer are what you were before, but a worthless moving number."[2]

1 The Croatian novelist Daša Drndić in *Trieste*, *Belladonna*, and *EEG* used lists of names, including the specific examples cited here, to make this very point. Her work is driven by the imperative to humanize and personalize various groups of participants in the Holocaust.

2 Jerzy Kosinski, *The Painted Bird*, 2nd ed. (New York: Grove Press, 1976), p. xii.

Names are also the key to knowledge of the perpetrators and enablers as individuals. Lists, such as this one of the caretakers appointed by the Győr city administration to care for dwellings stolen by the city from Jewish owners, identify those who enabled the crimes and who benefited from them, even in small ways. Such compilations, provided of course that they survive and that they are found, identify these custodians as respectable, educated citizens in positions of responsibility. They might even provoke conversations about the breadth of responsibility for and involvement in the systematic theft and deportation, as well as make accountability possible. These possible uses of lists like this one suggest reasons why everyone would not be eager to see them appear in print. Many are not likely to be interested in knowing that their grandparents or former neighbors played roles in the processes of dispossession, even if only as administrators or bureaucrats.

This list is compiled from reports published in the newspaper *Győr Nemzeti Hirlap*. The list appeared in eight separate issues starting on August 13, 1944, and ending on August 23, 1944. It is organized alphabetically by the surnames of caretakers. For caretakers, job titles are included if they were published in the newspaper. The translations reflect my ignorance of bureaucratic practices and jargon of the time and place, but I have tried to show as reasonably as possible the position titles of the individuals. When former property owners are identified by more than their names, English translations indicate widows, partnerships, and heirs. The suffix -né on names of caretakers or former owners indicates a married woman. Property addresses have been left in Hungarian. They are utca (street), út (avenue), tér (square), köz (alley), dűlő (ridge), and sétány (esplanade).

| Caretakers (117) | Owners | Property Addresses |
|---|---|---|
| Andorka László city executive | (widow) Reményi Sándorné | Akác tér |
| | Goldstein Józsefné | Akác tér 17 |
| | Brück Manó | Akác utca 5 |
| | Gross Zs. & heirs | Gyár utca 19 – 21 |
| | Grosz Dávid | Gyár utca 20 |
| | Klein Hermanné | Gyár utca 40 – 42 |

| | | |
|---|---|---|
| | Kohn Sándor & partners | Híd utca 17 |
| | Wachsler Dávid | Híd utca 19 |
| | Lőwinger Ilona & partners | Híd utca 14a |
| | Hercz Sándor | Akác tér 1 |
| Babos Tibor sales tax officer | Singer Alfrédné & partners | Deák Ferenc utca 25a |
| | (widow) Farkas Dezsőné | Domb utca 3 – 5 |
| | (widow) Fischer Edéné | Budai-u. 4 |
| | Lőwy Nándor | Deák Ferenc utca 16 |
| Bakoss Tibor municipal operations employee | Somló Sándor | Árpád út 71 |
| | Lusztig Zoltán | Árpád út 83 |
| | (widow) Kertész Józsefné | Külső-Árpád út-30 |
| | Kertész Ferenc | Külső-Árpád út 282 |
| | Meller Károly & heirs | Szt. István út 13 |
| | Gestettner Lajos | Híd utca 16 |
| | Heimberg Mór | Árpád út 85 |
| Balogh Zsigmond financial counselor | Gross József | Teleki utca 49 |
| Barants Viktor city tax officer | Appel Árpádné | Vörösmarty utca 11 |
| Barasits Viktor city tax officer | Fleischmann Miksa | Teleki utca 20 |
| | Rosenfeld Bernát | Teleki utca 27 |
| | Lukács Ferenc | Teleki utca 32 |
| | Neu Hermann | Vörösmarty utca 12 |
| | Weiner Izidor | Vörösmarty utca 13 |
| | Dr. Siklós Edéné | Vörösmarty utca 17 |
| | Gancz György | Újlak utca 2 |
| | Grosz Erzsébet | Teleki utca 15 |
| Bendzsel Ferenc sales tax officer (1st class) | Izraelite congregation | Andrássy út 24 |
| | Kőnigsberg heirs | Arany János utca 4 |
| | Lőwy Nándor | Andrássy út 23 |
| Boross Jenő city employee | Henrich Béla | Körkemence utca 24b |

| | | |
|---|---|---|
| Bors Károly alcohol monopoly official | D. Fehér Jenő | Andrássy út 86 |
| Bőhm Gusztáv company manager | Gestettner Lajos | Pápai út |
| Brantl Jenő sales tax officer (1st class) | Szántó Fülöpné | Kováts Pál utca 7 – 11 |
| | Fleischmann Mór | Kováts Pál utca 9 |
| | Steiner Benő | Arany János utca 22b |
| | Ganz György | Kováts Pál utca 1 |
| Csendes László sales tax officer | Szivós Ottóné | Árpád út 13 |
| Csodányi László sales tax officer | Mayer Ernő & partners | Árpád út 97 |
| | Rózsa József & partners | Árpád út 19b |
| | Frischmann Jenőné | Deák Ferenc utca 14 |
| | Szecsi Lászlóné & partners | Közép utca 21 |
| | Schwéd Miklós | Liezenmayer utca 17a |
| | Özv. Márkus Hermanné | Újlak utca 18 |
| | Donáth Nándor | Wennesz Jenő utca 11 |
| | Richter Béla & partners. | Árpád út 3 |
| | Kucsera Zsigmond & partners | Czuczor G. utca 21 |
| | Koch Mihályné heirs | Közép utca 10 |
| Deli Károly | Mendel S. Árminné | Megyeház utca 25 |
| | Fürst Ilus & partner | Munkácsy utca 10 |
| | Spielmann Mór | Rákóczi utca 30 |
| (vitéz) Dely Nándor ministerial department counselor | Holczer Nándor | Teleki utca 4 |
| Dobján Ádám retired sub-officer | Deutschlandker Rezső | Szt. Imre hg út 13 |
| | Weiner Rezső | Szt. Imre hg út 74 |
| | Deutsch Elemér | Kígyó utca 11b |
| | Margilusz Henrikné | Klétzár utca 6 |
| | Eckstein Salamon | Szt. Imre hg. út 10 |

| | | |
|---|---|---|
| Döbrentei Ferenc sales tax head officer | Dr. Klein Jenő & partners<br>Aldoz Kálmánné<br>Graltó Mór<br>Arany Dezső | Árpád út 23b<br>Andrássy út 25<br>Apáca utca 35<br>Apáca utca 38 |
| Erdélyi József city tax officer | Dr. Szekeres Oszkár<br>Fischer Imre | Árpád út 41<br>Árpád út 39 |
| Dr. Farkas Balázs financial draftsman | Koch Sándor<br>Bürger József & partners<br>Balogh Lajos & partners | Széchenyi tér 3.<br>Andrássy út 27a<br>Deák Ferenc utca 13 |
| Falláth Ferenc senior sales taxofficer | Kemény Károly | Árpád út 65 |
| Fehér Ferenc city tax officer | Dr. Wegl Andor<br>Dr. Reichenfeld Zsigmondné<br>(widow) Grosz Gyuláné<br>Salzer Andor<br>Kálics Simon<br>Baumel József | Jedlik Ányos utca 3<br>Jókai utca 9a<br><br>Kenyér köz 6<br>Kenyér köz 12<br>Kenyér köz 3<br>Iskola utca 5 |
| Dr. Ferentzy Gábor senior financial counselor | Dr. Kovács Jenő<br>Landler Samu<br>(widow) Dr. Korein Adolfné<br>(widow) Kardos Jenőné. | Andrássy út 34<br>Bisinger sétány 18<br>Szt. László király u. 20<br><br>Kisfaludy utca 20 |
| Folláth Ferenc senior sales tax officer | Dr. Kovács Jenő | Deák Ferenc utca 8 |
| Földessy Ference | Reif Elemér<br>Wollner Miksa<br>Herczberger Ignácné<br>(widow) Dr. Weisz Samuné | Kazinczy utca 5<br>Kisfaludy utca 19<br>Maros utca 16<br>Kazinczy utca 4 |

| | | |
|---|---|---|
| Fördős József city executive | Scheiber Pál | Opitz utca 24 |
| | Klein Ferenc | Pálffy utca 23 |
| | Klein Ignác | Várga utca 16 |
| | Eckstein Verona | Vasút utca 12 |
| | Gross Sándor | Opitz utca 15 |
| Galambos Béla senior state treasury officer | Singer Pál | Fecske utca |
| | Galambos Árpádné | Szt. Imre hg. út 84. |
| | Galambos Árpádné | Eperjes utca 21 |
| | Angyal Lajos & partners | Bisinger sétány 12 |
| | Heimler Ernő | Wennesz Jenő utca 39 |
| | Schwarcz Arnold | Álmos utca 4 |
| | Bakk Jenő | Liezenmayer utca 94 |
| Dr. Gerő Gyula deputy city clerk | Neufeld Izidor | Attila utca 16 |
| | Kántor Irén | Attila utca 26 |
| | Vogl Károly & partners | Attila utca 31 |
| | Fodor Istvánné | Attila utca 37 |
| | Strasser Emilné | Attila utca 15 |
| Geschwindt Andor sales tax officer | Knapp Gyula | Megyeház utca 30 |
| | Stern Miklós | Megyeház utca 26 |
| | Csillag Pálné | Árpád út 55. |
| Gyapay Antal sales tax officer | (widow) Kertész Edéné | Bástya utca 54 |
| | Singer Jakab | Bástya utca 73 |
| | (widow) Raab Gyuláné | Czuczor G. utca 7 |
| | Ziffer Miksáné | Kálvária utca 27 |
| | Kellner Marcell | Kálvária utca 3 |
| | Winkler Miklósné | Budai-u. 23 |
| | Klein heirs | Bástya utca 12 |
| Hámori Pálné | Dr. Hámori Ferenc & Partners | Árpád út 42 |
| Hanzély Gyula retired professor | Reich Ottó | Szél utca 6/8 |
| | Dr. Reisner Jenő | Árpád út 24 |
| | Dr. Elek Imre | Szt. László király u. 9 |

| | | |
|---|---|---|
| Hessky Sándor public prosecutor | Fleischmann Hermanné & partners | Andrássy út 1a |
| | Mayer Adolf & partners | Baross út 32 |
| Hidassi Kálmán financial officer | Deutsch Antal | Schwarzenberg utca 7a |
| | Blau Károlyné | Újkapu utca 27 – 29 |
| | Szőke Miklós | Újkapu utca 24 |
| | (widow) Bonyhárd Izidorné | Schwarzenberg utca 10 |
| | Hatschek Ede | Schwarzenberg utca 1 |
| Dr. Hodinka Dénes financial draftsman | Rosenberg László & partners | Bisinger sétány 10 |
| | Müller József | Fecske utca 3 |
| | Kellner Sándor | Batthyányi tér 13 |
| Honti János sales tax officer (2nd class) | Rosenfeld József | Budai utca 8 |
| | Csillag Ferenc | Budai utca 23 |
| | Világi József | Corvin utca 13 |
| | Ladány Gyula | Csaba utca 22 |
| | Özv. Hajós Sománé | Csaba utca 24 |
| | Csillag Jenő | Csaba utca 26 |
| | Kardos Imre & partners | Dugonits utca 18 |
| | Áldor Kálmán | Budai utca 4 |
| | Dr. Rosta Miklós | Corvin utca 12 |
| Horváth Antal customs officer | Springer József | Attila utca 39 |
| | Stern Miklós | Avar utca 15 |
| | Radványi Ernő & partners | Andrássy út 12 |
| | Abelesz Zsigmondné | Kisfaludy utca 3 |
| | Neuwirth Pál | Kisfaludy utca 25 |
| Dr. Horváth István city councilman | (widow) Fischer Edéné | Szt. István út 11 – 11a |
| | Schwarcz Márton & partners | Schwarzenberg u. 23 |
| Dr. Jeney Ferenc museum guard | Dr. Deutsch Béla | Czuczor G. utca 15. |
| | Szabó Márton & partners | Szt. László király u. 17 |

| | | |
|---|---|---|
| Juhász Ervin city tax office junior clerk | Braun József | Kisfaludy utca 15 |
| | Wittmann Samu heirs | Kisfaludy utca 26 |
| | Rosenberg Józsefné | Korona köz 10 |
| | Gestettner Lajos & partners | Híd utca 4 |
| | Gráncz János | Klétzár utca 7 |
| | Gráner János & partners | Híd utca 2 |
| | Rechberger Antal | Kisfaludy utca 11 |
| Dr. Kanabé László deputy cityclerk | Mendelshn Ármin | Megyeház utca 21 |
| | Kucsera Dávid | Megyeház utca 12 |
| Dr. Kardos Ferenc chief customs clerk | Szántó Jakab | Wennesz Jenő u. 10c |
| | Dr. Fekete Ernő & partners | Wennesz Jenő u. 10b |
| | Bürger Zoltán | Huszár utca 4 |
| Dr. Karikó Imre | Koch siblings | Lövőkert 16 |
| Kertész László city executive | Margulics Henrikné | Apátúr utca 8 |
| | Singer Gábor | Apátúr utca 14 |
| | Dr. Weiner István | Gárdonyi utca 7 |
| | Frankl Lajos | Homok utca 5 |
| | Weiler Viktorné | Homok utca 6a |
| | (widow) Rosen Samuné | Iskola utca 7 |
| | Bauer Jenő | Jedlik Ányos utca 12 |
| | Steiner Imre | Jókai utca 7. |
| | Steiner Ignác | Kisfaludy utca 7 |
| | Kőnigsberg sisters | Apáca utca 40 |
| | Braun József | Kazinczy utca 23 |
| | (widow) Pfeifer Gyuláné | Gárdonyi utca 5 |
| Kiczkó Gyula fashion merchant | Váradi & partners | Korona köz 2. |
| Dr. Koháry István attorney | Cseh Ernőné | Batthyányi tér 1 |
| | Strompf Hermann | Deák Ferenc utca 27 |
| Dr. Koller Jenő mayor | Dr. Krausz Mór | Apáca utca 28 |

| | | |
|---|---|---|
| Komka László sales tax officer | Adler Ferenc & partners | Újlak utca 14 |
| | Krausz Béláné | Felső-Nádor utca 16b |
| | Szűcs Magdolna | Fehérlaposi dűlő |
| | Heimler Ernő & partners | Felső-Nádor utca 6 |
| | Kopfstein Richárd | Pápai utca 4 |
| | Biringer János | Szt. Imre út 12 |
| Dr. Kondé Gyula chief state financial counselor | Dr. Erdős János | Árpád út 29 |
| | Dr. Brück Imre & partners | Wennesz Jenő utca 37 |
| Kovács István city accountant- counselor | Dr. Raáb Árpád & partners | Baross út 33 |
| Köppel József sales tax officer | Dr. Patak Endre & partners | Batthyányi tér 10 |
| | (widow) Steiner Hermanné | Hold utca 12 |
| | Hacker heirs | Batthyányi tér 8 |
| | Dr. Reisz Frigyes & partners | Kazinczy utca 20 |
| Kriván (Jr.) Elemér sales officer | Dr. Krausz Mór | Fürdő köz 11 |
| Kutálik Péter senior counselor | Adler Károly | Czuczor G. utca 11 |
| | Glaser Gyuláné & partners | Czuczor G. utca 9 |
| Dr. Láng Mihály financial counselor | Csillag Jenőné & partners | Arany János utca 6 |
| | Meller Ignác & partners | Árpád út 8 |
| Liliom István financial assistantofficer | Merkur knitting shop | Dugonits utca 22. |
| | Salzer Andorné | Eősy Péter utca 3 |
| | Dr. Rothauser György | Eősy Péter utca 9 |
| | Kóhn Ilona | Br. Jósika utca 5 |
| | Steiner Jenő | Bocskay utca 17 |
| Liliom János deputy financial officer | Deutsch Gyula | Közép utca 3 |
| Dr. Lipovits Gyula deputy city clerk | (widow) Hacker Richárdné | Deák Ferenc utca 25 |
| | Dr. Unger Gyula | Deák Ferenc utca 21 |

| | | |
|---|---|---|
| Lipocits Pál sales tax officer. | Schnabel Henrik | Teleszky utca 17 |
| | Pongrácz Tibor | Árpád út 50 |
| | Schlesinger Margit & partners | Árpád út 52 |
| Maróti János state treasury counselor | Dr. Magyar László & partners | Hunyadi utca 5c |
| Matuschek Imre foreign trade office director | Dr. Fekete Gyuláné | Munkácsy utca 18 |
| Mészáros József sales tax officer | Csillag Pálné | Budai-u. 2 |
| | Krausz siblings | Andrássy út 27 |
| Dr. Mondvay Jenő sales tax office director | Ländler Samu | Deák Ferenc utca 6 |
| | Schleisinger Endréné | Attila utca 20 |
| | Lengyel József | Dugonits Utca 6 |
| | Kádár Vilmos | Dugonits utca 8 |
| | Richter Imre | Dugonits utca 12 |
| | Lőwy Nándor & partners | Baross út 22 |
| | Rosinger and Osztovits | Bisinger sétány 2 |
| | Dr. Rothauser Lajos | Árpád út 22 |
| | Diamant Kálmán & partners | Árpád út 32 |
| Moravek Ferenc city executive | (widow) Kopfstein Mórné | Pápai út 2 |
| | (widow) Gestettner Náthánné | Pápai út 13 |
| | Engel Rózsa & partners | Rét utca 4 |
| | Ungár Fülöp Béla | Soproni utca 4 |
| | Dr. Deutsch Dávid & partners | Szt. György tér 16 |
| | Hercz Géza | Buda utca 14 |
| | Spielmann József | Kassai utca 23 |
| | Krausz Károly | Kassai utca 27 – 30 |
| | Fleischer Rezső and István | Buda utca 3 |
| | Kopfstein Richárd | Kálvária utca 23 |
| | Steiner Jenő | Attila utca 45 |

| | | |
|---|---|---|
| Dr. Morocz Mihály head l financial counselor | Szabó István. | Baross út 30 |
| | Schlauger Imréné & partners | Csaba utca 11 |
| | Kopfstein Richárd | Pápai utca 6 |
| | Sugár Árpád | Erzsébet tér 13 |
| Dr. Cs. Nagy Béla orphanage assessor | Steiner Margit | Opitz utca 9 |
| | Schneider Janka | Rákóczi utca 37 |
| | Hoch Gyuláné | Opitz utca 4 |
| | Staruss Gézáné | Opitz utca 21 |
| | Rothauser Lajos | Opitz utca 23 |
| | Gyárfás Zsigmond | Opitz utca 26 |
| | Spielmann Jenő | Corvin utca 56 |
| | Kardos Jenő & partners | Corvin utca 6 |
| | Wollner Adolf | Opitz utca 2 |
| Nagy Imréné clerk | Szántó Imre | Körkemence utca 24c |
| | Dr. Földes József | Körkemence utca 24a |
| Nagy József city executive | Haán József | Rákóczi utca 44 |
| | Neuhaus Márkus | Ország utca 7 |
| | Lefkovics Ármin | Ország utca 10 |
| | Frischmann Illés | Simor tér 3 |
| | Deutsch Ferenc | Klétzár utca 16 |
| | Galatzer József | Rákóczi utca 42 |
| Nauratyill József financial counselor | Kélisch Simon & partners | Vasút utca 8 |
| | Neumann Zsigmond | Zechmeister utca 4. |
| | Blau Pálné | Zechmeister utca 9 |
| | Neugebauer Pál | Újlak utca 6 |
| Némedi István city executive | Dr. Haller Tibor | Munkácsy utca 16 |
| | Steiner Hermanné | Munkácsy utca 6 |
| Dr. Németh Antal deputy city clerk | Eckmann Dávid | Andrássy út 63 |
| | Spiegel Samu | Rákóczi utca 9 |
| | Israelite Congregation | Andrássy út 43 |
| | Hermann siblings | Deák Ferenc utca 9 |
| | Angár Miksané | Deák Ferenc utca 11 |

| | | |
|---|---|---|
| Ódor János MÁV assistant executive | Ormos Ede | Szt. György tér 17 |
| | Neuwirth Sándorné | Szt. Imre hg. út 1 |
| | Salzer Magdolna | Soproni utca 36 |
| Pál Ferenc treasury officer 1st class | Kohn Sándor | Bocskay utca 15 |
| | Neumann Ferenc | Farkas Mátyás utca 13 |
| Pammer Ferenc waterworks administrator | Singer Jakab | Wennesz Jenő utca 46 |
| | Bartos Olga | Wennesz Jenő utca 59 |
| | Balogh Samu | Budai utca 30 |
| | Schwimmer György | Dr. Petz Lajos utca 6 |
| | Klopfer László | Wennesz Jenő u. 17c |
| Pásler György waterworks employee | Popper Vilma | Árpád út 20 |
| Pataki Miklós financial office director | Gross Sándor | Rákóczi u. 65. and 65a |
| | (widow) Blau Sándorné | Hunyadi utca 5b |
| | Neumann Sámuel | Wennesz Jenő utca 5 |
| | Fleischmann Árpád | Rákóczi utca 4 |
| | Holczer Nándor | Fecske utca 27 – 31 |
| | Csillag Pál | Dunaszer 18 |
| | Anhalzer Olga | Dunaszer 14 |
| Pávelcza Viktor financial office manager | Rosner Ottó & partners | Czuczor G. utca 24 |
| | Scheiber Pál | Czuczor G. Utca 19 |
| Péchy Kálmán deputy chief auditor | Róth Dezső | Rákóczi utca 23 |
| | Gottlieb Salamon | Rákóczi utca 26 |
| | Benedek Anna & partners | Rákóczi utca 33 |
| | Gold Samuné | Rákóczi utca 35 |
| | Singer Gábor | Rákóczi utca 44a |
| | Krausz Emánuel | Rákóczi utca 47 |
| | Kertész Imre | Rákóczi utca 61 |
| | Kallós Jenő | Rákóczi utca 13 |

| | | |
|---|---|---|
| Petényi Gyula head financial examiner | Stern Ernő | Kereszt u 16. and 18a |
| Piczek Sándor city auditor | Gross Dániel<br>Adler Pálné<br>Hacker Margit<br>Waldhauser Sándor<br>Lőwy Márton<br>Rajnát Ernőné<br>Grosz Sándor & partners | Arany János utca 3<br>Árpád út 36.<br>Megyeház utca 2.<br>Megyeház utca 9.<br>Megyeház utca 11<br>Andrássy út 70–72<br>Szt. István út 35b |
| Pilcz András sales tax officer | László Zsuzsanna<br>Wolf Károlyné & partners | Árpád út 95. and 191<br>Baross út 35 |
| Planka János financial administrator | Bing Géza & partners<br>Pelczer Elza<br>Grosz Henrikné<br>Drach Lajosné<br>Brenner Sándorné | Munkás utca 30<br>Sarkantyú köz 7<br>Saru köz 3<br>Szedres köz 4<br>Munkás utca 9 |
| Polcz Gyula financial auditor | Wittmann Miklós<br>Reiszfeld József<br>Nemsitz Lajosné<br>Perelesz heirs | Kisfaludy utca 36<br>Kisfaludy utca 38<br>Kisfaludy utca 44<br>Kisfaludy utca 34 |
| Dr. Pollák Károly city councilman | Adler Károly | Baross út 29 |
| Dr. Pongrácz Ödön deputy city clerk | Dr. Berndorfer Vilmosné<br>Dr. Wermes Ödön & partners | Rákóczi utca 2<br>Pálffy utca 29 |
| Pöttinger Gusztáv dental technician | Csillag Géza | Gyár utca 43. |
| Radnóti Elemér financial account inspector | Blau Sándorné<br>Bíró Hermann<br>Ungár József<br>Porjesz Albán<br>Goldstein Mór | Arany János utca 26<br>Arany János utca 28.<br>Arany János utca 29<br>Arany János utca 31<br>Erzsébet liget 4 |

| | | |
|---|---|---|
| | (widow) Spitzer Illésné | Arany János utca 23 |
| | Steiner siblings | Erzsébet liget 3 |
| Dr. Rajcsányi Lajos financial secretary | Gratte József | Dunaszer 26 |
| | Ganz György | Erdősor 3/5 |
| | Frankl József | Erzsébet tér 10 |
| Dr. Rajcsányi Mihály financial secretary partners | Dr. Földes József &. i | Erzsébet tér 11 |
| Rieger Antal Hungarian Royal Treasury employee | Engel Jenő | Régi Posta utca 57. |
| | Spitzer Samuné | Régi Posta utca 74. |
| | Deutsch Mariska | Régi Posta utca 62. |
| | Vajda Irén | Huszár utca |
| Samodai Elek city printing office director | Herczfeld Jakabné | Bástya utca 4 |
| | Berger József | Bástya utca 10 |
| | Fleischmann Árpád | Bástya utca 75 |
| | Stein László | Árpád út 48 |
| Sándor József financial counselor | Grosz Dávid & partners | Híd utca 10 |
| | Salczer Károlyné | Híd utca 8 |
| | Lőwy Nándor & partners | Andrássy út 15 |
| | (widow) Gestettner Náthánné | Híd utca 1 |
| Sáni Jenő savings bank office manager | Raab Malvin | Bercsényi liget 10 |
| Sári Erzsébet city employee | Molnár Béla | Csokonai utca 11 |
| Schőnberger János sales tax office manager | (widow) dr. Singer Emilné | Apáca utca 13 |
| | Waldhauser Sándor | Apáca utca 22 |
| | Füredi Lajos & partners | Apáca utca 3 |
| Sebestyén Géza city employee | (widow) Neufeld Sándorné | Arany János utca 11 |
| | Wohl Sándor | Arany János utca 15 |
| | Perl Sándor & partners | Batthyányi tér 9 |

| | | |
|---|---|---|
| | (widow) Braun Béláné | Arany János utca 10 |
| Dr. Sebestyén Miklós | Steiner Ernő<br>Deutsch Gyuláné | Opitz utca 11<br>Opitz utca 14 |
| Dr. Sipos Mihály dr. city head auditor (retired) | Dr. Perl László<br>Israelite Congregation<br>Flenk and Lőwy<br>(widow). Dr. Mayer Lajosné<br>Magyar Ferenc & partners | Szt. István út 15<br>Szt. István út 27<br>Andrássy út 31<br>Deák Ferenc utca 20<br><br>Dunaszer 10. |
| Dr Soós László deputy customs cllerk | Gerő Józsefné & partners | Szt. László király u. 12 – 14 |
| | Rosenberg László | Szt. László király u. 7 |
| Sulyok János businessman | Fischer Bernát<br>Dr. Merczel Félixné | Körkemence utca 12<br>Körkemence utca 6 |
| Szakács Jenő waterworks inspector | Berán Artúr<br>Hermann Dávid | Gőzmalom utca 5<br>Gőzmalom utca 4 |
| Dr. Szalkai Béla financial secretary | Schnabel siblings | Széchenyi tér 10 |
| Dr. Szalóky Sándor city councilman | Szóbel Sándor<br>Perl József<br>Neuhauser Ilona<br>Halmos Zsigmond | Szél köz 1<br>Szél köz 16<br>Szél köz 17<br>Arany János utca 7 |
| Szecsányi László Royal Court ofAppeals senior officer | Polgár Sándor & partners | Bisinger sétány 4 |
| Szép József retired senior customs officer | Knapp Gyula<br>Dr. Klein József & partners<br>Kallós Henrikné<br>Krausz Mór | Budai-u.<br>Gárdonyi Géza u. 12<br>Szt. István út 45.<br>Szt. László király u. 44 |

| | | |
|---|---|---|
| | Szántó Mór | Budai-u. 72 |
| | Kallós Henrikné | Árpád út 59 |
| Szigeti Imre sales tax officer | Anhalzer Olga | Baross út 5 |
| | Dr. Székely Gusztáv | Liezenmayer utca 23 |
| | László Imre | Marcal utca 11 |
| | Geister Sándor | Otthon utca 13 |
| | Spielmann Artúr | Liezenmayer utca 20b |
| | Wilkheim Sándor | Baross út 3 |
| Szörényi József senior counselor | Barcza A. Ernő | Endresz Gy. utca 3 |
| | (widow) Neuwirth Sándorné | Zrínyi utca 8b |
| Sztankovits József sales tax officer | Gestettner Lajos | Andrássy út 22 |
| | Balog Lajos | Andrássy út 28 |
| | (widow) Stein Bernátné | Kazinczy utca 18 |
| Takács József sales tax officer | Fleischmann Miksáné | Árpád út 12 |
| | Szász Zsigmondné | Rákóczi utca 20 |
| | Halász Lászlóné & partners | Kígyó utca 9a |
| Temesváry Antal tax office head financial counselor | Weisz Benő | Bisinger sétány 22 |
| | Atlasz Márkus | Teleki utca 29 |
| Dr. Tomaj Ferenc customs counselor | Drach Dezső | Szél köz 20. |
| | Wollner Mór | Teleki utca 3. |
| | Lőwy Márton | Teleki utca 8. |
| | (widow) Salzer Jenőné | Teleki utca 16. |
| | Deutsch Irén & partners | Teleki utca 19 |
| | Fenyő Gyuláné | Szél köz 18 |
| Tóth Péter | Simon Endre | Kenyér köz 2 |
| Töllössy Zoltán | Bérczi Dezső | Ecet utca 3 |
| | Lőwinger Samu | Gőzmalom utca 5a |
| | Grünzweig Józsefné | Gyár utca 14 |
| | Pál László & partners | Gyár utca 15 |

| | | |
|---|---|---|
| | Perl Józsefné | Kálvária utca 27 |
| | Mosonyi siblings | Kálvária utca 35 |
| Tölössy Imre sales tax officer 1st class | Schőnberger & partners | Liezenmayer utca 5 |
| | Waldhauser Dezső | Attila utca 1 – 3 |
| | Krausz Vilmos & partners | Andrássy út 9 |
| | Frankl József & partners | Kazinczy utca 18 |
| | Barcza Arnold | Árpád út 17 |
| Treitli Sándor customs official | Leipnicker Imre | Domb utca 8b |
| Dr. Turcsán Mihály tax office senior financial officer | Székely Jenő | Levente utca 22 |
| | Weisz Hugó | Levente utca 18 |
| | Spiegel Henrik | Levente utca 4 |
| Dr. Turnán Mihály state treasury senior officer | Szántó Ödönné & partners | Bisinger sétány 16 |
| Dr. Veöreös Imre retired customs head prosecutor | Dr. Csillag József | Árpád út 18 |
| Vojacsek Ferenc city head auditor | Dr. Krausz Mór & partners | Baross út 7 |
| | Dr. Szelényi Ferenc | Csillag utca 1 |
| Wessely Géza city chief engineer | Neubrun Géza | Dr. Petz Lajos utca 11 |

# Bibliography


*A Frigyes-laktanyától a Leier City Center-ig: Történelmi etűdök egy városrész életéből* (Leier City Center Kft., 2011).

Achenbach, Michael, and Dieter Szorger, "Der Einsatz ungarischer Juden am Südostwall im Bauabschnitt Niederdonau 1944/45," unpublished manuscript in author's files.

Alford, Henry, "Return Trips," review of *The Time Traveler's Handbook: 18 Experiences, From the Eruption of Vesuvius to Woodstock*, by James Wyllie, Johnny Acton, and David Goldblatt, *New York Times Book Review*, June 5, 2016, p. 18.

Ascherson, Neal, "How Could They?" *New York Review of Books*, 61, October 23, 2014, pp. 35–7.

Bana, József, *A Lövöldöző "Level hordozó": Jegyzetek Győr történetének lapjaihoz*. Városi Levéltári füzetek 3 (Győr: Győr Megyei Városi Levéltára, 2001).

Bánffy, Miklós, *The Phoenix Land: The Memoirs of Count Miklós Bánffy*. Patrick Thursfield and Katalin Banffy-Jelen, trans. (London: Arcadia Books, 2003).

Batthanyi, Sasha, *A Crime in the Family*. (New York.: DaCapo Press, 2017)

Baumgartner, Gerhard, and Florian Freund, *Roma Policies in Austria* (Vienna: Cultural Association of Austrian Roma, 2007).

Bayer, Pia, and Dieter Szorger, *Der Weg Zum Anschluss: Burgenlandshicksal 1928–1938*, Wissensschaftliche Arbeiten aus dem Burgenland, Band 125 (Eisenstadt: Landesmuseum, 2008).

Benjamin, Walter, *Illuminations*, edited with an introduction by Hannah Arendt, trans. Harry Zohn (New York: Schocken, 1969), pp. 257–8, quoted in Susan Handelman, "Walter Benjamin and the Angel of History," *Cross Currents*, Fall 1991, p. 345.

Berkes, Timea, "A Győr-Moson-Pozsony vármegyei zsidok története 1944-ben," *Holocaust Füzetek* 5 (1996), pp. 6–42.

Braham, Randolph, *The Politics of Genocide: The Holocaust in Hungary*. 2 vols. (New York: Columbia University Press, 1981).

—, ed., *Magyarországi Holokauszt Földrajzi Enciklopédiaja*. 2 vols. (Budapest: Park Konyvkiado, 2006).

Brettl, Herbert, and Michael Hess, *NS-Euthanasie im Burgenland*, Wissenschaftliche Arbeiten aus dem Burgenland, Band 136 (Eisenstadt: Burgenlandischen Lanndesmuseum, 2015).

Burghardt, Andrew F., *The Political Geography of Burgenland*. Publication 587. (Washington, D.C.: National Academy of Sciences – National Research Council, 1958).

Cesarani, David, *Final Solution: The Fate of Jews 1933–1949* (New York: St. Martin's Press, 2016), e-book.

Cole, Tim, *Traces of the Holocaust: Journeying in and out of the Ghettos* (London: Continuum, 2011).

Csapody, Tamás, *Bori Munkaszolgálatasok: Fejezetek a bori munkaszolgálat történenéből* (Budapest: Vince Kiadó, 2012).

—, *Bortól Szombathelyig: Tanulmányok a bori munkaszolgálatról és a bori munkaszolgalátosok részleges névlistája* (Budapest: Zrinyi Kiadó, 2012).

Czirók, Zoltán, *"Tegnap istenitélet volt Szombathelyen …": Légitamadások a vasi megyeszékhely ellen 1944–1945* (Szombathely: A Vasi Muzeumbarát Egylet, 2015).

Deák, István, *Europe on Trial: The Story of Collaboration, Resistance, and Retribution During World War II* (Boulder, CO: Westview Press, 2015).

Dean, Martin, *Robbing the Jews: the Confiscation of Jewish Property During the Holocaust* (New York: Cambridge University Press, 2008, 2010).

Douglas, R. M., *Orderly and Humane: The Expulsion of the Germans after the Second World War* (New Haven: Yale University Press, 2011).

Drndic, Dasa, *EEG*, trans. Celia Hawkesworth (New York: New Directions, 2018).

Egy Rongyos, *A Rongyos Gárda Harcai 1919–1939* (Budapest: Magyar Ház, 1999).

Etschmann, Wolfgang, Tamara Scheer, and Erwin A. Schmidl, *An der Grenze: Der erste Einrückungstermin des Bundesheeres und der Einsatz während der Ungarnkrise 1956* (Graz: Vehling Verlag GmbH, 2006).

Faludi, György, *My Happy Days in Hell*, trans. Kathleen Szasz (London: Penguin Classics, 2010).

"The Fascination of the Metropolis," *Lost in the City: Urban Life in the IVAM* [Institut Valencia d'Art Modern] *Collection*, May 18, 2016–June 4, 2017.

Gábor, Kádár, and Vági Zoltán, *A Végső Döntés: Berlin, Budapest, Birkenau 1944* (Budapest: Jaffa, 2013).

Gárdonyi, Maté, "Veszprémi püspöki rendeletek a zsidótörvények árnyékában," in Judit Molnár, ed., *Nagypolitikától a Hétköznapokig: A Magyar Holokauszt 70 Év Távlatából* (Budapest: Balassi Kiadó, 2016), pp. 126–36.

Gerencsér, Miklós, *Fekete Tél* (Budapest: Szépirodalmi Könyvkiadó, 1973).

Germanova, Miroslava, Boryana Dzhambazova, and Helene Bienvenu, "Vigilantes Patrol Where Few Migrants Set Foot," *New York Times*, DL: Bratislava, June 10, 2016, published June 11, 2016, https?/www.nytimes.com/2016/06/11/world/europe/vigilante-patrols-inparts-of-europe-where-few-migrants-set-foot-html, accessed February 26, 2024.

Giller, Joachim, Hubert Mader, and Christina Seidl, *Wo sind sie geblieben ...? Kriegerdenkmäler und Gefallenenehrung in Österreich* (Vienna: Österreichischer Bundesverlag, 1992).

Graf, Maximilian, Alexander Lass, and Karlo Ruzicic-Kessler, eds., *Das Burgenland als international Grenzregion im 20. und 21. Jahrhundert* (Vienna: Neue Welt Verlag, 2012).

Hanebrink, Paul A., *In Defense of Christian Hungary: Religion, Nationalism, and Antisemitism 1890–1944* (Ithaca: Cornell University Press, 2006).

Héjjas, Jenő, *A Nyugat-Magyarorszägi Felkelés: Kecskemetiek az 1921. Évi Nyugat-Magyarorszägi Harcokban* (Budapest: Magyar Ház, 2006).

Herczl, Moshe Y., *Christianity and the Holocaust of Hungarian Jewry*, trans. Joel Lerner (New York: New York University Press, 1993).

Hilberg, Raul, *Perpetrators Victims Bystanders: The Jewish Catastrophe 1933–1945* (New York: HarperCollins, 1992).

Holtzinger, Gregor, ed., *Das Drama Südostwall am Beispiel Rechnitz: Daten, Taten, Fakten, Folgen*. Burgenländische Forschungen, Band 98. (Eisenstadt: Burgenland State Museum, 2009).

Horváth, Ferenc, and L. Kiss Csaba, *Végjáték a határon: Kőszeg 1944–1945* (Szombathely: Szűlöföld Könyvkiado, 2015).

Jagadics, Peter, *Savaria katonai története* (Budapest: HM Hadtörténeti Intézet és Múzeum, 2010).

Joskowicz, Ari, *Rain of Ash: Roma, Jews, and the Holocaust* (Princeton: Princeton University Press, 2023).

Juhász, László, *Ausztria magyar emlékei* (Lakitelek: Antológia, 2005).

Karsai, László, *A cigánykérdés Magyarországon 1919–1945: Út a cigány holocausthoz* (Budapest: Cserépfalvi Könyvkiadó, 1992).

—, *Szálasi Ferenc: Politikai életrajz* (Budapest: Balassi Kiado, 2016).

Kelbert, Kriszina, *Szemből Szemben: Képek az elhurcolt Szombathelyi zsidóság tőrténetéből* (Szombathely: Savaria Megyei Hátókörű Városi Múzeum, 2014).

Klay, Phil, "What Defines a Modern Warrior?" *New York Times* online, December 9, 2015, <http://www.nytimes.com/2015/12/09/opinion/what-defines-a-modern-warrior.html?emc=eta1&_r=0>, accessed December 14, 2015.

Kosinski, Jerzy, *The Painted Bird*, 2nd ed. (New York: Grove Press, 1976), p. xii.

Kovács, Tamás, "A Nemzeti Számonkérő Különítmény," *Múltunk* 3 (2006), pp. 71–100.

Kovács, Zoltan András, "A Szálasy Kormány Belügyministeriuma: Rendvédelem, Állambiztonság, Közigazgatás A Nyilas Korszakban" (Ph. D. Dissertation, Pécsi Tudományegyetem-Bölcsészettudomanyi Kar, 2008).

Krisch, András, *A Soproni Németek Kitelepítése* (Sopron: Escort, 2006).

Lacsó, Balázs, "Mögöttük lépdel a remény," Zsidóüldözás a folyók városában, 3. Rész, *Kisalföld K2*, August 19, 2017, p. 6.

Lénárt, András, "Csillagos házak Budapesten, 1944–2014," in Judit Molnár, ed., *A Nagypolitikától a Hétköznapokig: A Magyar Holokauszt 70 Év Távlatából* (Szeged: Balassi Kiadó, 2016), pp. 373–88..

Litchfield, David R., *The Thyssen Art Macabre* (London: Quartet Books, 2007).

Magris, Claudio, *Journeying*, trans. Anne Milano Appel (New Haven: Yale University Press, 2018).

Manoschek, Walter, *Der Fall Rechnitz: Das Massaker an Juden im März 1945* (Vienna: Braumüller, 2009).

Marquand, David, *The End of the West* (Princeton: Princeton University Press, 2011).

Mask, Deirdre, *The Address Book: What Addresses Reveal about Identity, Race, Wealth, and Power* (New York: St. Martin's Press, 2020).

Molnár, Ernő, *Munkásmozgalmi emlékhelyek Győr-Sopron megyében* (Győr: Győr Megyei Lapkiado Vállalat, 1986).

Murber, Ibolya, "Az 1956-os magyar menekűltek Ausztriában: Menekűltlét és integráció," *Multunk* 3 (2016), pp. 123–59.

Nagy, István, *A Mi Utcánk Kisfaludy Utca* (Győr: Győri Ipartestulet, 2008).

—, *Győr vértanú püspöke, Apor Vilmos* (Győr: Győri Egyházmegyei Levéltár, 2012).

—, *Húsvéttól húsvétig: Győr harmincöt bombazása* (Győr: Győr-Moson-Sopron Megye Győri Levéltára, 2007).

—, *Quiritatio. Sikoly. Győri zsidő tragédia 1938–1945* (Győr: A Győri Zsidő Hitközség, 2010).

Neiman, Susan, *Learning from the Germans: Race and the Memory of Evil* (New York: Farrar, Strauss and Giroux, 2019).

Orbánné, Horváth Márta, *Győri Emlékhelyek és Köztéri Alkotások* (Győr: Gálgócsi Erzsébet Városi Könyvtár, 2006).

Ormos, Mária, *Civitas Fidelissima: Népszavazás Sopronban 1921* (Győr: Gordiusz, 1990).

Paksy, Zoltán, "A veszkorszak Zalaegerszegen," in Judit Molnár, ed., *Nagypolitikától a Hétköznapokig: A Magyar Holokauszt 70 Év Távlatából* (Szeged: Balassi Kiadó, 2016), pp. 273–87.

Perger, Gyula, *A Pusztulás Képei: Dobos Vilmos Felvételei Győr 1944-es Bombázásairol* (Győr: Xántus János Múzeum, 2010).

Pingitzer, Norbert, *Der Anschluss 1938 Burgenland* (Schwarzach: Heimat-Verlag, 2018).

Pnomarev, Sergey, "They Let 71 People Die in a Stifling Truck. They Got 25 Years," *New York Times* online, June 14, 2018, <https://www.nytimes.com/2018/06/14/world/europe/austria-migrants-truck.htm>.

Prónáy, Pál, *A határban a Halál kaszál ...: Fejezetek Prónáy Pál Naplójából*. Szabó Ágnes and Pamlényi Ervin, eds. (Budapest: Kossuth Könyvkiado, 1963).

Quittner, Eva, *Pebbles of Remembrance* (Balmain, Australia: Kerr Publishing, 1993).

Reiss, Johannes, *"... Because our love for our home town has been drained from us ...": A Walk through the Jewish History of Eisenstadt*, trans. Serge Claus (Eisenstadt: Österreichisches Jüdisches Museum, 2001).

Reiter, Johannes, ed. *Ein Mantel Des Schweigens* (Köln, Germany: Bohlau Verlag, 2022).

Romsics, Ignác, *Hungary in the Twentieth Century*, trans. Tim Wilkinson (Budapest: Corvina Osiris, 1999).

Samer, Helmut, *Roma von Oberwart: zur Geschichte und aktuellen Situation der Roma in Oberwart* (Oberwart: Edition Lex Liszt 12, 2001).

Ifj. Sarkady Sándor, *Légiharcok és Légiesemények 1944–1945-ben Sopron Vármegyében* (Sopron: Edutech Kiadó, 2004).

—, "The West Hungarian Uprising and the Sopron Referendum," *Sopron a Népszavazás Idején 1921–1922*, Schäffer Ármin, fotograáfiái, Ifj. Sarkady Sándor, Tóth Imre, és Kincses Károly tunulmányával. (Sopron: Edutech Kiado, 2001).

Schmidl, Erwin A., ed., *Die Ungarnkrise 1956 und Österreich* (Vienna: Böhlau Verlag, 2003).

Schubert, Frank N., *Hungarian Borderlands: From the Habsburg Empire to the Axis Alliance, the Warsaw Pact, and the European Union* (London: Continuum, 2011).

Schwarzmayer, Eva, Herbert Brettl, Tamás Koloszár, Edit Balázs, and Lajos Szarka, *Zsidó emlékek a Nyugat-Pannon Eurégióban/Jüdische Errinerungen in der West-Pannonischen EuRegion* (Szombathely: Magyar-Israeli Baráti Társaság, 2008).

Sebald, W. G., *On the Natural History of Destruction*, trans. Anthea Bell (New York: Modern Library, 2003).

Söptei, Imre, *Kőszeg turizmusának története 1949-ig* (Kőszeg: Írottkő Natúrparkért Egyesület, 2003).

Stach, Reiner, *Kafka: The Early Years*, trans. Shelley Frisch (Princeton: Princeton University Press, 2017).

Szabo, Robert, ed., "Szabo, Jenő, a Hajtomű̈gyár Munkástanácsának titkára emlékezik 1956-ról," *Ghyőri Tanulmányok*, 28 (2006).

Szakolczai, Attila, *Forradalom és Szabadságharc Győr-Sopron Megyeben* (Győr: Megyei Jogú Város Levéltára, 2006).

Székely, László, *Kőszegi krónika, 1938–1952: Székely László apátplebános feljegyzése*. (Szombathely: Szülőföld, 2015).

Szita, Szabolcs, *A Gestapo Tevékenysége Magyarországon 1939–1945* (Budapest: Corvina, 2014).

—, *Haláreről: A munkaszolgálat és a hadimunka történetéhez* (Budapest: Kössuth Könyvkiado, 1989).

Tárkanyi, Sandor, and Tarkányi Eszter, *Faces, Fates, Victims, Chapters from the History of the Jewry of Sopron*, trans. Koltai Bálint, Szakonyi Janka, and Tárkányi Eszter (Sopron: Hungarian-Israeli Fellowship of Sopron, 2014).

Tavernise, Sabrina, "When History's Losers Write the Story," *New York Times*, "Sunday Review," September 17, 2017 (published online September 15, 2017).

Thullner, István, *Hegyeshalom nagyközség története*. Vol. II. (Hegyshalom: Palatia, 2004).

*Top 50 Látnivaló a Kisalföldön* (Győr: Lapcom.Zrt., 2017).

Torma, Attila, *Győr a II, világháború sodrásban.* Győri Tanulmányok Füzetek 2014/15. (Győr: Győr Megyei Jogú Város Levéltára, 2014).

—, *Győr Vármegye Főispánjai* (Győr: Dr. Kovács Pál Megyei Győr Megyei Könyvtár, 2017).

Várga, Ervin, *Living and Dying in Hungary: Jewish Psychiatrist Looks Back* (Bloomington, IN: Xlibris, 2012).

Vihár, Béla, ed., *Sárga Könyv: Adatok a magyar zsidóság háborús szenvedéseiből, 1941–1945* (Budapest: Hechaluc, 1945).

Vonnegut, Kurt, *Breakfast of Champions*, 1973, in Vonnegut, *Novels and Stories 1963–1973*, Sidney Offit, ed. (New York: the Library of America, 2011).

Weiss, Petra, *TÜPL Bruckneudorf: 150 Jahre Brucker Lager. Eine Geschichte in Bildern* (Bruck an der Leitha: Stadtgemeinde, 2008).

Weiss, Petra, and Irmtraut Karlsson, *Die Toten von Bruck* (Berndorf, Austria: Kral-Verlag, 2008).

Werfel, Franz, *Cella oder die Überwinder* [*Cella, or the Survivors*], trans. Joachim Neugroschell (New York: Henry Holt and Company, 1989).

Young, James E., *The Texture of Memory: Holocaust Memorials and Meaning* (New Haven: Yale University Press, 1993).

Zimmermann, Berndt, "Die Sudtiroler Siedlung in Oberwart," *Osterreich in Geschichte and Literatur*, 35/5b (1991), p. 430.

# Index

# CULTURAL MEMORIES

SERIES EDITOR

Dr Katia Pizzi
Institute of Languages, Cultures and Societies,
School of Advanced Study, University of London

*Cultural Memories* is the publishing project of the Centre for the Study of Cultural Memory at the Institute of Languages, Cultures and Societies, University of London. The Centre is international in scope and promotes innovative research with a focus on interdisciplinary approaches to memory.

This series supports the Centre by furthering original research in the global field of cultural memory studies. In particular, it seeks to challenge a monumentalizing model of memory in favour of a more fluid and heterogeneous one, where history, culture and memory are seen as complementary and intersecting. The series embraces new methodological approaches, encompassing a wide range of technologies of memory in cognate fields, including comparative studies, cultural studies, history, literature, media and communication, and cognitive science. The aim of *Cultural Memories* is to encourage and enhance research in the broad field of memory studies while, at the same time, pointing in new directions, providing a unique platform for creative and and forward-looking scholarship in the discipline.

Vol. 1 Margherita Sprio
Migrant Memories: Cultural History, Cinema and the Italian Post-War Diaspora in Britain
2013. ISBN 978-3-0343-0947-9

Vol. 2 Shanti Sumartojo and Ben Wellings (eds)
Nation, Memory and Great War Commemoration: Mobilizing the Past in Europe, Australia and New Zealand
2014. ISBN 978-3-0343-0937-0

Vol. 3 Cara Levey
Fragile Memory, Shifting Impunity: Commemoration and Contestation in Post-Dictatorship Argentina and Uruguay
2016. ISBN 978-3-0343-0987-5

Vol. 4 Katia Pizzi and Marjatta Hietala (eds)
Cold War Cities: History, Culture and Memory
2016. ISBN 978-3-0343-1766-5

Vol. 5 Renata Schellenberg
Commemorating Conflict: Models of Remembrance in Postwar Croatia
2016. ISBN 978-3-0343-1901-0

Vol. 6 Stephen Wilson and Deborah Jaffé (eds) Memories of the Future: On Countervision
2017. ISBN 978-3-0343-1935-5

Vol. 7 Patrizia Violi
Landscapes of Memory: Trauma, Space, History
2017. ISBN 978-3-0343-2202-7

Vol. 8 Samuel Merrill
Networked Remembrance: Excavating Buried Memories in the Railways beneath London and Berlin.
2017. ISBN 978-3-0343-1919-5

Vol. 9 Dirk Göttsche (ed.)
Memory and Postcolonial Studies: Synergies and New Directions.
2019. ISBN 978-1-78874-478-2

Vol. 10 Clara Rachel Eybalin Casséus
Geopolitics of Memory and Transnational Citizenship: Thinking Local Development in a Global South
2019. ISBN 978-1-78707-978-6

Vol. 11 Borut Klabjan (ed.)
Borderlands of Memory:
Adriatic and Central European Perspectives
2019. ISBN 978-1-78874-134-7

Vol. 12 Edward Saunders
Kaliningrad and Cultural Memory:
Cold War and Post-Soviet Representations of a Resettled City
2019. ISBN 978-1-78707-274-9

Vol. 13 Pamela Krist
Memory and the Trevi Fountain:
Flows of Political Power in Media Performance
2020. ISBN 978-1-78874-014-2

Vol. 14 Egon Pelikan
Hitler and Mussolini in Churches:
The Church Painter's Subversion of Fascism. The Ideological Marking of Space along the Slovene–Italian Border
2020. ISBN 978-1-78997-149-1

Vol. 15 Sally Debra Charnow (ed.)
Artistic Expressions and the Great War, A Hundred Years On
2020. ISBN 978-1-78997-404-1

Vol. 16 Matteo Cassani Simonetti, Roberta Mira and Daniele Salerno (eds)
The Heritage of a Transit Camp. Fossoli: History, Memory, Aesthetics
2021. ISBN 978-1-78997-904-6

Vol. 17 Struan Gray
Picturing Ghosts:
Memories, Traces and Prophesies of Rebellion in Postdictatorship Chilean Film
2022. ISBN 978-1-80079-119-0

Vol. 18 Susanne Baackmann
Writing the Child:
Fictions of Memory in German Postwar Literature
2022. ISBN 978-1-78707-722-5

Vol. 19 Matteo Cassani Simonetti and Roberta Mira (eds)
Camps of Transit, Sites of Memory:
European Perspectives in the Twentieth Century
2023. ISBN 978-1-80079-389-7

Vol. 20 Jaynie Anderson, Bernardino Branca and Fabio Tononi (eds)
Edgar Wind:
Art and Embodiment
2024. ISBN 978-1-80079-952-3

Vol. 21 Mark Stuart-Smith
Juan Muñoz:
The Politics of Silence
2024. ISBN 978-1-80374-247-2

Vol. 22 Frank N. Schubert
The Past is not Past: Confronting the Twentieth Century in the
Hungarian-Austrian Borderlands
2024. ISBN 978-1-80374-359-2

Printed by
CPI books GmbH, Leck